The First Original Unexpurgated Authentic
Canadian
Book
of Lists

Pierre Berton, co-author of The Canadian Food Guide, *admits, "I remember once we tried to roast a beaver. I'm afraid we didn't much care for it!"*

The First Original Unexpurgated Authentic Canadian Book of Lists

by

JEREMY BROWN AND DAVID ONDAATJE

Pagurian Press Limited

TORONTO

ISBN: 0-88932-072-1 paper
0-88932-097-7 cloth

Printed and bound in Canada

CONTENTS

*The authors, Jeremy Brown and David Ondaatje, interview
Toronto's diminutive ex-mayor David Crombie for* The Canadian
Book of Lists.

INTRODUCTION

At the conclusion of the gathering of the lists which make up this book, my co-author David Ondaatje and I retired to a corner and counted the number of lists we had compiled in coming to grips with this venture. There were 487.

We started with one Master List. Then we started making lists of who was going to call whom to produce lists for us. As these lists became onerously long, we organized a list of the various lists, by category. These Category Lists spread themselves about the office, so we compiled a Master List of the Sub-Master Category Lists. Then lists started pouring in from friends and acquaintances who had become enchanted with the idea of *The Canadian Book of Lists*. We were then forced to meld these fresh lists into the Sub-Master Category Lists, cross-referenced and correlated with the Master List.

From this exercise flowed various lists of people to call back to check certain points, called the Call-Back List. The Call-Back List was naturally integrated into the Master List, which went through 17 typings.

One day, in desperation, we started throwing out the lists from the previous day, and began each day with a fresh list — the Fresh Daily List. This list was a conglomerate of the unassigned ideas from the previous day, plus what had occurred to us overnight. As the project gathered momentum, we devised a Hurry-Up List, a list of the various people who had promised *faithfully* to deliver a list but hadn't yet delivered. The title was later adjusted to the Hurry-Up Panic List.

One afternoon we realized that the new Fresh Daily List bore similarities to some of the earliest ideas which had already been assigned and submitted. We then had to check the new Fresh Daily List with the Master List of Received Lists and criss-cross.

Lists arrived in bizarre fashion. Lists from senior executives would arrive after a prim phone call from an efficient secretary ("Are you there to receive it?"), by messenger or courier. A list arrived scratched on the back of notepaper from Yellowknife. People would telephone their lists in from Vancouver (Bill Cameron), or Northern Ontario (Charles Templeton), or Wawa, or Briar's Bend. Gordon Sinclair sent a list from his island in Muskoka.

One day we realized we were swamped with lists. David took two days off to reconcile the latest Master List with the Table of Contents, and then divide the lists into folders, stapling a list of the lists therein contained on each folder, and concluded by making a list of the folders — the Folder List. Now we were organized.

As each list came in it was recorded on the Folder List and scratched off the Master List (and of course the Sub-Master Referral List and the Panic List). In the achingly frantic days nearing publication, we devised the Critical List. This list was of the absolutely imperatively critically important lists. One day we organized a Search. The Search was to check over all the lists to see if anything had been lost during the List Reconciliation Period.

We can now say with some confidence that we are, perhaps, the definitive list makers in Canada.

A lot of people can suggest lists but only a few have the ultimate genius to produce the *right* title. Johnny Wayne, the comedian, threatened to produce the following list: 11 REASONS WHY METRICATION WILL FAIL IN CANADA. With such a title, who needs the actual list?

Premier William Davis wrestled with his list during weekends at his cottage; Premier René Lévesque said he might consider the second edition; Harold Town kept leaving his list at his farm; and Anne Murray telephoned her list in from the Maritimes.

A lot of people did NOT number their lists. Remember, a list isn't a list unless it's numbered. Numbering itself is fun. Terry O'Malley, the advertising genius, was the most prodigious producer. He was asked for two lists and sent along sixteen. Some of them we couldn't understand.

Making a list is a catharsis, as good as jogging three miles in twelve minutes. Instead of running three miles tonight, sit down and write a list. We may publish it in the next edition, and you will feel a lot better. In the meantime have fun studying the following pages. You will find a prodigious amount of information coupled with some strange insights into the Canadian condition.

Jeremy Brown
Toronto, September 1978

P.S. A very special thank you to the following who provided photographs for *The Canadian Book of Lists:* Air Canada, Association of Canadian Television and Radio Artists, Bell Canada, The Canadian Broadcasting Corporation, Canadian National, Canadian Pacific, Imperial Oil Limited, The Lobster Cove, Metropolitan Toronto Police College, National Air Photo Library, The Office of the Lieutenant-Governor of Ontario, Ontario Amateur Basketball Association, Ontario Department of Travel & Publicity, The Ontario Film Institute, Ontario Hydro, Ontario Ministry of Industry & Tourism, The Public Archives of Canada, Henry Roxborough, *The Toronto Star, The Toronto Sun,* and the University of Toronto. Without them the book would not have been possible.

To the hundreds who gave of their time to compile lists,
and to Karen-Sue Miyashita who unravelled the tangled
web of lists which daily flooded her desk.

"We are devil-worshippers, we Canadians, half in love with easeful Death. We flog ourselves endlessly, as a kind of spiritual purification."

W. Robertson Davies,
Governor-General Award winning author

1
PEOPLE

10 GREAT CANADIAN
QUOTATIONS ON CANADIANS

1. We are devil-worshippers, we Canadians, half in love with easeful Death. We flog ourselves endlessly, as a kind of spiritual purification.

    Robertson Davies, *Tempest-Tost*, 1951

2. Never has any people been endowed with a nobler birthright, or blessed with prospects of a fairer future.

    Lord Dufferin, a speech

3. Historically, a Canadian is an American who rejects the Revolution.

    Northrop Frye, *Letters in Canada,* 1952

4. Nobody understands one damn thing except that he's better than everyone else.

    Hugh MacLennan, *Two Solitudes*, 1945

5. The trouble with Canadians is they spend half their time convincing the Americans they're not British, and the other half convincing the British they're not Americans — which leaves them no time to be themselves.

    McGill's Red & White Review, *My Fur Lady*, 1957

6. The Canadian people are more practical than imaginative. Romantic tales and poetry would meet with less favour in their eyes than a good political article from their newspapers.

    Susanna Moodie, Introduction to *Mark Hurdlestone*, 1853

7. There are as many ways of being Canadian as there are of being French or British, and many more than there are of being American or Irish.

    Lister Sinclair, *The Canadian Idiom*, 1960

8. We have often been told of our necessary dullness because we had no Revolutionary War, no French Revolution, no War Between the States.

    Milton Wilson, *Other Canadians and After,* 1958

9. Canadians will buy anything stamped indigenous. . . .

    John Carroll, *On Richler & Ludwig*, 1963

10. Many a Canadian can trace lineage back to a United Empire Loyalist woman who planted the first crop by hand with a hoe and reaped the first crop by hand with a sickle.

    Agnes C. Laut, *Canada, the Empire of the North,* 1909

10 CANADIANS
WHO DIED TOO YOUNG

1. NORMAN BETHUNE (1890-1939) — 49 YEARS OLD — SURGEON

From 1937-39 Bethune served in China as a surgeon with the Eighth Route Army. He died of a disease he contracted while working on infected patients.

2. BILL BARILKO (1927-1951) — 24 YEARS OLD — HOCKEY PLAYER

Barilko played for the Toronto Maple Leafs from 1946-51. He was a member of Stanley Cup winning teams in 1946-47, 1947-48, 1948-49, and in the Stanley Cup final of the 1950-51 season he scored the winning goal in overtime, to help Toronto defeat the Montreal Canadiens 4 games to 1. He died in a plane crash almost immediately after the game.

3. WILLIAM KURELEK (1927-1977) — 50 YEARS OLD — PAINTER

Canada's best-loved painter was frequently compared to the famous Dutch painter Brueghel. Kurelek's primitive style reflected many aspects of the joys and sadness of the Canadian people. His output was prolific, and, before death overtook him at 50, he had also produced a number of brilliantly original books. His paintings hang in many public galleries and important private collections.

4. TIM HORTON (1930-1974) — 44 YEARS OLD — HOCKEY PLAYER

Horton was a defenceman for the Toronto Maple Leafs from 1953-69, and appeared on all-star teams no less than 6 times. On Stanley Cup teams in Toronto in 1961-62, 1962-63, 1963-64, and 1966-67, in 1969 he was traded to the Rangers in New York, and from 1971-72 he played for the Pittsburgh Penguins. He was traded to the Buffalo Sabres at the end of the 1971-72 season. He died in an automobile accident in September 1974.

5. JOHN McCRAE (1872-1918) — 45 YEARS OLD — POET

McCrae wrote the famous poem "In Flanders Fields." At 45 he died of pneumonia in the hospital in Boulogne, France, where he was the officer in charge of medicine.

6. GEORGE McCULLAGH (1905-1952) — 47 YEARS OLD — NEWSPAPER PUBLISHER

George McCullagh merged the *Toronto Globe* and the *Mail and Empire* to form the *Globe and Mail*, Canada's first national daily newspaper. He became President of the *Globe and Mail* in 1936 and was one of the most powerful political influences of the day. In 1949 he purchased the *Toronto Evening Telegram*. He died in a drowning accident in 1952.

Dr. Norman Bethune died in China when he was only 49 years old.

Bill Barilko, cheered by his teammates after scoring the winning goal to help Toronto defeat the Montreal Canadiens in the 1951 Stanley Cup final. He died in a plane crash almost immediately after the game.

7. LOUIS RIEL (1844-1885) — 41 YEARS OLD — REBEL LEADER

Riel was the secretary of the *Comité national des Métis*, an organization formed to fight the establishment of Canadian authority in the Northwest. He led the rebellion of 1885, which he lost. On his capture he was tried, found guilty, and hanged.

8. SIR JOHN SPARROW DAVID THOMPSON (1844-1894) — 50 YEARS OLD — PRIME MINISTER OF CANADA

Thompson was Prime Minister from 1892-94. On December 12, 1894, he was attending a luncheon at Windsor Castle when he fainted and was rushed from the table. A few minutes later he fell dead in the arms of the Royal physician.

9. TOM THOMSON (1877-1917) — 40 YEARS OLD — PAINTER

A bushranger in Algonquin Park, Ontario, Thomson was inspired to paint the scenery there, and, posthumously, became a member of the Group of Seven. He drowned in Algonquin Park on July 8, 1917. The exact cause of his death is one of Canada's great mysteries.

10. PIERRE LAPORTE (1921-1970) — 49 YEARS OLD — QUEBEC MINISTER OF LABOUR AND IMMIGRATION

Pierre Laporte was murdered by extremists of the Front de Libération de Québec during the 1970 FLQ crisis in Quebec.

10 PEOPLE MOST LIKELY TO INFLUENCE THE COURSE OF EVENTS IN CANADA

1. JOHN TURNER

The only Liberal besides Pierre Trudeau who has maintained his own individual constituency within the Liberal party; he is tough, bright, and has an instinct for power.

2. CONRAD BLACK

A rare combination of scholar and tycoon, he is a student of the exercise of power and has learned his lessons well.

3. BRIAN MULRONEY

Bicultural, brilliant, and beautiful, he is the dream incarnation of the Conservative party. Some day they'll realize it and he will become Prime Minister of Canada.

4. FRED EATON

Has managed to live down his upbringing and can be expected to take on increasing corporate power outside the family empire.

5. DAVID CROMBIE

Articulate yet street-wise, he has natural leadership qualities which will find growing expression during the next decade.

6. NORMAN WEBSTER

This *Globe and Mail* columnist is the best journalist of his generation and can be expected to influence all of our thoughts.

7. CLAUDE FRENETTE

One of French Canada's most enlightened and imaginative entrepreneurs whose vision has international dimensions.

8. MICHAEL McCABE

A civil servant with balls. He will revive Canada's film industry as he has everything else he touches.

9. ROSALIE ABELLA

Canada's youngest woman judge, she is handing out a mixture of compassion and insight from the bench.

10. JENNIFER ASHLEY NEWMAN

Because she's the smartest 14-year-old I know.

Peter C. Newman
Editor
Maclean's Magazine

John Turner is one of the very few current political leaders likely to influence the future course of events in Canada.

THE 10 MOST EXCLUSIVE MEN'S CLUBS IN CANADA

1. YORK CLUB, 135 St. George St., Toronto
   Established in 1909.
2. ST. JAMES CLUB, 1145 Union Ave., Montreal
   Established in 1857.
3. TORONTO CLUB, 107 Wellington St. W., Toronto
   Established in 1835.
4. UNION CLUB OF BRITISH COLUMBIA, 805 Gordon St., Victoria
   Established in 1879.
5. HALIFAX CLUB, 1682 Hollis St., Halifax
   Established in 1862.
6. RIDEAU CLUB, 84 Wellington St., Ottawa
   Established in 1865.
7. NATIONAL CLUB, 303 Bay St., Toronto
   Established in 1874.
8. MOUNT ROYAL CLUB, 1175 Sherbrooke St. W., Montreal
   Established in 1899.
9. VANCOUVER CLUB, 915 West Hastings St., Vancouver
   Established in 1893.
10. CALGARY PETROLEUM CLUB, 319 5th Ave. S.W., Calgary
    Established in 1913.

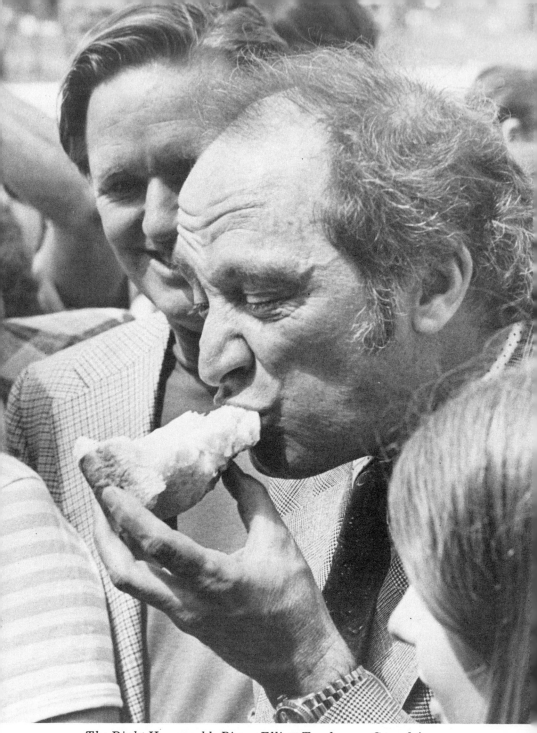

The Right Honourable Pierre Elliott Trudeau — Canada's best-known separated Canadian.

10 WELL-KNOWN DIVORCED OR SEPARATED CANADIANS

1. PIERRE ELLIOTT TRUDEAU, prime minister
2. RENÉ LÉVESQUE, Quebec premier
3. FRANCIS FOX, former Solicitor-General
4. GORDON LIGHTFOOT, singer
5. PETER WORTHINGTON, Editor-in-Chief, *The Toronto Sun*
6. ADRIENNE CLARKSON, television performer, author
7. CAROLE TAYLOR, former television star
8. PETER C. NEWMAN, Editor, *Maclean's* Magazine
9. LYNNE GORDON, broadcaster, head of Ontario Women's Task Force
10. JOYCE DAVIDSON, television broadcaster

10 CORPULENT CANADIANS

1. JUDY LaMARSH, lawyer
2. SAM SHOPSOWITZ, restaurateur
3. BARBARA HAMILTON, actress, comedienne
4. JOE PICCININNI, Toronto Alderman
5. E.P. TAYLOR, industrialist
6. HARRY BRAY, Vice-Chairman, Ontario Securities Commission
7. RON BASFORD, Solicitor-General of Canada
8. LORNE 'GUMP' WORSLEY, hockey player
9. RAYMOND BURR, actor
10. LARRY ZOLF, T.V. commentator

10 LEAN CANADIANS

1. JOHN KENNETH GALBRAITH, economist
2. ROBERT BOURASSA, politician
3. GREG JOY, athlete
4. DAVID BROADFOOT, comedian
5. CAROLE TAYLOR, T.V. commentator
6. MARSHALL McLUHAN, visionary
7. FRANCES HYLAND, actress
8. JOHN EVANS, politician
9. GUY LAFLEUR, hockey player
10. JEROME DRAYTON, marathon runner

10 GREAT CANADIAN QUOTATIONS ON WOMAN

1. Youth and charm in a woman makes any deviation from ordinary conduct doubly reprehensible.

   Robertson Davies, *Leaven of Malice*, 1954

2. No woman wants to be loved; she only wants to love.

   James de Mille, *A Strange Manuscript*, 1888

3. A woman wants to be taken, not adored.

   Frederick P. Grove, *Settlers of the Marsh*, 1925

4. I have always found that the way to a woman's heart lies through her child.

   T.C. Haliburton, *Sam Slick*, 1836

5. The woman who enriches her husband with her admiration and her ready response gets her reward on earth, from her husband.

   Marion Hilliard, *A Woman Doctor Looks at Love and Life*, 1956

6. At certain moments, even an ugly woman, if she has lived for some time with the wind and the sun, can be sexually attractive.

   Irving Layton, *Vacation in la Voiselle*, 1946

7. In point of intellect, the average woman cannot reason and think. But she can argue.

   Stephen Leacock, Preface to *Winnowed Wisdom*, 1926

"In point of intellect, the average woman cannot reason or think. But she can argue!"

Stephen Leacock
Winnowed Wisdom, 1926

Irving Layton, the controversial Canadian poet, observes that "At certain moments, even an ugly woman, if she has lived for some time with the wind and the sun, can be sexually attractive."

8. When a woman closes her lips up tight, you may depend on it she is going to bite.

   J.J. Proctor, *The Philosopher in the Clearing*, 1897

9. The heart of a woman is seldom cold to those who cherish her offspring.

   Catharine Parr Traill, *Canadian Crusoes*, 1850

10. Get all the lasting things out o' men you can. Small, costly things like joolery that is easy to carry 'round, and can always be pawned, if necessary.

    Mazo de la Roche, *Delight*, 1926

THE 10 MOST IMPORTANT WOMEN IN CANADA

1. PAULINE McGIBBON

First woman chancellor of the University of Toronto, first woman Lieutenant-Governor (Ontario).

2. MARGARET ATWOOD

Writer of international acclaim.

3. DORIS ANDERSON

Masterminded *Chatelaine* magazine to new heights of appeal (and profitability) as its editor, now an author.

4. SYLVIA OSTRY

Chairman, Economic Council of Canada, former head of Statistics Canada, a formidable achiever (and hostess) in the highest levels of the civil service.

5. DR. PAULINE JEWETT

Politician, now President of Simon Fraser University, Vancouver.

6. JEANNE SAUVÉ

Writer, politician, now Minister of Communications, Ottawa.

7. KATE REID

Canada's foremost actress.

The Honourable Pauline McGibbon, the first woman Lieutenant-Governor of Ontario, holds one of Canada's most important posts.

8. FLORA MacDONALD

Dyed-in-the-wool politician, leadership contender, Member of Parliament for Kingston and the Islands.

9. IONA CAMPAGNOLO

Exuberant Minister of Fitness in Ottawa, taking health to the people.

10. KAREN KAIN

Prima ballerina of international calibre, beauty, and style.

Barbara Hamilton
Actress, Comedienne

Karen Kain — Canadian prima ballerina of international calibre, beauty, and style.

Laura Secord.
History proves
that she is one of
Canada's most
admirable
women.

10 OF CANADA'S
MOST ADMIRABLE WOMEN

1. LAURA SECORD

In 1813, in one night she walked 20 miles through the bush to warn Colonel James Fitzgibbon that American troops were planning a 600-man surprise attack on a British outpost.

2. MME PAULINE VANIER

Deeply involved in charitable works. As the wife of the Governor-General, the late Georges Vanier, Mme Vanier's charm, tact, and graciousness will not soon be forgotten.

3. MADELINE DE VERCHERES

In 1692, when she was 14 years old, she was alone with two younger brothers, two soldiers, an old servant, and several women with infants. The young girl held off marauding Iroquois for eight days until help arrived.

4. DR. EMILY HOWARD STOWE

In 1880 Emily Howard Stowe was permitted to practice medicine in Ontario, thus becoming Canada's first woman doctor.

5. EMILY CARR

One of Canada's foremost West Coast impressionist artists. For many years she lived alone in poverty in a small shack in the woods in British Columbia. She died in 1945.

6. MRS. AGNES MACPHAIL

A school teacher from Owen Sound, Ontario, Agnes Macphail became the first woman in Canada to be elected to Parliament.

7. MRS. CAIRINE WILSON

The first woman appointed to the Canadian Senate (in 1930). An active member of a group of suffragettes, she argued that 'persons' covered both sexes, and that women were people.

8. NELLIE McCLUNG

By the time she was 16 she had finished her schooling in Winnipeg and was teaching. Largely self-educated, she was a lecturer, teacher, and politician — a member of the Alberta Legislature. As a social reformer she fought for the vote for women and other women's issues. Author of *In Times Like These* and the novel *Sowing Seeds in Danny*, Nellie McClung died in 1951, at the age of 79.

9. MRS. ADELAIDE HOODLESS

In 1897 she founded the now world-wide Women's Institute and helped establish the Victorian Order of Nurses, the Young Women's Christian Association of Canada, the Macdonald Institute at Guelph, and the National Council of Women.

10. MRS. LOUISE McKINLEY

The first woman elected to a legislature in the British Empire — in Alberta, in 1917.

10 WAYS CANADIANS CAN RECOGNIZE A BRITISH IMMIGRANT

1. Washes and polishes his car in his driveway on Sundays.

2. Wears suspenders with his belt.

3. Drinks beer only out of a mug.

4. Prefers tea to coffee.

5. Wears brown shoes and blue socks with knee-high shorts.

6. Monotonously deplores the fact that the beer ain't like it was at 'ome.

7. Wisely prefers his dog to his wife.

8. Wisely complains about all fish and chips.

9. Pretends he's a Canadian by barbecuing (abominably).

10. Showers or bathes infrequently, claiming it's bad for the skin.

David Scott-Atkinson
Public Relations Executive
and Canadian Trend Observer

Barbara Amiel — the most beautiful woman in Canada.

THE 10 MOST BEAUTIFUL WOMEN IN CANADA

1. MS. BARBARA AMIEL, Toronto
   Sensual, purring, and feminine

2. MISS JULIE AMATO, Toronto
   Gorgeous, humorous, and sexy

3. MRS. JOHN BASSETT, Toronto
   A wonderfully expressive face, either on television or in private

4. MRS. DENNIS BLACK, Montreal
   Regal, beautiful, and utterly feminine

5. MS. ELANOR CALBES, Toronto
   Dynamite

6. THE HONOURABLE IONA CAMPAGNOLO, Ottawa
   Fantastic mixture of strength and femininity

7. MRS. W. M. HATCH, Toronto
   Classic beauty with humour just beneath the surface

8. MRS. JULIAN PORTER, Toronto
   The ultimate in sexy femininity

9. MRS. GERALD REGAN, Halifax
   Warm, smiling, and a delight

10. MRS. CAROLE TAYLOR, Vancouver
    Just plain gorgeous

John W. H. Bassett
Chairman and President
Baton Broadcasting Incorporated

*René Simard, popular singer, and one of the most attractive young
men in Canada.*

THE 10 MOST ATTRACTIVE
MEN IN CANADA

1. LANFRANCO AMATA
Director of Special Projects and Associate of Bregman & Hamann, Honorary Chairman of the Board and Director of Olivetti Canada Ltd.

2. PETER DUNCAN CURRY
President, Power Corporation of Canada Ltd.

3. JACQUES COURTOIS
Montreal lawyer

4. JOHN C. LOCKWOOD
Chairman, Carling O'Keefe Limited

5. PETER LOUGHEED
Premier of Alberta

6. GORDON PINSENT
actor, producer, director, writer

7. DONALD HARRON
actor, comedian, author

8. BORA LASKIN
Chief Justice, Supreme Court of Canada

9. MURRAY B. KOFFLER
Chairman, Koffler Stores Ltd.

10. RENÉ SIMARD
popular singer

Joan Sutton
Columnist, *The Toronto Sun*
Author, *Lovers and Others,*
Once More with Love

CANADA'S 10 WORST-DRESSED CELEBRITIES

1. RENÉ LÉVESQUE, politician
2. CHARLES TEMPLETON, author
3. PETER SWANN, cultural advisor
4. LARRY ZOLF, broadcaster
5. JUDY LaMARSH, instant authority
6. MARILYN BROOKS, designer
7. ANNE MURRAY, songster
8. JOANNE KATES, restaurant reviewer
9. ADRIENNE CLARKSON, broadcaster
10. BRYAN VAUGHAN, communications consultant

David Scott-Atkinson
Public Relations Executive
and Canadian Trend Observer

René Lévesque, Premier of Quebec — and probably Canada's worst-dressed celebrity.

5 PROMINENT CANADIANS WITH HANG-UPS

1. GLENN GOULD, agora and other phobias
2. MACKENZIE KING, fey spiritualist
3. TERRY SAWCHUCK, sick before games
4. FRANK MAHOVLICH, gentleman hockey player
5. CARL BREWER, fear of flying

Dr. Daniel Cappon
Professor in Environmental Studies
York University

Glenn Gould — a brilliant musician, but a Canadian with a hang-up.

THE 10 MOST PREVALENT CANADIAN HANG-UPS

1. AGORAPHOBIA
Fear of the vast Canadian spaces

2. OTHER PHOBIAS
Thanato — of death; lysso — of madness; claustro — of enclosed spaces; fear of flying, etc., etc.

3. BOREDOM
Producing anxiety

4. INVOLUTIONAL ENNUI
In women who don't know what to do with themselves and menopause

5. INVOLUTIONAL ENNUI
In men who don't know what to do with themselves and retirement

6. WEEDINESS
A combination of hirsuitism, acid, and other drug-headedness, lost horizons — generally infesting the West Coast

7. JUVENILE AND OTHER DELINQUENCIES

8. SEXUAL FAILURES AND DEVIANCES

9. PSYCHOSOMATIC STRESS REACTIONS
From head to belly aches

10. IDENTITY CRISIS
Personally, culturally, and nationally — except in Quebec

Dr. Daniel Cappon
Professor in Environmental Studies
York University

10 FAMOUS FOREIGN-BORN CANADIANS

1. GEORGE BELANEY (ALIAS GREY OWL—1888-1938)—BORN IN ENGLAND
Belaney emigrated to Ontario in 1903 where he became a trapper, guide, and forest ranger. He served in France in World War I for the Canadi-

George Belaney was born in England in 1888, but lived his life in Canada as an Indian under the name of "Grey Owl."   31

an Expeditionary Force. In 1918 he returned to Canada and lived the life of an Indian under the name "Grey Owl." He died on April 13, 1938.

2. ALEXANDER GRAHAM BELL (1847-1922)—BORN IN SCOTLAND

In 1874 he first transmitted sound through a telephone wire. He patented his invention and founded the Bell Telephone Company.

3. SIR MACKENZIE BOWELL (1823-1917)—BORN IN ENGLAND

Became the Prime Minister of Canada in 1894 after the death of Sir John Thompson. His term ended in 1896 when he resigned because of dissatisfaction in his Cabinet. He referred to them as a "nest of traitors."

4. TIMOTHY EATON (1834-1907)—BORN IN IRELAND

In 1869 he founded the firm of T. Eaton and Company. The company since then has become one of the largest department stores in North America.

5. SIR JOHN A. MACDONALD (1815-1891)—BORN IN SCOTLAND

The first Prime Minister of Canada, from 1867 to 1873 and again from 1878 to 1891.

6. JAMES McGILL (1744-1813)—BORN IN SCOTLAND

A member of the North West Company. From 1792 to 1796 and from 1800 to 1804 he represented the west ward of Montreal in the Legislative Assembly in Lower Canada. When he died in 1813 a large part of his estate went to found McGill University.

7. SIR ALEXANDER MACKENZIE (1822-1892)—BORN IN SCOTLAND

Prime Minister of Canada from 1873-1878. He defeated Sir John A. Macdonald in the election of 1873 because of the controversial Pacific Scandal.

8. EUGENE O'KEEFE (1827-1913)—BORN IN IRELAND

In 1861 he founded the Victoria Brewery, later the O'Keefe Brewery, of which he was president.

9. STEPHEN ROMAN (1921-   )—BORN IN SLOVAKIA

Director of: Denison Mines Ltd., Roman Corp Ltd., Lake Ontario Cement Ltd., Romandale Farms Ltd., Crown Life Insurance Co., Canadian Nuclear Assoc., Guarantee Trust Co. of Canada, Mogul of Ireland Ltd., Pacific Tin Corp., and Resperin Corp. Ltd. One of Canada's great industrialists and philanthropists.

10. ROBERT WILLIAM SERVICE (1874-1958)—BORN IN ENGLAND

Came to Canada in 1894 and worked for the Canadian Bank of Commerce in Victoria, Vancouver, and Kamloops, as well as in Yellowknife and Dawson. It was in the Yukon that he published his first book of poetry, *Songs of a Sourdough*. His best-known poems are "The Shooting of Dan McGrew," and "The Cremation of Sam McGee."

Alexander Graham Bell was born in Scotland and founded the Bell Telephone Company in Canada. 33

Marshall McLuhan set the world ablaze with his understanding that the electronic world was different from the print world.

THE 10 GREATEST THINKERS IN CANADA

1. RICHARD MAURICE BUCKE, M.D.

Bucke published a book called *Cosmic Consciousness* in 1901. A medical doctor and psychiatrist from Montreal and a graduate of McGill University, the book is subtitled, "a study in the evolution of the human mind." It was and is a pivotal work in the consciousness movement of the twentieth century.

2. WILDER PENFIELD, M.D.

A superb neurosurgeon, administrator, author, and public speaker. His last book before he died, *The Mystery of the Mind,* based on his empirical experience with a thousand brain operations, is the first scientific work to make the distinction between mind and brain. He suggests that while the brain is the hardware, the mind, is in reality, the software or even the programmer!

3. HUGH MacLENNAN

Thirty-three years ago, when he wrote *Two Solitudes,* he even then understood the rumblings that were to erupt in the October 1970 confronta-

The late Wilder Penfield, author of The Mystery of the Mind — *one of Canada's greatest thinkers.*

tion in Quebec. A man with great foresight, a good tennis player, but an enigmatic Latin teacher.

4. MARSHALL McLUHAN

He set the world ablaze with his understanding that the electronic world was different from the print world and might be causing a metamorphosis of the human species. His ideas are clear and precise, but cleverly masked with baffling prose. The roots of his ideas come from H. A. Innis, another great Canadian thinker.

5. HUMPHREY OSMOND

This thinker and catalyst of thinkers has been responsible for the flowering of innumerable ideas. He introduced Aldous Huxley to the mescaline world, causing him to write books which became the hallmark of the flower generation. He coined the term "psychedelic." He initiated, with Dr. Abram Hoffer, the field of nutritional medicine and orthomolecular psychiatry which has stirred Linus Pauling into action in his investigations of Vitamin C. His research in human typology could provide humanity with a better key to harmonious existence. He was born in England but lived in Saskatchewan.

6. GEORGE GRANT

Our most profound and provocative conservative philosopher. Lamenter of our lost nationhood and sturdy opponent of an arrogant and irreverent technology.

Northrop Frye —
Canada's foremost
literary scholar.

7. NORTHROP FRYE

Canada's foremost literary scholar. Achieved an international reputation with his *Anatomy of Criticism*. Profoundly influenced several generations of Canadian writers and critics. A legendary teacher.

8. ETIENNE GILSON

Head of the Institute of Pontifical Studies in Toronto for many years, Etienne Gilson had a magnificent perspective of ancient and medieval philosophies which he made relevant to modern man.

9. JOHN KENNETH GALBRAITH

Although his ideas have attracted great attention and he has become a prominent economist, time could very well be unkind to him. There are many of us who hope so.

10. ALEXANDER GRAHAM BELL

His invention — the telephone — has far exceeded his expectations and is now becoming essential to the use of computers. We hope it may soon free us from the lethargic grasp of Canada's Post Office.

Donald C. Webster
President
Helix Investments Limited

THE 10 MOST DISGUSTING CANADIAN HABITS

1. Drinking beer and other burp-making beverages out of bottles.

2. Chewing gum.

3. Men — not shaving on holidays and inflicting the eyesore on others.
   Women — wearing curlers in public and inflicting the eyesore on others.

4. Men — leaving the toilet seat up.
   Women — leaving the toilet seat down.

5. Public exploration of the contents of noses and ears, coupled with inspection of results.

6. Sticking gum under restaurant tables.

7. Parking in no-parking areas.

8. Leaving public washrooms in a mess.

9. Reducing below reasonable levels the use of the words "please" and "thank you."

10. Desecrating Scotch with Coke.

> David Scott-Atkinson
> Public Relations Executive and
> Canadian Trend Observer

THE 10 MOST INTERESTING PEOPLE IN CANADA

1. DR. JOHN KOVACH

Supernatural diagnostic skills coupled with supernatural mathematical brilliance and a lacing wit make this man compelling. Sadly, his battles with Establishment medicine and his intellectual restlessness have hampered his career.

2. PETER C. NEWMAN

The most interesting people are usually driven, and Peter C. Newman is a driven man. While some of his actions rankle his journalistic subordinates at *Maclean's* where Newman is Editor, he was a principal combatant in ousting *Time* from Canada and making *Maclean's* weekly. His books on fellow power brokers are remarkable.

3. HENRY SEARS

This Toronto-based architect is a brilliant theoretician and has taken his discipline to new heights, embracing sociology and psychology in helping others to design buildings and institutions which serve the soul as well as the eye.

4. MARSHALL McLUHAN

His aphorisms on the media, which roll forth in an unending stream, have crystallized much of our thinking about television, radio, and the printed word. While some still struggle with his most famous phrase "the medium is the message," who can fail to respond to his description of a newspaper as "climbing into a warm bath?"

5. CONRAD BLACK

The accumulation of wealth and power is constantly fascinating, especially so when combined with a literary flair. Using his own multi-millions, then his family's multi-millions, he gained control of Argus Corporation in a bold and sure manoeuvre. And his book *Duplessis* is one of the best.

6. PIERRE JUNEAU

When he was head of the government regulatory agency on broadcasting, Pierre Juneau towered over his fellow commissioners. His mistimed run at elective politics failed and today his usefulness to Canada is not lost but submerged in mandarin Ottawa.

7. ALLAN FOTHERINGHAM

One of the few people virtually unlurable from the easy pleasures of Vancouver, Fotheringham has parlayed his arrogance and wicked pen to preeminence in the field of journalism. His regular columns in *Maclean's* distress and provoke.

8. GARTH DRABINSKY

While Canada can produce international-calibre actors, actresses, directors, and composers, it has failed miserably in producing *producers*, the people who can meld the artistic with the financial. Perhaps it will be Garth Drabinsky, lawyer, author, and entrepreneur.

9. JOHN J. ROBINETTE

Jonathan Swift said lawyers only prove black is white and white is black. John J. Robinette surpasses Swift; as Canada's most outstanding *avocat*, his mere presence on either side of a case greatly elevates its importance.

10. MOLLY LAMB BOBAK

Far from the corridors of power and money, Molly Lamb occupies a special place in the artistic fabric of the nation. Formerly a war artist, this wisp of a lady bops around the country, frequently by bus, painting flowers, teaching, and spreading gentleness and a joyful exuberance.

Jeremy Brown
Author
Dining Out in Toronto

Peter C. Newman, the outspoken editor of Maclean's Magazine.

10 ADVANTAGES
OF BEING LEFT-HANDED

1. Taking off jar tops.

2. Losing less at one-armed bandits because we tire quicker — they're made for right-handers.

3. Winning more fencing and tennis matches because our opponents are not used to left-handers, but then again neither are we.

4. Playing baseball, because 30 per cent of the pitchers, 32 per cent of the batters, and 48 per cent of the first basemen are left-handed (15 per cent of the average population is left-handed).

5. As designers we have a better sense of design, space, and proportion.

6. We have an advantage if we have strokes. Because of the position of our speech centre we recover faster.

7. Typewriters are made for left-handed people.

8. Toilets are made for left-handed people.

9. Hebrew is a left-handed language.

10. Driving in Europe. (British cars are made for left-handed people.)

Lawrie Weiser
The Sinister Shoppe, Toronto

10 DISADVANTAGES OF
BEING LEFT-HANDED

1. Shaking hands.

2. Having dinner in a Moslem country.

3. Learning how to do up a brassiere.

4. Learning how to cut with scissors.

5. Playing a saxophone.

6. Writing in big binders.

7. Using power tools.

8. Knitting.

9. Coping with prejudice — newspaper articles that insist that left-handed people are born with brain damage and other uncomplimentary traits.

10. Right-handed people.

Lawrie Weiser
The Sinister Shoppe, Toronto

THE 10 MOST EXCLUSIVE YACHT CLUBS IN CANADA

1. ROYAL NEWFOUNDLAND YACHT CLUB, Box 214, St. John's
   Founded in 1932

2. ROYAL NOVA SCOTIA YACHT SQUADRON, Box 156, Halifax
   Founded in 1873

3. ROYAL KENNEBECASIS YACHT CLUB, Box 801, Saint John
   Founded in 1894

4. ROYAL ST. LAWRENCE YACHT CLUB, 1350 Lakeshore Dr., Dorval
   Founded in 1888

5. BRITTANIA YACHT CLUB, Box 6073, Station 'J', Ottawa
   Founded in 1887

6. KINGSTON YACHT CLUB, 13 Maitland St., Kingston
   Founded in 1896

7. ROYAL HAMILTON YACHT CLUB, Foot of McNab St., Hamilton
   Founded in 1888

8. ROYAL CANADIAN YACHT CLUB, 94 Hayden St., Toronto
   Founded in 1852

9. ROYAL VANCOUVER YACHT CLUB, 3811 Pt. Grey Rd., Vancouver
   Founded in 1903

10. ROYAL VICTORIA YACHT CLUB, 3475 Ripon Rd., Victoria
    Founded in 1892

Margaret Trudeau, the estranged wife of the Canadian Prime Minister, was born under the sign of "Virgo"!

Sir John A. Macdonald was born on January 11, 1815.

BIRTHDAYS AND ASTROLOGICAL SIGNS
OF 10 FAMOUS CANADIANS

1.	SIR JOHN A. MACDONALD	Capricorn	January 11th	(1815)
2.	SIR WILLIAM STEVENSON	Capricorn	January 11th	(1896)
3.	BOBBY ORR	Pisces	March 20th	(1948)
4.	GENEVIEVE BUJOLD	Cancer	July 1st	(1942)
5.	PIERRE BERTON	Cancer	July 12th	(1920)
6.	RUSS JACKSON	Leo	July 28th	(1936)
7.	RENÉ LÉVESQUE	Virgo	August 24th	(1922)
8.	MARGARET TRUDEAU	Virgo	September 10th	(1948)
9.	GUY LAFLEUR	Virgo	September 20th	(1951)
10.	PIERRE ELLIOTT TRUDEAU	Libra	October 18th	(1919)

THE 10 MOST
OUTSTANDING CANADIANS

1. SIR FREDERICK BANTING
   Discoverer of insulin and saviour of countless lives.

2. AIR MARSHALL WILLIAM AVERY BISHOP, V.C., D.S.O., M.C., D.F.C., French Legion of Honour and Croix de Guerre
   For creating the ideal of Canadian courage which inspired so many.

3. JACQUES CARTIER
   Who gets credit for starting it all.

4. THE GROUP OF SEVEN
   Who collectively expressed in living colour a new realization of Canadian beauty.

5. THE HONOURABLE JOSEPH HOWE
   The first Canadian to formalize the concept of freedom of the press.

Sir Frederick Banting, the discoverer of insulin — certainly one of Canada's most outstanding achievements.

6. HIS EMINENCE PAUL EMILE LEGER

Who gives Canadians an ideal of service, which, if followed, could create a soul for this nation.

7. SIR JOHN A. MACDONALD

For all the obvious reasons.

8. SIR GEORGES-ETIENNE CARTIER

For making all the obvious conditions acceptable and workable in French Canada.

9. JUDGE EMILY MURPHY

Who led the battle to declare women persons.

10. SIR WILLIAM STEPHENSON

For doing one or two of the most important war jobs in the world with dignity, modesty, and courage.

John W. H. Bassett
Chairman and President
Baton Broadcasting Incorporated

Dr. Charles H. Best had an I.Q. of 155.

ESTIMATED IQ's
OF 10 FAMOUS CANADIANS *

1.	CHARLES H. BEST	155
2.	LESTER B. PEARSON	124
3.	FREDERICK BANTING	123
4.	NORMAN BETHUNE	120
5.	STEPHEN LEACOCK	120
6.	WILLIAM LYON MACKENZIE KING	119
7.	LOUIS RIEL	118
8.	SAMUEL DE CHAMPLAIN	113
9.	SIR JOHN A. MACDONALD	112
10.	LAURA SECORD	111

*Genius is 140 and above. Normal is 85-115.

David L. Streiner
Associate Professor of Psychiatry
McMaster University

Don Harron (Charlie Farquharson) — a well-known left-handed Canadian.

10 FAMOUS LEFT-HANDED CANADIANS

1. DON HARRON (CHARLIE FARQUHARSON), actor

2. BARBARA FRUM, radio reporter

3. MARION ENGEL, writer

4. GORDON PINSENT, writer, actor, director, singer, producer

5. WARNER TROYER, investigative reporter, TV & radio personality

6. JAMES JEROME, Speaker of the House of Commons

7. DOUGLAS CREIGHTON, Publisher of the *Toronto Sun*

8. PAUL RIMSTEAD, columnist, *Toronto Sun*

9. MARIE DIONNE, one of the Dionne quintuplets

10. JOHNNY WAYNE, TV personality

Lawrie Weiser
The Sinister Shoppe, Toronto

Charles Templeton, author of Act of God, *is an instant authority on almost any subject.*

Adrienne Clarkson — an instant authority on any subject.

CANADA'S 10 GREATEST INSTANT AUTHORITIES ON ANY SUBJECT

1. CHARLES TEMPLETON, author, broadcaster

2. ADRIENNE CLARKSON, author, broadcaster

3. RICHARD ROHMER, author, lawyer

4. DORIS ANDERSON, author, former editor of *Chatelaine*

5. PIERRE BERTON, author, broadcaster

6. MORTON SHULMAN, author, doctor, former politician

7. PIERRE ELLIOTT TRUDEAU, author, Prime Minister of Canada

8. JOE CLARK, politician

9. GORDON SINCLAIR, author, broadcaster

10. LAURA SABIA, former chairman of the Task Force on Women

David Scott-Atkinson
Public Relations Executive
and Canadian Trend Observer

THE 10 PROVINCES WITH
THE LARGEST POPULATION GROWTH

	Percent of Population Growth 1967-1977
1. ONTARIO	36.0
2. QUEBEC	27.0
3. BRITISH COLUMBIA	10.7
4. ALBERTA	8.0
5. MANITOBA	4.4
6. SASKATCHEWAN	4.0
7. NOVA SCOTIA	3.6
8. NEW BRUNSWICK	3.0
9. NEWFOUNDLAND	2.4
10. PRINCE EDWARD ISLAND	0.5

Note:

NORTHWEST TERRITORIES	0.2
YUKON TERRITORY	0.1

Statistics Canada

10 PRAISEWORTHY
CANADIAN CHARACTERISTICS

1. Tolerance, to a fault.

2. Cautiousness, to a fault.

3. Self-criticism, to go along with the smugness.

4. Independently minded and hitherto enterprising.

5. Moderate in judgments.

6. Would rather parley than fight.

7. Brave in war.

8. Tendency to egalitarianism.

9. Technologically adept, good at "do-it-yourself."

10. Loyal to European heritage.

Dr. Daniel Cappon
Professor in Environmental Studies
York University

THE 10 MOST DEPLORABLE
CANADIAN CHARACTERISTICS

1. Smugness without much cause.

2. Over-earnestness.

3. Socially gauche — still.

4. A greater and silenter majority than in most nations.

5. Politically ambiguous (consistently Liberal federally and Conservative provincially).

6. Identity confusion (we don't know who we are and couldn't care less).

7. Regionally over-aware of the four points of the compass.

8. Much deflowered (ripped off economically) nation of virgin minds about to come into its own artistically.

9. Butchers of both parental languages.

10. Over-cautious, especially in praising others.

Dr. Daniel Cappon
Professor in Environmental Studies
York University

2
GEOGRAPHY

THE 10 GREATEST CANADIAN EXPLORERS

1. WILLIAM BAFFIN (1584-1622) — BORN IN ENGLAND

While attempting to discover the Northwest Passage aboard the *Discovery*, he discovered the island that now bears his name.

2. JACQUES CARTIER (1491-1557) — BORN IN FRANCE

Cartier was commissioned by King Francis I to explore the St. Lawrence River. He made three voyages. On the second, in 1535, he went as far as present-day Montreal.

3. SAMUEL DE CHAMPLAIN (1567-1635) — BORN IN FRANCE

In 1603 Champlain landed at the mouth of the St. Lawrence. In 1608 he founded the post of Quebec and spent the rest of his life attempting to make the settlement there a success. In 1627 he was appointed Governor of New France.

4. SIR JOHN FRANKLIN (1786-1847) — BORN IN ENGLAND

In 1819 he commanded an expedition to explore the Arctic coast of North America east of the Coppermine River. On his second voyage from 1825 -1827 he explored the Arctic coast both east and west of the Mackenzie River. Finally, on his last voyage in 1845, he attempted to sail from the Atlantic to the Pacific via the Northwest Passage. His ship became immobilized in ice and all the members of his expedition died.

5. SIMON FRASER (1776-1862) — BORN IN NEW YORK

Fraser was in charge of the operations of the North West Company beyond the Rocky Mountains. He explored the river that now bears his name from the Rockies to its mouth on the Pacific.

6. SIR MARTIN FROBISHER (died 1594) — BORN IN ENGLAND

Frobisher, too, sought to discover a Northwest Passage to China. During the course of his three expeditions he explored Frobisher Bay and Frobisher Strait. He was knighted for his services in the defeat of the Spanish Armada in 1588.

7. HENRY HUDSON (died 1611) — BORN IN ENGLAND

While trying to discover a Northwest Passage to Asia, Hudson explored the river that now bears his name, as well as Hudson Bay. Returning in 1611 from Hudson Bay, his crew mutinied and set him, his son, and a few others adrift aboard a small open boat. That is the last we know of him.

8. SIR ALEXANDER MACKENZIE (1764-1820) — BORN IN SCOTLAND

In 1787 he became a partner of the North West Company. In 1789 he voyaged from Fort Chipewayan at Lake Athabaska to the Arctic Ocean on the river that now bears his name.

9. JOHN PALLISER (1807-1887) — BORN IN IRELAND

In 1857 he commanded a northern expedition for the British Government, exploring Palliser Strait.

10. PIERRE ESPRIT RADISSON (1636-1710) — BORN IN FRANCE

He made several voyages west of the Great Lakes between 1654 and 1660. In 1665 he led a trading expedition to Hudson Bay, which resulted in the forming of the Hudson's Bay Company.

THE 10 LONGEST RIVERS IN CANADA

		Length
1. MACKENZIE	Begins at Great Slave Lake, runs through the western part of the Northwest Territories, and joins the Arctic Ocean in the most northwesterly corner of the Northwest Territories.	2,635 miles
2. YUKON	Begins in southern Yukon, runs through Yukon's western border and central Alaska until it meets the Pacific Ocean on the west coast.	1,979 miles
3. ST. LAWRENCE	Begins at Lake Ontario and defines Ontario's southern border with the United States. It runs east to the Atlantic Ocean.	1,900 miles
4. NELSON	It meets the Saskatchewan River on Manitoba's western border and runs north through Manitoba to Hudson Bay on Manitoba's east coast.	1,600 miles
5. COLUMBIA	Begins on British Columbia's east coast in the Rockies and runs south to the United States where it meets the Pacific Ocean on the southwest coast of Washington.	1,243 miles

The Mackenzie River, the longest river in Canada, runs for 2,635 miles.

6. SASKATCHEWAN	Meets with the North and South Saskatchewan rivers in central Saskatchewan and runs north through Manitoba to Hudson Bay on Manitoba's northeastern coast.	1,205 miles
7. PEACE	Begins on Alberta's western border in the Rockies and runs north through Alberta into Lake Athabasca.	1,195 miles
8. CHURCHILL	Begins at Lac la Rouge in central Saskatchewan and runs northeast through northern Manitoba to Hudson Bay.	1,000 miles
9. SOUTH SASKATCHEWAN	Begins in southern Alberta and runs north, where it meets the Saskatchewan River at the Saskatchewan border.	865 miles
10. FRASER	Begins in middle-eastern British Columbia in the Rockies at Williston Lake and runs southwest to the most southwestern corner of B.C., where it meets the Pacific Ocean.	850 miles

Ellesmere Island, one of Canada's largest islands, has an area of 75,767 square miles.

THE 10 LARGEST ISLANDS IN CANADA

		Area (Sq. Miles)
1. BAFFIN ISLAND	Northwest Territories	195,928
2. VICTORIA ISLAND	Northwest Territories	83,896
3. ELLESMERE ISLAND (Queen Elizabeth Islands)	Northwest Territories	75,767
4. NEWFOUNDLAND (main island)	Newfoundland	42,031
5. BANKS ISLAND	Northwest Territories	27,038
6. DEVON ISLAND	Northwest Territories	21,331
7. AXEL HEIBERG ISLAND	Northwest Territories	16,671
8. MELVILLE ISLAND	Northwest Territories	16,274
9. SOUTHAMPTON ISLAND	Northwest Territories	15,913
10. PRINCE OF WALES ISLAND	Northwest Territories	12,872

Statistics Canada

THE 10 HIGHEST
MOUNTAINS IN CANADA

		Elevation (Feet)
1. MOUNT LOGAN (St. Elias Mountains)	Yukon Territory	19,524
2. MOUNT ST. ELIAS (St. Elias Mountains)	Yukon Territory	18,008
3. MOUNT LUCANIA (St. Elias Mountains)	Yukon Territory	17,147
4. KING PEAK (St. Elias Mountains)	Yukon Territory	16,971
5. MOUNT STEELE (St. Elias Mountains)	Yukon Territory	16,644
6. MOUNT WOOD (St. Elias Mountains)	Yukon Territory	15,885
7. MOUNT VANCOUVER (St. Elias Mountains)	Yukon Territory	15,700
8. FAIRWEATHER MOUNTAIN (St. Elias Mountains)	British Columbia	15,300
9. MOUNT HUBBARD (St. Elias Mountains)	Yukon Territory	15,015
10. MOUNT WALSH (St. Elias Mountains)	Yukon Territory	14,780

Statistics Canada

10 AMAZING FACTS ABOUT
CANADIAN GEOGRAPHY

1. Middle Island, Lake Erie, Ontario, is farther south than the California–Oregon border.

2. Canada has more fresh water than any other country in the world — 290,000 square miles of it.

3. There are 30 changes of crew on a freight train travelling from Vancouver to Halifax. Why? Because of a union rule that allows a workspan of only a hundred miles per worker.

4. Forty-eight per cent of Vancouver's inhabitants have not completed Grade Ten!

5. Ninety per cent of Canadians are wedged within two hundred miles of the U.S.-Canadian border.

6. Canada has the world's largest freshwater island — Manitoulin Island in Lake Huron.

7. Canada has the highest tides in the world. The Bay of Fundy, which separates New Brunswick from Nova Scotia, has average tides of 36 feet. They can, however, rise as high as 56 feet.

8. Canada has only six people per square mile. (The United States has 50; Europe has 80.)

9. Only 13 per cent of Canada's population are actually bilingual; that is, English and French speaking.

10. There are 36 cities in the world that are colder than Canada's coldest city. Canada's coldest is Regina, and it ranks 37th.

THE 10 LARGEST NATIVE CANADIAN TREES

	Maximum Height	Average Height	Average Diameter	Where Found
1. Douglas Fir	300 ft.	150-200 ft.	6-8 ft.	PC
2. Sitka Spruce	280 ft.	150-200 ft.	3-6 ft.	PC
3. Western Red Cedar	200+ ft.	150-200 ft.	3-8 ft.	PC
4. Western Larch	200 ft.	150-180 ft.	3-4 ft.	PC
5. Western White Pine	200 ft.	100-150 ft.	2-5 ft.	PC
6. Sycamore	150 ft.	100-120 ft.	3-8 ft.	LGLR
7. Engelmann Spruce	180 ft.	100-120 ft.	1-3 ft.	PC
8. Eastern White Pine	175 ft.	75-100 ft.	3 ft.	LGLR
9. White Oak	100+ ft.	75-100 ft.	3-4 ft.	LGLR/LEC
10. White Spruce	120 ft.	75- 90 ft.	2-3 ft.	All over

PC   Pacific Coast

LGLR   Lower Great Lakes Region

LGLR/LEC   Lower Great Lakes Region and Lower East Coast

All over   Found in most parts of Canada

THE 10 LARGEST NATIVE LINGUISTIC GROUPS IN CANADA

		Number of persons
1.	ALGONKIAN	153,594
2.	ATHAPASCAN	22,657
3.	IROQUOIAN	22,304
4.	SALISHAN	20,989
5.	WAKASHAN	8,217
6.	TSIMSHIAN	7,730
7.	SIOUAN	6,212
8.	HAIDA	1,367
9.	TLINGIT	491
10.	KOOTENAY	446

Department of Indian Affairs and Northern Development

THE 10 MOST POPULOUS PROVINCES IN CANADA

		Population
1.	ONTARIO	8,394,000
2.	QUEBEC	6,285,000
3.	BRITISH COLUMBIA	2,512,000
4.	ALBERTA	1,867,000
5.	MANITOBA	1,033,000
6.	SASKATCHEWAN	945,000
7.	NOVA SCOTIA	836,000
8.	NEW BRUNSWICK	694,000
9.	NEWFOUNDLAND	558,000
10.	PRINCE EDWARD ISLAND	122,000
Note: Northwest Territories and Yukon		60,000

Statistics Canada

Toronto, Canada's largest city, has a population of almost 3,000,000.

THE 10 LARGEST CITIES
IN CANADA

	Number of Persons
1. TORONTO, Ontario	2,803,101
2. MONTREAL, Quebec	2,802,485
3. VANCOUVER, British Columbia	1,166,348
4. WINNIPEG, Manitoba	578,217
5. EDMONTON, Alberta	554,228
6. QUEBEC, Quebec	542,228
7. HAMILTON, Ontario	529,371
8. OTTAWA, Ontario	521,341
9. CALGARY, Alberta	469,917
10. ST. CATHARINES-NIAGARA, Ontario	301,921

Statistics Canada

THE 10 LARGEST FRESHWATER LAKES IN CANADA

	Canadian Area (square miles)	Total Area (square miles)
1. LAKE HURON (Ontario, U.S.)	13,675	23,010
2. GREAT BEAR LAKE (NWT)	12,275	
3. LAKE SUPERIOR (Ontario, U.S.)	11,200	32,159
4. GREAT SLAVE LAKE (NWT)	11,031	
5. LAKE WINNIPEG (Manitoba)	9,417	
6. LAKE ERIE (Ontario, U.S.)	5,094	9,940
7. LAKE ONTARIO (Ontario, U.S.)	3,727	7,540
8. LAKE ATHABASCA (Alberta, Saskatchewan)	3,064	
9. REINDEER LAKE (Manitoba, Saskatchewan)	2,568	
10. SMALLWOOD RESERVOIR (Newfoundland)	2,500	

Statistics Canada

As much as 13,675 square miles of Lake Huron lie within the Canadian border. The Lake's total area is 23,010 square miles.

THE 10 MOST SIGNIFICANT
MAPS OF CANADA

1. WORLD MAP   BY JUAN DE LA COSA   (1500 A.D.)

Manuscript map in Naval Museum, Madrid. *Earliest map known to show discoveries of any part of Canada.* Five English standards, and the words "Sea discovered by the English," indicate the explorations of the Cabots in 1497 and 1498.

2. WORLD MAP   BY JOHN RUYSCH   (1508 A.D.)

Printed map from the 1508 edition of Ptolemy. Shows Cabot's discoveries joined to Asia. The peninsula, which represents part of Newfoundland, bears the name "Terra Nova." *First map to contain any name for what was to become Canada.*

3. WORLD MAP   BY DIEGO RIBERO   (1529 A.D.)

Printed map in Weimar Library. Shows the explorations of Giovanni da Verrazano along eastern coast of North America in 1524. First explorer to be sent out by France to New World; first to discover entrance to Gulf of St. Lawrence.

4. WORLD MAP   BY PIERRE DESCELIERS   (1550)

Manuscript in British Museum. Perhaps the most beautiful of a group of World maps made at Dieppe from about 1540. Shows the discoveries of Jacques Cartier. These maps were apparently the first to use the word "Canada" to represent the area around the St. Lawrence. Before that a number of names had been used — Terra Nova, Baccalearum, Francisca.

5. WORLD MAP   BY FURLANI AND CAMOCIO   (1562)

The second state of this map is probably the first *printed map* to bear the name "Canada." Also shows the American continent joined to Asia.

6. MAP OF NEW FRANCE   BY SAMUEL DE CHAMPLAIN (1632)

Champlain's final map which clearly shows the water systems of northeastern America — the St. Lawrence River, the Ottawa River, the Hudson River, and Hudson Bay. Although Champlain had only seen two of the Great Lakes, he has included four, correctly placed on this map. Only Lake Michigan is missing.

7. MAP OF CANADA   BY NICHOLAS SANSON   (1658)

First map to show all five Great Lakes, although two (Michigan and Superior) are left open-ended. The prototype for most maps of this area for the next 50 years.

8. MAP OF NORTH AMERICA, PACIFIC OCEAN, AND COAST OF RUSSIA   BY W. DE L'ISLE   (1754)

Most notable for its fantastic conception of Canada's West Coast, which includes a huge "Sea of the West" and many lakes and rivers stretching from the Pacific to Hudson Bay. It started a world-wide controversy about the American West Coast which finally resulted in James Cook's third voyage and subsequent charting of the West Coast.

9. JAMES COOK'S MAPS OF CANADA

Cook mapped much of the East Coast and the St. Lawrence during the 1750s. His is the first really accurate mapping and the best done until the middle of the nineteenth century. Years later he was the first to map the West Coast of Canada. No one map can be singled out as the most important, so they have been grouped together here as one item.

10. DAVID THOMPSON'S MAP OF NORTH WEST TERRITORY OF THE PROVINCE OF CANADA   (1792-1812)

A magnificent map, pieced together gradually over a period of 20 years of wide-ranging travels and explorations by David Thompson. The intricate river systems of northern and western Canada were mapped with incredible accuracy for the first time. The basis of mapping and exploration of the West for almost a century.

E. N. Rutherford
Map Historian

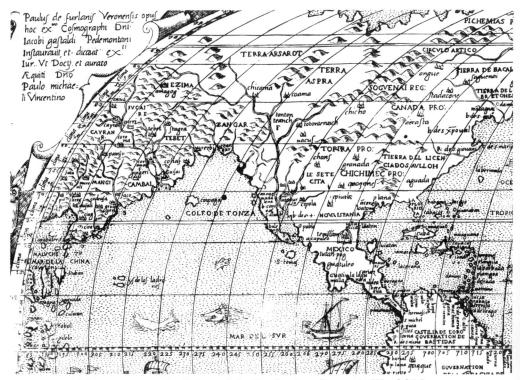

The rare second edition of the Furlani – Camocio World Map, published in 1562, showed the word Canada *for the first time on any map.*

60

THE 10 HIGHEST TEMPERATURES EVER RECORDED IN EACH OF CANADA'S PROVINCES

Province	City	Temperature	Date
1. Saskatchewan	Regina	110° F	July 5, 1937
2. Manitoba	Winnipeg	108° F	July 11, 1936
3. British Columbia	Kamloops	107° F	July 27, 1939
4. Ontario	Toronto	105° F	July 8, 1936
5. Nova Scotia	Halifax	99° F	July 10, 1912
6. Alberta	Edmonton	99° F	June 29, 1937
7. Prince Edward Island	Charlottetown	98° F	August 19, 1935
8. Quebec	Montreal	97° F	July 1, 1931
	Quebec City	97° F	July 17, 1953
9. New Brunswick	Saint John	93° F	August 8, 1945
10. Newfoundland	St. John's	93° F	August 14, 1976

Note:

Yukon	Whitehorse	94° F	June 14, 1969
Northwest Territories	Yellowknife	90° F	June 14, 1969

Statistics Canada

61

THE 10 LOWEST TEMPERATURES
EVER RECORDED
IN EACH OF CANADA'S PROVINCES

Province	City	Temperature	Date
1. Quebec	Schefferville	-59°F	Feb. 7, 1950
2. British Columbia	Prince George	-58°F	Jan. 2, 1950
3. Saskatchewan	Regina	-58°F	Jan. 1, 1885
4. Alberta	Edmonton	-57°F	Jan. 19, 1886
5. Manitoba	Winnipeg	-54°F	Dec. 24, 1969
6. Ontario	Port Arthur–Fort William	-42°F	Jan. 30, 1951
7. New Brunswick	Saint John	-34°F	Feb. 11, 1948
8. Prince Edward Island	Charlottetown	-23°F	Jan. 18, 1922
9. Nova Scotia	Halifax	-21°F	Feb. 18, 1922
10. Newfoundland	St. John's	-21°F	Feb. 16, 1975

Note:

Yukon	Whitehorse	-62°F	Jan. 31, 1947
Northwest Territories	Yellowknife	-60°F	Jan. 31, 1947

Statistics Canada

3
CRIME

THE 10 MOST FAMOUS CANADIAN CRIMINALS

1. NORMAN (RED) RYAN

A Toronto gang leader and bank robber of the late 1920s, Ryan was sentenced to life imprisonment and escaped from Kingston Penitentiary. Captured and sent back, he became Canada's most written-about prisoner. He was proclaimed as an example that our prison system *was* working and was released mostly because of the personal intervention of the then prime minister, R.B. Bennett. Ryan came out in a blaze of glory and went down in a blaze of police gunfire in a Sarnia liquor store in 1936 after he killed a policeman (with other members of a gang with whom he had served time in Kingston). He returned to crime despite the front page stories ghosted under his byline that crime didn't pay.

2. ALBERT GUAY

From Quebec City, Guay was hanged for organizing the first airline bombing in 1948. He had a jeweller (who was also hanged) make a time bomb to blow up the plane so he could collect the insurance on his wife's life. She was on the plane, which blew up, not over the St. Lawrence where it would have sunk, but on land, where experts detected the smell of dynamite.

3. EDWIN ALONZO BOYD

The son of a Toronto policeman, he masterminded a gang of bank robbers and eventual killers of a Toronto detective in 1952. Boyd, together with his gang, twice broke out of the Toronto jail where he was serving his sentence.

4. GERRARD DENNIS

A St. Catharines man, he became the famous "Raffles," the man who stole millions of dollars in diamonds from the homes of Hollywood millionaires and movie stars. He also robbed homes in the best areas of Westchester County, New York. His exploits were made into a movie about a jewel thief. He started his crime career in Toronto.

5. EVELYN DICK

A comely young Hamilton woman, she was convicted of manslaughter and eventually served a life-term in Kingston Penitentiary. In 1946 she was arrested and charged with the torso murder of her husband, a case which caused a sensation in the press, after her baby was found encased in a bag of cement in her bedroom cupboard. She was sentenced to hang, but the jury's

Norman (Red) Ryan — the notorious Toronto Gang leader and bank robber.

verdict was upset on appeal because police hadn't warned Mrs. Dick that she was being charged with murder before taking down her rambling statements in which she tried to explain John Dick's death. The life term was for killing the baby.

6. PETER DEMETER

A millionaire contractor in Mississauga, just outside Metropolitan Toronto, Demeter was sentenced to life imprisonment in 1974 for arranging the murder of his wife so he could collect $1 million life insurance. His beautiful wife was battered to death in their garage. Demeter thought he had a foolproof alibi of being away shopping with friends. Demeter's case inspired a book and a fictional movie.

7. LUCIUS (CHRISTMAS TIME) PARMALEE

Probably the greatest forger Canada has ever produced, Parmalee also plied his trade in large U.S. cities. He got the name "Christmas Time" because in the festive season he often used clergymen's garb and became friendly with bank tellers, persuading them to put over rubber cheques for large sums of money. Year after year, bank tellers were warned about him, but invariably he was successful in making them believe he was a kindly minister helping the poor at Yuletide.

8. STANLEY BUCKOWSKI

A Toronto criminal, Buckowski was involved in a bizarre double murder after killing a man who chased him after a supermarket hold-up in 1950. He was put to death in San Quentin for killing a woman in Los Angeles during a house robbery. He made headlines when he confessed to a Toronto *Star* reporter that he had killed two people just north of Toronto because he wanted their car to make good his escape.

9. WILBERT COFFIN

Executed in a controversial case in the late 1940s after two American hunters were murdered in the woods, Coffin was arrested after the dead men's effects were traced to a second-hand store and after a woman friend informed on him. But many thought he was innocent and that he had been framed in order to persuade U.S. hunters to come back to Quebec to hunt. A book was written on the case, one of the most publicized cases of the era.

10. STEPHEN TRUSCOTT

As a 14-year-old boy, he was convicted and sentenced to death at Goderich in 1958 for the rape-murder of a nine-year-old girl. Word that Canada was going to put to death a child of such tender years went around the world; the sentence was commuted and he was taken out of the penitentiary to a reformatory. A book was written casting doubt on the boy's guilt and eventually the case was referred to the Supreme Court of Canada in a precedent-setting move. They ruled 8 to 1 on his guilt. He has served his term and is now free.

Gwynn (Jocko) Thomas,
Police Reporter
Toronto Star

7 FAMOUS CANADIAN CRIMES

1. AMBROSE J. SMALL, 1919

The disappearance and assumed death by foul play of Ambrose Small in 1919 resulted in newspaper headlines that continued right up to the 1940s. The case became internationally famous because Small sold his theatrical interests for a million dollars and was never seen again. His private secretary, a man, was arrested in a lumber camp in Oregon and charged with embezzling Small's bonds, a large sum, and sentenced to imprisonment. However, neither Small nor his body was ever seen again.

2. JOHN LABATT, 1936

The kidnapping of John Labatt, the London, Ontario, brewer, was the first ransom kidnapping in Canada after numerous ones had made headlines in the United States, including the kidnapping of the Charles A. Lindberg baby. He was abducted from his car near London while on his way to his office and then held in a Muskoka cottage while his kidnappers sought to get $50,000. He was eventually released without any ransom being paid.

3. THE BLACK DONNELLYS, 1880

The barbaric Donnelly feud was an almost endless series of depredations exemplifying human depravity at its worst. Lasting for nearly thirty-three years — a succession of murders, gang wars, robberies, mass arson, derailed trains, mutilations, and barbarisms — it resulted in the slaughter of the entire "Black" Donnelly family at Lucan in Ontario by citizens of the town.

4. ROCCO PERRI, 1944

The disappearance and assumed underworld murder of Rocco Perri, one-time king of the bootleggers and top Ontario Mafia gangster remains a mystery. Perri was interned when Italy invaded France and entered World War II on the side of the Axis. He was released from internment on the condition that he report weekly to the RCMP in Hamilton where he lived. He vanished in 1944 and was never seen again. Police believe he was killed and thrown into Hamilton Bay in "cement shoes" because they could not take the chance or investigate into the possibility that he had made a deal with legal authorities in order to get his release from the internment camp.

5. TORONTO UNION STATION ROBBERY, 1928

The $250,000 railway mail car robbery at the Toronto Union Station in 1928 resulted in several arrests. Although a similar sum has been stolen in a bank robbery in recent years, the $250,000 in those days ranked with the largest amount ever stolen in a North American robbery. It was a daring midnight raid.

6. CHRISTINE KETTLEWELL, 1947

The strange death of Christine Kettlewell in 1947, while she was on her honeymoon with her husband Jack, resulted in macabre headlines. She was found with head injuries at the edge of the Severn River near the remains of the cottage where she and her husband were staying. Her husband's friend, Ronald Barrie, a New Toronto builder, owned the cottage and actually went on the honeymoon with the newlyweds. He was in the cottage when it burned down. Kettlewell was injured, but Barrie somehow escaped without harm. The ensuing inquest was covered extensively by the press and resulted in a verdict that Christine was murdered by a person or persons unknown. This verdict was returned despite a suicide note written in her handwriting, and the startling evidence that double indemnity insurance had been taken out in case of accident — with Barrie as the beneficiary.

7. THE "HOT STOVE" MURDER, 1940

The "Hot Stove" murder case in Flanders near Atikokan, in northwestern Ontario in 1940, revealed that Beatrice Casnig had been cruelly tortured on a stove in an attempt to make her reveal the hiding place of money she had buried — proceeds from bootlegging. Three of four men were found guilty of the murder and were hanged in Fort Frances after a sensational trial. One was the husband of the slain woman's daughter who had actually planned the killing.

Gwynn (Jocko) Thomas
Police Reporter
Toronto Star

THE 10 CRIMES MOST COMMONLY COMMITTED IN CANADA

	Number of Offences
1. Theft of $200 or under	459,192
2. Provincial Statutes (except traffic)	368,716
3. Other Criminal Code (except traffic)	366,714
4. Breaking and Entering	233,362
5. Assaults (not indecent)	94,750
6. Theft, Motor Vehicle	83,309
7. Municipal By-laws (except traffic)	81,306
8. Theft over $200	79,745
9. Fraud	75,873
10. Narcotics Control Act (Federal Statutes)	53,030

Statistics Canada

THE 5 MOST FAMOUS
MODERN CANADIAN SWINDLES

1. THE RACAN FRAUD

Undoubtedly Canada's best — carried out with flair, impudence, and total effrontery. International swindler Elias Rabbiah came to Canada in 1959 just one jump ahead of the police of Italy, Israel, and South Africa. In 1962 Rabbiah announced the discovery of a wonderful new photocopy machine that would copy anything for pennies on plain paper, but the machine never existed except in his imagination. He conned the newspapers, the business world, and numerous Toronto luminaries into investing tens of millions of dollars — all of which disappeared with him when the truth came out. When last heard of he was leading the good life on the Riviera.

2. ATLANTIC ACCEPTANCE

Outwardly a highly respectable finance and trust company until June 1965, when a cheque that they issued for five million dollars bounced. When the smoke cleared it turned out that Atlantic had been the front for dozens of frauds and swindles, all of which were desperately being manipulated by President C. Powell Morgan. Thousands of people lost their life savings. Powell died of leukemia before he could be charged.

3. WINDFALL

In 1963 the Texas Gulf Company made a massive base metal discovery in Northern Ontario and kept it a secret for months, while insiders of that firm bought up the stock. This massive chicanery was followed by dozens of promoters buying up land around the Texas Gulf discovery and peddling stock on the basis of proximity. The greatest hysteria surrounded a tiny company called "Windfall," owned by prominent prospector and promoter Viola MacMillan. The stock went from pennies up to over $5 on rumours that a huge find had been made, but in actual fact the drill-hole results, which had shown nothing, had been kept secret while the stock hysteria proceeded. Mrs. MacMillan was subsequently convicted of wash trading and was sentenced to nine months in prison, but after a few weeks she was quietly released.

4. PAN AMERICAN MINES

A case of Howard Hughes and the promoters. Frauds in Toronto are carried out by outsiders despite the law; in Montreal the criminals combine with the lawmakers to swindle the public. Pan American was a classic example, whereby millions of dollars of worthless stock was issued using the name of Howard Eckersley, Hughes's personal assistant. Behind the company was Andy McNaughton and an assortment of thugs and prominent officials. The public lost everything, and numerous charges were later laid but no one went to jail. Andy McNaughton has since gone on to greater glories in the promotion of laetrile.

5. THE I.O.S. COLLAPSE

The I.O.S. collapse was the world's greatest swindle. Founded in the mid-1960s by superpromoter Bernie Cornfeld, this huge fund collapsed in 1970 because of imprudent investments and poor management. In the midst of the company's travails, super-swindler Robert Vesco used the I.O.S. nominal Toronto headquarters to grab control of the firm. When the smoke had cleared, Vesco had departed for Costa Rica, taking some 260 million dollars with him and leaving the shareholders and the Canadian authorities piles of worthless paper. As of this writing, Vesco has not served a day in jail and is living like a king in Central America.

Morton Shulman
Author
Anyone Can Make a Million

THE 10 MOST COMMON RELATIONSHIPS OF MURDERERS TO VICTIMS

	Percentage of Murders
1. Immediate family	22.6
2. Unsolved	17.5
3. Casual acquaintance	15.3
4. During commission of another criminal act	9.4
5. Common-law family	9.0
6. No known relationship	8.6
7. Close acquaintance	8.2
8. Kinship	5.6
9. Lover's quarrel and/or triangle	2.6
10. Business relationship	1.2

Statistics Canada

THE 16 GREATEST PROBLEMS FACING LAW ENFORCEMENT AGENCIES IN CANADA

1. Deterioration of any consensus on moral norms — too many differences of opinion on what is right and what is wrong.

2. People's general apathy about disturbances, maladjustments, or injustices in their community as long as their ox is not being gored.

3. The adoption by many people of an obnoxious and offensive attitude when caught committing even a minor legal offence, such as parking in a prohibited area or exceeding the speed limit.

4. The demand by most people of their "rights," with a complete neglect of their "obligations" or "duties."

5. The "facts" as presented by their multi-faceted different forms, content, and emphasis by the various media.

6. The rise in importance, influence, and volubility of the paid mercenaries in many new public and semi-public citizens' groups and agencies that have sprung up in recent years.

7. The consistent weakening of laws, which are supposed to be designed to benefit the weak and innocent, but which work to the advantage of the experienced wrong-doer.

8. The extreme leniency in the courts and inconsistency of sentencing.

9. Lack of a proper diversion program system — rather than just keeping offenders locked up.

10. Constant threats of budgetary restraints from one side, and demands for higher remuneration and benefits from the other.

11. The difficulty of determining a proper role for the police to follow during the course of a public demonstration or strike which gets out of control.

12. The problem of how to invoke an effective, impartial, unbigoted, non-racist immigration policy which screens out immigrants and visitors with criminal propensities.

13. The problem of dramatizing the seriousness of the white-collar crime and placing more emphasis and resources on its solution, prosecution, and conviction.

14. The problem of training a special breed of police officer to match in skill, acumen, and brilliance, that of the computer crime rip-off artist.

15. The laying of a groundwork of defence against the kind of senseless "red brigade" terrorism extant in various Western European democracies.

16. The increase of economic discontent and political divisiveness in the country, with a resultant loss in confidence in all properly constituted authority which hampers law enforcment and tranquility in the community.

His Honour Judge Philip Givens
Chairman
Board of Commissioners
Metropolitan Toronto Police Force

THE 10 MOST COMMON VICTIM-TO-ATTACKER RAPE RELATIONSHIPS

Rape is technically defined under the Criminal Code of Canada, section 143, as follows:

"A male person commits rape when he has sexual intercourse with a female person who is not his wife,
a) Without her consent
b) With her consent if the consent
    i) is extorted by threat or fear of bodily harm
    ii) is obtained by impersonating her husband, or
    iii) is obtained by false and fraudulent representation
    as to the nature and quality of the act."

1. Stranger	32%	6. Relative*	8%
2. Platonic Friend	12%	7. Co-Worker	2%
3. Casual Acquaintance	12%	8. Neighbour	2%
4. Trusting Initial Meeting	12%	9. Ex-Spouse/Boyfriend	2%
5. Friend of Friend	8%	10. Spouse	2%

*Includes parents and siblings

Toronto Rape Crisis Centre

71

THE 10 MOST COMMON CIRCUMSTANCES OF RAPE ATTACK *

1. An unexpected attack during a normal course of events with family, friends, etc.	35%
2. A trusting initial meeting after an outing other than at a pub.	13%
3. A surprise attack at a location other than on the street.	13%
4. A surprise attack on the street	11%
5. Breaking and entering the victim's home	7%
6. Related to a party	7%
7. A trusting initial meeting after an outing at a pub	5%
8. Hitch-hiking	3%
9. Other	3%
10. Letting in a serviceman, telephone user, etc.	2%

*It was noted that 40 per cent of all rapes were committed between 6 p.m. and 12 a.m. Thirty-nine per cent of all rapes occurred during the summer months.

Toronto Rape Crisis Centre

THE 10 MOST COMMON LOCATIONS FOR RAPE

1. Victim's Home	33%		6. Park/Field	3%
2. Attacker's Home	15%		7. Campus	3%
3. Street/Alley	15%		8. Parking Lot	2%
4. Car	7%		9. Office Building	2%
5. Home other than attacker's or victim's	6%		10. Rural Area	2%

Toronto Rape Crisis Centre

4
MONEY

10 GREAT CANADIAN QUOTATIONS ON MONEY

1. If genius means extraordinary energy allied to extraordinary originality, the great financier is undoubtedly a genius.

   Robertson Davies, Introduction to *Moonbeams from the Larger Lunacy* (Stephen Leacock), 1964

2. All around us there are all kinds of people prostituting their souls and their principles for money.

   Morley Callaghan, *Such Is My Beloved,* 1934

3. Make money and the whole nation will conspire to call you a gentleman.

   Robert C. Edwards, *Summer Annual,* 1920

4. There are more fortin's got by savin' than by makin'.

   T. C. Haliburton, *Sam Slick,* 1835

5. The great way to inspire brotherly love all round is to keep on getting richer and richer till you have so much money that everyone loves you.

   Stephen Leacock, *Further Foolishness,* 1916

6. Today, money speaks in much louder tones, and learning in much humbler, while both law and medicine have cut down their own status by leaning too far towards the cash.

   Arthur R. M. Lower, *Canadians in the Making*, 1958

7. Money is one of the most important elements in modern literature.

   Jack Ludwig, *Fiction for the Majors,* 1960

8. Your family may increase, and your wants will increase in proportion. Out of what fund can you satisfy their demands?

   Susanna Moodie, *Roughing It in the Bush,* 1852

9. There's too strong a smell of money here. I confess it never bothered me before. Now it does.

   Thomas H. Raddall, *A Muster to Arms*, 1954

10. What's the good of money if you can't have a little fun with it?

    Nellie L. McClung, *Sowing Seeds in Danny*, 1911

10 PIECES OF ADVICE TO CANADIANS ON HOW TO MAKE MONEY

There are three lessons for all investors and would-be investors which can be considered and stated as axiomatic rules for investment in shares.

One: While sound, selected shares are likely to be fine investments, they are just as likely to prove risky when purchased purely for speculation. To put it another way, investors are individuals who bank on the climate, while speculators bet on the weather. The climate follows an established and predictable pattern year after year and decade after decade. The weather is notoriously temperamental and changeable.

The investor buys for the long pull and reaps his profit from dividends and through the gradual growth of his capital. He banks on the historical fact that the overall trends of living costs, wages, and almost everything else are up. He calmly waits out the dips, slumps, and recessions — and even depressions — and holds on to his stocks.

The speculator buys in the hope that he can make big, short-term profits and is blind to the fact that short-term developments are highly unpredictable and are generally governed by countless variable and imponderable elements, factors, and forces.

Two: Shares should be purchased when their prices are low, not after they have risen to high levels during soaring bull market spirals. It is illogical to buy when stock, or any other, prices are at or near their peaks.

Three: An investor should know as much as he possibly can about the companies which issue the stocks in which he invests his money. Among the questions that every prospective investor should ask — and to which he should obtain clear and satisfactory answers — before buying any share are these ten:

1. What is the history of the company which issues the stock — is it a solid firm with a good reputation and seasoned, efficient management?

2. Is the company producing or dealing in goods or services for which there will be a continuing demand in the foreseeable future?

3. Is the company operating in a field which is not overcrowded, and is it in a satisfactory competitive position within that field?

4. Are company policies and operations farsighted and aggressive without calling for or involving unjustified or unreasonably hazardous expansion?

5. Will the company balance sheet stand up to close scrutiny by a critical and impartial accountant?

6. Does the company have a satisfactory earnings record, and does the price of its stock bear a reasonable relationship to those earnings?

7. Have reasonable dividends been paid regularly, and if some dividends were missed, were there good and sufficient reasons and explanations for missing them?

8. Is the company well within "safe" limits insofar as both long- and short-term borrowings are concerned?

9. Has the course followed by the price of the company's shares over the last several years been fairly regular, without any violent, wide, and apparently inexplicable swings?

10. Does the per-share value of the company's net realizable assets bear a favourable relationship to the per-share value of its stock?

Far too many people disregarded these basic investment rules during the stock-buying spree of the Roaring Twenties. I hope that present-day investors will take an example from their mistake and apply the rules in their own stock-buying operations.

J. Paul Getty
The Financial Post

THE 10 MOST COMMON PERSONAL FINANCIAL-PLANNING MISTAKES

1. Buying too much on credit.

2. Borrowing at the wrong places; for example, borrowing from a finance company when the loan would be cheaper at a bank.

3. Not paying off debt as quickly as possible, particularly credit cards and charge accounts, where the interest expense is exorbitant.

4. Owning a car when you really don't need one, or buying one more expensive than you can afford.

5. Renting instead of buying living accommodation.

6. Not budgeting for expenditures which arise irregularly, such as insurance, vacation, Christmas, TV cable, subscriptions.

7. Not budgeting at all.

8. Buying on impulse instead of shopping around and evaluating alternatives.

9. When investing, trying to make a quick buck instead of going for a slower but surer return.

10. Making investments such as savings accounts or whole life insurance policies, on which the interest rate does not keep pace with inflation, with the result that one is actually losing money.

J. Lyman MacInnis
Accountant
Touche Ross & Co.

THE 10 BEST-PERFORMING
CANADIAN EQUITY FUNDS *

	Millions	Capital Appreciation Over Last 3 years %
1. Canada Cumulative Fund	4.0	23.3
2. Growth Equity Fund	27.3	20.5
3. Industrial Equity Fund	12.4	20.2
4. Canadian Gas & Energy Fund	33.6	20.0
5. Dynamic Fund of Canada	2.4	19.6
6. Tradex Investment Fund	2.6	17.4
7. Harvard Growth Fund	2.4	17.9
8. Xanadu Fund Ltd.	1.9	16.4
9. Principal Growth Fund	16.3	14.8
10. Corporate Investors Stock Fund	4.1	14.6

*Canadian stocks only.

W. Robert Farquharson
Vice-President and Director
AGF Management Limited

THE 10 BEST-PERFORMING EQUITY FUNDS IN CANADA

		Assets in Millions	Capital Appreciation Over Last 3 years %
1.	Taurus Fund Ltd.	5.2	33.7
2.	MD Growth Investment Ltd.	n/a	33.6
3.	Templeton Growth Fund	183.6	32.5
4.	Eaton/Bay International Fund	11.7	28.8
5.	Cundill Value Fund Ltd.	10.4	28.1
6.	Principal Venture Fund Ltd.	5.3	25.9
7.	Eaton/Bay Venture Fund	12.8	24.6
8.	Canada Cumulative Fund	4.0	23.3
9.	NW Equity Fund Ltd.	1.9	22.0
10.	Industrial Equity Fund	12.4	20.7

W. Robert Farquharson
Vice-President and Director
AGF Management Limited

6 IMPRINTS ON CURRENT CANADIAN COINS

Coin	Name	Imprint
1. One cent	Penny	Maple twig
2. Five cents	Nickel	Beaver
3. Ten cents	Dime	Fishing schooner — the *Bluenose I*
4. Twenty-five cents	Quarter	Caribou
5. Fifty cents	50¢ piece	Canadian coat of arms
6. One dollar	Silver dollar	Voyageur

THE 10 BEST PERFORMING
CANADIAN STOCKS

Who says you can't make money in Canadian stocks? If you had bought the following stocks, listed on Canadian exchanges, at their 1974 lows, you would have had the following gains, based on the price as on the date of writing (June 9, 1978).

Stock	1974 Low	Current Price	Percent Rise	Industry
1. Amalgamated Bonanza Petroleum	0.95	34³/₄	3558	Oil and gas
2. Nowsco Well Service	2.125	41¹/₂	1853	Oil and gas service
3. Wainoco Oil	1.00	19¹/₄	1825	Oil and gas
4. Harlequin Enterprises	0.944	11³/₄	1145	Publishing
5. Daon Development	0.75	8¹/₂	1033	Construction and real estate
6. Woodsreef Minerals	0.05	.55	1000	Mining mainly asbestos in Australia
7. BX Development	0.45	4.60	922	Mining mainly quick-lime in Arizona
8. Quasar Petroleum	1.20	12.00	900	Oil and gas
9. OPI Ltd.	1.20	11⁷/₈	890	Oil field equipment
10. Stampede Int'l Resources	0.50	4.95	890	Various, especially as holder of "Explosafe" patent

Needless to say, Canadians have benefited greatly from the oil and gas discoveries in the last few years. If one goes back to 1970, however, Harlequin Enterprises would be the leader, with a gain of 5,994 per cent! And it's still rising.

John E. Mahoney
Author,
Buy Low Sell High
Analyst, A. E. Osler, Wills, Bickle

Sir Robert Borden is one of only four Canadians whose image appears on Canadian paper currency.

THE 8 PORTRAITS ON CANADIAN PAPER CURRENCY

		Denomination
1.	QUEEN ELIZABETH II	$1
2.	QUEEN ELIZABETH II	$2
3.	SIR WILFRID LAURIER	$5
4.	SIR JOHN A. MACDONALD	$10
5.	QUEEN ELIZABETH II	$20
6.	WILLIAM LYON MACKENZIE KING	$50
7.	SIR ROBERT BORDEN	$100
8.	QUEEN ELIZABETH II	$1,000

Bank of Canada

THE 10 BEST TAX SHELTERS IN CANADA

1. REGISTERED RETIREMENT SAVINGS PLANS

Invest the maximum the law allows. Contributions are deductible and you only pay tax when the funds are drawn down on retirement. A dollar of tax deferred ultimately becomes a dollar of tax saved.

2. REGISTERED HOME OWNERSHIP SAVINGS PLANS

Up to $1,000 per year can be deductible, to a life-time maximum of $10,000. You pay no tax when you draw the funds out of the plan if you use the funds for buying or furnishing your home, which could include your summer cottage.

3. DON'T RENT, BUY YOUR OWN HOME

Real estate is appreciating, and the profit you make when you sell your home is one of the few tax-free capital gains left.

4. HAVE YOUR WIFE PURCHASE A SECOND HOME

A condominium in the sun or a summer cottage. It will qualify as a principal residence for her, and any profit on the sale will be tax-free.

5. INVEST IN A MURB (MULTIPLE UNIT RESIDENTIAL BUILDING)

The depreciation can be used to shelter all of your other income, as well as the income from the investment itself.

6. INVEST IN FILMS OR TELEVISION PRODUCTION SYNDICATES

Your total liability, which may exceed the amount of cash you have actually laid out, can be written off against all your other income very rapidly.

7. INVEST IN OIL AND GAS DEVELOPMENT SYNDICATES

Here again there are generous tax sheltering opportunities recently introduced by the Federal Government.

8. PAY OFF YOUR HOUSE MORTGAGE AS FAST AS POSSIBLE

The interest you are paying is not deductible, but any interest you earn from outside investments is fully taxable. There is no better investment than a clear title home.

9. INVEST IN "DEEP DISCOUNT" BONDS

The interest you earn may be small, but it is fully taxable, whereas the capital gain you make when the bond is redeemed or matures will be only half taxed as capital gain.

10. FINALLY, INVEST IN LOTS OF LOTTERY TICKETS

All prizes are capital gain and tax free!

Putting aside emotional considerations, the best personal tax plan is this: divorce your wife and make her your mistress. Make a generous alimony settlement in the divorce, because the alimony you pay her is deductible by you and taxable in her hands at her personal rates. Thus you effectively split your income in half and effectively get dramatically lower tax rates (the only trouble is your wife may start to enjoy her new-found freedom and the whole thing can come unscrewed.)

I.H. Asper
Chairman and Chief Executive Officer
Can West Capital Corporation

THE 10 MOST UNUSUAL REQUESTS FOR INSURANCE MADE TO A CANADIAN INSURANCE BROKER

1. A shark fighter in enclosed lagoon with shark. Request came from American Samoa.

2. The nose of prominent Canadian hockey star and entertainer.

3. Face of model against scars. Request came from California.

4. Daredevil motorcyclist jumping Grand Canyon, Colorado.

5. Failure of TV signal from satellite for Ali/Foreman boxing match; from Zaire.

6. New York daredevil acrobat descending exterior of skyscraper suspended by teeth.

7. Failure of three trained dogs to°perform through complete, full-length movie due to accident or illness; from Hollywood.

8. To pay prize in event golfer achieves hole-in-one on predetermined hole. (Several requests for this one.)

9. To idemnify promoter of outdoor rock concert, if cancelled because of rain; from Ontario.

10. To indemnify contractor if gas systems, including oxygen in hospital, installed incorrectly; from Toronto.

Walter A. Knox
Robert H. Bradshaw Associates
Insurance Brokers

THE 10 LARGEST INSURANCE CLAIMS MADE IN CANADA

1. DIANE TENO

Five years old at time of accident, 1969, Windsor, Ontario. Crossed street to visit Good Humour truck. Struck by car. Permanently crippled. Initial award by Supreme Court of Ontario — $950,000. Appeal Court reduced award to $875,000 and judged mother to be 25 per cent at fault. Supreme Court of Canada set final award of $540,000.

2. GARY THORNTON

Fifteen years old at the time of accident, 1971, Prince George, British Columbia. Hit head in gym class. Became a quadriplegic. Lower court awarded $1.5 million. Found school board negligent in not providing adequate matting. British Columbia Appeals Court cut it to $642,000. Supreme Court of Canada had been asked to restore the $1.5 million. Supreme Court set final award of $859,628.

3. J. A. ANDREWS

Twenty-one years old at time of accident, 1972, Edmonton, Alberta. Motorcycle struck by van. Became a quadriplegic. Lower court awarded slightly more than $1 million. Provincial appeal court reduced to $516,000 and found he was 25 per cent at fault. Supreme Court of Canada set final award of $613,000.

4. BONNIE MCLEOD

Fourteen years old at time of accident, 1973, Scarborough, Ontario. Hit and run accident. Became a quadriplegic. Supreme Court of Ontario awarded $1,041,197.

5. ANDREW GAUVIN

About forty-seven years old at the time of accident, 1974, Princeton, Ontario. Struck from behind while stopped at light. Spinal cord injuries and impaired vision. Confined to wheelchair. Was paid $401,000.

6. MARY MULLINS

Forty-six years old at time of accident, 1973, Delhi, Ontario. Collided with another car at country road intersection; thrown from car. Brain damage and impaired movement on left side of body. Ontario Supreme Court awarded $257,601. Original award was reduced by 10 per cent to the above amount because she wasn't wearing seat belt.

7. BRIAN LINDEL

Nineteen years old at time of accident, 1975, Vancouver, British Columbia. No details. He was incapacitated. British Columbia Supreme Court awarded $454,000. No details as to current status.

8. TEN PEOPLE

1973, Barrie, Ontario. Bus collided with lumber-laden truck and caused 32-car pile up. 12 killed and 40 injured. Award of $297,500.

9. CORRINE LISSELL

About sixteen years old at time of accident, 1972, Courtenay, British Columbia. Passenger on motorcycle which collided with car. Paralyzed from waist down and in left arm. British Columbia Supreme Court awarded $1.1 million.

10. DR. MARISSA ZORZITTO

1975, Hamilton, Ontario. Her car was struck. Confined to wheelchair. Awarded $350,000 by county court but driver at fault was uninsured and almost penniless and so she won't collect the total amount.

U.S.A. CASES

TOM GARHAR
1974, Fort Lauderdale, Florida. Hit rock placed as deterrent to motorists. Paralyzed. Awarded $4.95 million.
RICHARD GRIMSHAW
Thirteen years old at the time of accident, 1972, San Bernadino, California. Stalled car hit from behind and gas tank exploded. Burned over 90 per cent of body. Driver was killed and her family was awarded $666,000 in damages against Ford.
SANDRA HAVLICK
1972, West Palm Beach, Florida. Car struck from behind and gas tank exploded. Circuit court awarded $3 million in damages against Ford Motor Co.

Heidi Palmer
Insurance Bureau of Canada

THE 10 HIGHEST AVERAGE WAGE-EARNING CITIES IN CANADA*

		Average Wage
1.	Sept-Iles, Que.	$12,592
2.	Oakville, Ont.	12,212
3.	Port Alberni,B.C.	11,659
4.	Mississauga, Ont.	11,298
5.	Sarnia, Ont.	11,204
6.	Ottawa, Ont.	11,099
7.	Prince George, B.C.	11,004
8.	Montreal, Que.	10,872
9.	Whitby, Ont.	10,849
10.	Swift Current, Sask.	10,781

*1977 statistics

Statistics Canada

THE 10 MOST EXPENSIVE CITIES IN CANADA FOR PURCHASING HOUSES

	City/Province	*($)*
1.	KERRISDALE (VANCOUVER), B.C.	93,000
2.	NORTH VANCOUVER, B.C.	73,000
3.	EDMONTON, ALTA.	71,000
4.	MISSISSAUGA (TORONTO), ONT.	69,000
5.	CALGARY, ALTA.	69,000
6.	SCARBOROUGH (TORONTO), ONT.	66,000
7.	VICTORIA, B.C.	66,000
8.	MONT ROYAL (MONTREAL), QUE.	65,000
9.	REGINA, SASK.	62,000
10.	OTTAWA, ONT.	62,000

Statistics Canada

THE 10 CHEAPEST CITIES IN CANADA FOR PURCHASING HOUSES *

City/Province	($)
1. CHATEAUGUAY (MONTREAL), QUE.	27,000
2. TROIS-RIVIÈRES, QUE.	30,000
3. LAVAL (MONTREAL), QUE.	33,000
4. MONCTON, N.B.	38,000
5. POINTE CLAIRE (MONTREAL), QUE.	39,000
6. CHARLOTTETOWN, P.E.I.	40,000
7. HULL, QUE.	40,000
8. SAINT JOHN, N.B.	42,000
9. ST. JOHN'S, NFLD.	45,000
10. STE. FOY (QUEBEC CITY), QUE.	45,000

*House prices are based on estimates of the "Fair Market Value"
of a comparable house. The estimates were supplied by Royal Trust
Real Estate managers across Canada. The survey house is a detached
bride bungalow, five to eight years old with three bedrooms, one-
and-one-half bathrooms, an attached garage, and full basement, but no
recreation room, fireplace, or appliances. The total area of the house
(using outside dimensions) is 1,200 sq. ft. and the dwelling is
situated on a fully serviced 6,000 sq. ft. lot. There are no
mortgages on the house.

Statistics Canada

"The world is out of work for the simple reason that the world has killed the goose that laid the golden eggs of industry."

Stephen Leacock

5
BUSINESS

10 GREAT CANADIAN
QUOTATIONS ON WORK

1. Work is a great thing to make you forget who you are entirely.

   Nathaniel A. Benson, *The Patriot,* 1930

2. When you get the feel of it there's nothing to compare with the satisfaction of hard work.

   Harry J. Boyle, *Jezebel Jessie*

3. It is necessary, in order to secure good work, that we should throw ourselves into it wholeheartedly.

   Bliss Carman, *The Kinship of Nature,* 1904

4. A man's home is where his heart is, and his heart is where his work lies.

   Ralph Connor, *The Prospector,* 1904

5. When a man's working he wants to work. Work and booze don't mix.

   M. Allerdale Grainger, *Woodsmen of the West,* 1908

6. Work, and plenty of it, saves every man.

   S. Frances Harrison, *The Forest of Bourg-Marie*, 1898

7. The world is out of work for the simple reason that the world has killed the goose that laid the golden eggs of industry.

   Stephen Leacock, *My Discovery of England,* 1922

8. No matter how good his work might be...it would never be good enough to satisfy him.

   Hugh MacLennan, *Each Man's Son,* 1951

9. If you haven't no pride in your work you haven't no pride in yourself.

   John Metcalf, *Our Mr. Benson,* 1969

10. In this country honest industry always commands respect: by it we can in time raise ourselves, and no one can keep us down.

    Catharine Parr Traill, *The Canadian Settler's Guide,* 1855

THE 10 MOST IMPORTANT WARNINGS TO ANYONE CONSIDERING BUYING COMMON STOCKS IN CANADA

1. BE SURE THAT YOUR INVESTMENT PROGRAM IS SUITED TO YOUR OVERALL FINANCIAL POSITION

Buying stocks entails a risk, and many people are in no position to take the risks involved. For instance, if you are considering how to invest your savings and you are going to need those savings, don't gamble, but rather put the money into something safe. Taxes also are an important consideration. In Canada there are real benefits to the private investor in having dividend income and there are other ways of minimizing taxes. The important thing is to assess your overall investment and tax situation carefully.

2. MAKE SURE THAT YOU DO NOT GO TO THE WRONG PEOPLE FOR INVESTMENT ADVICE

Fortunately there are laws in Canada to prevent unscrupulous stock promoters from bilking unwary investors, so chances are good you will not be exposed to out-and-out fraud. But, even among the ranks of those who are supposedly professionally qualified, there are a great many individuals who do not make money for their clients. In considering a broker or investment advisor, be sure that you go to somebody who is trustworthy, has clearly demonstrated "market feel," feels personally responsible for seeing that your portfolio does well, and is not "too busy" to pay attention to it.

3. DO NOT OVER-DIVERSIFY

If you spread your investments around and just "buy the averages," you will only do as well as the averages which, after allowing for the effects of inflation, will mean that over the past 10 years you will have lost money. At any given point only relatively few stocks show good performance. The important thing is to concentrate your efforts in the areas of greatest opportunity.

4. DON'T FORGET THAT EARNING POWER IS WHAT MAKES COMPANIES SUCCESSFUL

In the long run, what investors want from their investments is either dividends or the capital gains that result from increased values. To achieve either one the company you invest in must have good basic earning power. One thing to look for is a steady progression of increasing earnings.

5. DO NOT OVERLOOK THE FINANCIAL POSITION OF THE COMPANY YOU INVEST IN

Balance sheets are very important too. If the company's financial position is rocky, a downturn in business may create enormous problems. Furthermore, if the company has sizeable debts to pay off, it will be in no position to pay meaningful dividends.

6. DO NOT OVERLOOK THE IMPORTANCE OF GOOD MANAGEMENT

The essence of any business is a combination of money, people, and systems. If a company's management is incompetent, the company is headed for trouble, and its stock will not do well.

7. DO NOT PAY TOO MUCH FOR A STOCK

When a company has good earning power, a sound financial position, and first-class management, there is a risk that investors may, from time to time, pay a sizeable premium for the stock, a premium that may evaporate at some future date. Be sure that you are not paying too much in relation to the values that are there.

8. AVOID UNMARKETABLE SITUATIONS

You will find that if the market for a stock is thin you may have to pay up to buy it and then when you want to sell you may find that the bids have evaporated and you must take a fire-sale price.

9. DO NOT IGNORE THE PSYCHOLOGY OF THE MARKETPLACE

The interaction of the forces of supply and demand — and of greed and fear in the marketplace — can be sensed by those familiar with the market and, indeed, can be shown graphically on charts. It is important to have a feel for what is known as "the technical factors" when buying and selling stocks.

10. STICK TO YOUR GUNS AND DON'T LOSE YOUR NERVE

Having committed your funds to the marketplace, have confidence in your decision and stick with it. A classic rule is to cut one's losses when a stock goes down by more than 10 per cent of one's purchase price, but to let one's gains run. All too often investors, amateur and professional alike, are deprived of handsome profits because they sell too early.

Charles B. Loewen and Christopher Ondaatje
Loewen, Ondaatje, McCutcheon & Company Ltd.

THE 10 AREAS STILL LEFT FOR FREE ENTERPRISE IN CANADA

1. THE INVESTMENT BUSINESS

Although there have been many mergers and problems, it is still possible to operate a profitable "no frills" brokerage house.

2. TAX COUNSELLING

As the tax system and the tax burden become more complicated and more punitive, there will be a continued demand for tax advice.

3. ROCK GROUPS

Totally unregulated — can charge what they wish. If they are lucky, they can roll their successes over into T-shirts, souvenirs, etc.

4. GAS IN THE GROUND

Natural gas already discovered but not currently saleable due to Canada's temporary gas glut. If you can buy it, then at some point you can sell it — at a profit.

5. LEASING OF PERSONAL EFFECTS

Cars, furniture, paintings, jewellery — particularly jewellery — because of high insurance rates and fear of loss.

6. COMPUTER SOFTWARE AND PERIPHERAL EQUIPMENT

Good write-offs. All sorts of scientific grants.

7. COURIER SERVICES

Essentially a reflection of poor postal services. Many new services have started up; more are likely.

8. LIFE INSURANCE BROKERAGE

We are all going to die some day, and life insurance will continue to be a part of family protection and investment planning.

9. PUBLISHING

Regional newspapers. Look for possible nationalistic restrictions.

10. PROSTITUTION

Richard Robinson
President
Martonmere Securities Ltd.

Bay Street in Toronto — perhaps the last stronghold of free enterprise remaining in Canada.

There is no doubt that Robert Blair must now be listed among the 10 most powerful businessmen in Canada today.

THE 10 MOST POWERFUL BUSINESSMEN IN CANADA*

1. S. ROBERT BLAIR,
President and Chief Executive Officer, Alberta Gas Trunk Line Co.

With his $10 billion Alaska Highway gas pipeline project and his dazzling 1978 open-market acquisition of Husky Oil (outmanoeuvring both state-owned Petro-Canada and Occidental Petroleum Corp. of Los Angeles), Bob Blair suddenly and boldly emerged as a warrior to be reckoned with on the corporate warfare front. Blair and AGTL have good government connections, and he used his better understanding of the political process to win his bid to build the northern pipeline, an enormous undertaking, over powerful eastern financial establishment rivals.

2. CONRAD BLACK,
President, Argus Corporation

After Bud McDougald's death in 1978, Black — at 33 — Canada's youngest comer to the corporate power game — quickly and assertively wrested control of Toronto's fabled Argus Corporation from some of the most prominent members of the Canadian business establishment. This gave him and brother Montegu control over commercial and industrial assets worth $4 billion, with holdings that touch the life of just about every Canadian (Dominion Stores, Massey-Ferguson, Hollinger Mines, Domtar, and Standard Broadcasting), and a spectacular power base for striking out in new directions.

*1978

3. PAUL DESMARAIS,

Chairman and Chief Executive Officer, Power Corporation of Canada

French Canada's most dynamic businessman, Sudbury-born Desmarais took a run at Argus and failed, but he has built and acquired a remarkable corporate empire, the lynchpin of which is Power Corporation, the Montreal holding, management, and transportation company. In the Desmarais fold are Investor's Group, Montreal Trust, Great-West Life, Imperial Life, Laurentide Financial, Canada Steamship Lines, Davie Shipbuilding, Consolidated-Bathurst, plus other companies, broadcasting outlets, and newspapers (among them *La Presse*). His bid to take over Argus triggered the Royal Commission on Corporate Concentration.

4. K.C. IRVING,

Founder and (in his late 70s) still *patrone* of the Irving Group of companies (about 100 of them)

Perhaps Canada's last genuine tycoon and certainly one of the richest, New Brunswick industrialist Irving now lives outside Canada, presumably for tax reasons, but is said to still call the shots in the privately held Irving empire headed by his three sons. The Irving interests represent the most powerfully concentrated regional force in Canada, predominant in the Maritimes in oil refining and distribution, pulp and paper, timber, shipbuilding, newspapers, and broadcasting. K.C. and his companies have a penchant for privacy, even thumbing their noses at the Royal Commission on Corporate Concentration (and getting away with it).

5. CHARLES BRONFMAN,

Chairman of the Executive Committee of the Seagram Co.

Debonair Edgar Bronfman, as Seagram's New-York-based chief executive officer, has a publicly disclosed salary nearly twice as large as his Montreal-based brother Charles ($325,000 *vs.* $171,500). But the Bronfman family's corporate and investment clout lies with quiet, shy Charles, who, as well as being chairman of Seagram's executive committee and the chief executive officer of the House of Seagram, also heads up Cemp Investments, the thrusting Bronfman family trust, runs the Montreal Expos baseball club, gets deeply involved in many charities, and has all the power to act or not act that flows from being the pivotal force in a very rich family.

6. IAN SINCLAIR,

Chairman and Chief Executive Officer of Canadian Pacific Ltd.

At $330,000 a year, this blunt-spoken lawyer from Winnipeg is not quite the highest-paid executive in Canada (he bet a columnist a $200 dinner that his salary would never be disclosed, but lost when the U.S. Securities & Exchange Commission made it public in 1978). But he is rated as one of the best, running the world's largest transportation complex. And he is the driving force behind CP's transformation into a huge and highly diversified conglomerate (oil and gas, steel, mining; and in terms of assets, $7.5 billion, Canada's largest industrial company). Sinclair's power base is his corporate information network — he's on the boards of more than 20 blue-chip Canadian companies.

7. A. EPHRAIM DIAMOND,
Chairman and Chief Executive Officer, Cadillac Fairview Corp.

Son of a Montreal shoemaker, "Eph" Diamond graduated in engineering from Queen's University, served three war years as a Royal Canadian Navy radar officer, and now runs Canada's (and one of North America's) largest publicly owned real estate development company (assets $1.4 billion). The Reichmann family's privately owned Olympia & York Developments Ltd. may have just as much clout and be just as big, or bigger, but it keeps its financial dimensions to itself. So Diamond, more visible, more accessible, and said to be a "man without enemies," makes the list as one whose decisions in a fragmented, temperamental industry can and do have a mighty influence on the physical shape of our cities and countryside.

8. THOMAS J. BATA,
President, Bata Ltd.

Born in Czechoslovakia where his father founded the company at the turn of the century, Tom Bata now rules as the world's largest shoe manufacturer from Don Mills, Ontario (factories in 94 countries, 85,000 employees, 350 million pairs of footwear a year). And, he rules it tightly, much like a private dukedom (smoking in the head office isn't allowed). Bata, who has built whole towns around his factories, operates largely outside the glare of public company scrutiny, but he and his wife Sonya, who's on the Bata board, are quietly involved in many community-minded philanthropic activities.

9. JOHN HENDERSON MOORE,
Chairman and Chief Executive Officer, Brascan Ltd.

With Brascan ($3.3 billion in assets), Jake Moore aggressively directs one of Canada's few major pools of active corporate investment capital through what's known as the Brascan-Jonlab-Labatt "troika." A former partner in Establishment accountants Clarkson Gordon & Co., he repatriated control of Labatt's from the U.S., fought off an attempted U.S. takeover of Brascan itself, and is determined to diversify Brascan's Canadian interests (most of its assets are still tied up in Brazil). Well connected in business and banking circles, Moore's next corporate assault could create another wave of change in the Canadian business community.

10. JOHN PATRICK GALLAGHER,
Chairman and Chief Executive Officer, Dome Petroleum Ltd., Calgary

In the second half of 1978, Jack Gallagher was making a strong run to contest fellow Calgarian Bob Blair for the title of Canada's most dynamic and acquisitive oil and gas man. A frenzied round of corporate moves brought Siebens Oil & Gas Ltd. into the Gallagher fold and gave him a big chunk of TransCanada PipeLines Ltd. Born in Winnipeg, Gallagher went into the oil industry in 1937 after graduating in geology from the University of Manitoba. He built Dome Petroleum from a one-man operation (himself) to a $1.2 billion asset enterprise which, among other things, has spearheaded northern frontier exploration.

Neville J. Nankivell
Editor
The Financial Post

CANADA'S 10 MOST
SELF-RIGHTEOUS INSTITUTIONS

1. *The Toronto Star*

2. *The Globe and Mail*

3. The Canadian Broadcasting Corporation

4. Robertson Davies

5. The Liberal Party

6. The Conservative Party

7. The Liquor Control Board of Ontario

8. The Postal Workmen's Union

9. The Canadian Council of Churches

10. Dominion Stores

David Scott-Atkinson
Public Relations Executive and
Canadian Trend Observer

The Toronto Star — one of Canada's most self-righteous institutions.

THE 10 LARGEST CORPORATE
UNDERWRITINGS IN CANADA

Amount	Issuer	Date of Issue
1. $175,000,000	Bell Canada 7.84% Cumulative Redeemable Convertible Preferred Shares, Par value $25.00 per share	May 4, 1978
2. $150,000,000	Bell Canada 9.40% Debentures due February 15, 2002, at $100.00	February 15, 1977
3. $150,000,000	Inco Limited $75,000,000 — $7^{1}/_{2}\%$ Debentures due June 30, 1978, at $100.00 $75,000,000 — $8^{5}/_{8}\%$ Debentures due June 30, 1991, at $100.00	June 30, 1971
4. $145,000,000	Canada Development Corp. 8% Cumulative Redeemable Convertible Voting Class B Preferred Shares, Par value $100.00 per share	October 1, 1975
5. $140,000,000	TransCanada PipeLines Limited $8^{3}/_{4}\%$ First Mortgage Bonds (Series A & B) due July 2, 1992, at $100.00	July 11, 1972
6. $125,000,000	Bell Canada $2.28 Cumulative Redeemable Convertible Voting Preferred Shares, Par value $25.00 per share	June 26, 1975

The Bell Telephone Company raised $175,000,000 on May 4, 1978 — the largest corporate underwriting in Canada.

7. $125,000,000   IAC Limited   June 5, 1978
9$^3/8$% Secured Notes due
June 5, 1985, at $99.50

8. $125,000,000   Inco Limited   December 15, 1977
7.85% Preferred Shares, Par
value $25.00 per share

9. $125,000,000   The Seagram Company Limited   June 1, 1975
$65,000,000 — 9$^1/2$% Debentures
due June 1, 1980, at $100.00
$60,000,000 — 10$^7/8$% Debentures
due June 1, 1995, at $99.75

10. $125,000,000   Shell Canada Limited   January 19, 1978
9$^3/8$% Debentures due   .
March 15, 2003, at $100.00

David W. Kerr,
McLeod, Young, Weir Limited

THE TOP 10 MERCHANDISERS
IN CANADA RANKED BY SALES

Company (Head Office)	1977/1978 $'000
1. George Weston Ltd.* (Toronto)	4,590,090
2. Canada Safeway Ltd. (Winnipeg)	2,581,893
3. Dominion Stores Ltd. (Toronto)	2,215,836
4. Simpsons-Sears Ltd. (Toronto)	2,093,378
5. Steinberg Inc. (Montreal)	1,767,687
6. Hudson's Bay Co. (Winnipeg)	1,411,296**
7. F.W. Woolworth Co. (Toronto)	1,209,792
8. Oshawa Group Ltd. (Toronto)	1,205,805
9. Provigo Inc. (Montreal)	1,201,953
10. Canadian Tire Corporation Ltd. (Toronto)	718,114

*Corporate secrecy and corporate concentration keep some names off the merchandisers' list:

T. Eaton Co. (private) — sales probably $1.2 billion.
Loblaw Co. ($3.7 billion), Kelly Douglas & Co. ($1 billion) and Westfair Foods Ltd. ($505 million) are all included in sales figure of parent George Weston Ltd.

**Excludes fur consignments $283 million.

The Financial Post

Galen Weston, when he was married in 1966. He now heads George Weston Limited — Canada's largest merchandising company.

CANADA'S 10 LARGEST ORE
BODIES AND WHO OWNS THEM

Producers	Ore/Short Tons	Metal Content	
1. INCO Limited	407,000,000	6,900,000	nickel
		4,300,000	copper
2. Lornex Mining Corp. Ltd.	400,000,000	1,600,000	copper
		56,000	molybdenum
3. Rio Algom Ltd.	170,000,000	125,000	uranium
4. Denison Mines Ltd.	170,000,000	125,000	uranium
5. Brunswick Mining and Smelting Corp. Ltd.	122,000,000	11,163,000	zinc
		4,502,000	lead
6. Texas Gulf Inc. — Kidd Creek	119,000,000	5,986,000	zinc
		3,332,000	copper
7. Cominco Ltd. —Sullivan Mines	55,000,000	3,000,000	zinc
		3,000,000	lead
8. Cyprus Anvil Mining Corp.	41,000,000	2,132,000	zinc
		1,394,000	lead
9. Valley Copper Mines Ltd. (undeveloped)	800,000	3,840,000	copper
10. Gibraltar Mines Ltd.	300,000	1,020,000	copper

Henry Reimer
Loewen, Ondaatje, McCutcheon & Company Ltd.

Inco Limited owns Canada's largest ore body, estimated to be 407,000,000 short tons.

THE 10 MOST PROFITABLE INDUSTRIAL COMPANIES IN CANADA RANKED BY NET INCOME

Company (Head Office)	1977/1978 $'000
1. Imperial Oil Ltd. (Toronto)	289,000
2. Bell Canada (Montreal)	286,208
3. Canadian Pacific Ltd. (Montreal)	239,862
4. Alcan Aluminium Ltd. (Montreal)	214,302*
5. Gulf Canada Ltd. (Toronto)	185,000
6. General Motors of Canada Ltd. (Oshawa)	180,640
7. Shell Canada Ltd. (Toronto)	154,587
8. Brascan Ltd. (Toronto)	154,420*
9. Inco Ltd. (Toronto)	106,200*
10. IBM Canada Ltd. (Toronto)	98,167

*Accounts stated in U.S. Funds. Converted at average rate during fiscal year.

The Financial Post

Imperial Oil Limited has earnings of over $289,000,000 — Canada's most profitable industrial company.

THE 10 LARGEST INDUSTRIAL COMPANIES IN CANADA RANKED BY ASSETS

Company (Head Office)	1977/1978 $'000
1. Canadian Pacific Ltd. (Montreal)	7,357,419
2. Bell Canada (Montreal)	7,330,694
3. Inco Ltd. (Toronto)	4,460,516*
4. Alcan Aluminium Ltd. (Montreal)	3,724,332*
5. Imperial Oil Ltd. (Toronto)	3,401,000
6. Brascan Ltd. (Toronto)	3,271,928*
7. Massey-Ferguson Ltd. (Toronto)	2,874,861*
8. Gulf Canada Ltd. (Toronto)	2,573,600
9. Seagram Co. (Montreal)	2,189,517*
10. Noranda Mines Ltd. (Toronto)	2,152,881

*Accounts stated in U.S. funds. Converted at fiscal year-end rate.

The Financial Post

Headquarters of the mighty Canadian Pacific Limited. The company has the largest assets of any industrial company in Canada.

THE 10 INDUSTRIAL COMPANIES IN CANADA WITH THE LARGEST SALES OR OPERATING REVENUE

Company (Head Office)	1977/1978 $'000
1. General Motors of Canada Ltd. (Oshawa)	6,115,434[1]
2. Ford Motor Co. of Canada (Oakville)	5,725,000[1]
3. Imperial Oil Ltd. (Toronto)	4,970,000[2]
4. Canadian Pacific Ltd. (Montreal)	4,700,136[3]
5. Bell Canada (Montreal)	3,559,887
6. Alcan Aluminium Ltd. (Montreal)	3,220,704[4]
7. Chrysler Canada Ltd. (Windsor)	3,119,063[1]
8. Massey-Ferguson Ltd. (Toronto)	2,935,987[4]
9. Shell Canada Ltd. (Toronto)	2,349,295[2]
10. Gulf Canada Ltd. (Toronto)	2,322,100[2]

1. Figures include sales to parent and affiliated companies:
   General Motors $2,753 million;
   Ford $2,339 million (also consolidates $1,257 million sales of overseas subsidiaries);
   Chrysler, unstated.
2. Excise taxes deducted.
3. After eliminating inter-company transactions.
4. Accounts stated in U.S. funds. Converted at average rate during fiscal year.

The Financial Post

General Motors of Canada Limited has sales of more than $6,000,000,000 — more than any other company in Canada.

THE TOP 10 PETROLEUM AND MINING PRODUCERS IN CANADA RANKED BY SALES OR OPERATING REVENUE

		1977/1978 $'000
1.	Texaco Exploration Canada. Ltd. (Calgary)	1,012,298
2.	Amoco Canada Petroleum Co. (Calgary)	668,713
3.	Mobil Oil Canada Ltd. (Calgary)	572,899
4.	Dome Petroleum Ltd. (Calgary)	521,433
5.	Hudson's Bay Oil & Gas Co. (Calgary)	342,952
6.	Kaiser Resources Ltd. (Vancouver)	299,005
7.	Ashland Oil Canada Ltd. (Calgary)	228,058
8.	Great Canadian Oil Sands Ltd. (Toronto)	178,685
9.	Placer Development Ltd. (Vancouver)	177,100
10.	Consolidated Natural Gas Ltd. (Calgary)	172,119

Not shown: PanCanadian Petroleum ($295 million) consolidated with parent company Canadian Pacific Ltd.

The Financial Post

10 OCCUPATIONS OF PEOPLE IN CANADA WITH IQ'S IN THE TOP 2 PERCENT OF THE POPULATION *

1. Cod De-wormer

2. Mushroom Grower

3. Swimming Pool Consultant

4. Truck Driver

5. Letter Carrier

6. Carpet Installer

7. Taxi Driver

 8. Firefighter

 9. Commercial Salmon Troller

10. Waitress

*Having an IQ of over 140.

Mensa Canada Society, Toronto. (Mensa is a society
for the top 2 per cent of the population as established by standard IQ tests.)

THE 10 LARGEST CANADIAN
OIL DISCOVERIES

Field	Initial Estimate of Reserves (millions of barrels)
1. PEMBINA 1953	1,742
2. SWAN HILLS 1957	1,315
3. REDWATER 1948	818
4. LEDUC–WOODBEND 1947	601
5. JUDY CREEK 1959	540
6. RAINBOW LAKE 1965	517
7. BONNIE GLEN 1952	516
8. SOUTH SWAN HILLS 1957	404
9. KAYBOB 1957	383
10. GOLDEN SPIKE 1949	321

Gint Berius
Loewen, Ondaatje, McCutcheon & Company Ltd.

6
NATURE AND WILDLIFE

10 FAVOURITE CANADIAN FLOWERS

1. DANDELION
Comes very early and lasts right through until the early winter.

2. MAYFLOWER
Found under the snow. They have a fantastic smell, even in winter.

3. WILD DAISIES
A beautiful white colour. Wonderful to look at alongside the road.

4. COSMOS
A wonderful spindly elegance.

5. TANSY
A glorious healing smell. Their intense deep yellow colour makes them a joy to paint.

6. WILD COMPANULA
An intense violet-blue, quite similar to bluebells. They grow near washed out golden lilies and emphasize their colour wonderfully.

7. POPPY
Their fragile colour and shape make this my very favourite flower to paint.

8. ASTERS
Asters remind me of my childhood. In the fall the spiders would weave their webs between them, and in the morning drips of dew would hang from the webs.

9. MOOSEWOOD
This is a bush. It is the first flower that comes out, but you must take it into the house in January.

10. BLOODROOT
They come up before the snow goes, and their beautiful white colour against the thawing snow is incredibly picturesque.

Molly Lamb Bobak
Artist

THE 10 MOST COMMON REASONS
FOR DISASTER IN THE CANADIAN BUSH

1. PANIC
People confronted with an unfamiliar situation in the bush will panic if fear is not checked in time.

2. DEHYDRATION
Forgetting to drink water or eating snow can result in serious dehydration problems.

3. HYPOTHERMIA
Over-exertion in wet or cold weather causes deep body temperatures to drop.

4. BURNS
Often caused by carelessness in handling fires and cooking utensils.

5. INSECT BITES
They can be so bad as to drive a person into a state of panic.

6. IMPROPER CLOTHING
Neglect in selecting proper clothing for the season of the year can easily be avoided.

7. CUTS AND BRUISES
Lack of know-how when using sharp tools often causes severe cuts and bruises.

8. FOOD
Not knowing how to recognize and prepare the most common emergency foods can result in disaster.

9. FIRE AND MATCHES
Not knowing how to start a fire in wet weather or not keeping matches in a water-tight container is dangerous.

10. OVERLOADING
People often overload themselves, their boat, or their canoe — with the inevitable disastrous results.

Berndt Berglund
Author
Wilderness Survival

THE 10 MOST POISONOUS
WILD PLANTS IN CANADA

1. WATER HEMLOCK

    Leaves, stem, and roots are poisonous. No known antidote.

2. DEATH CAMAS

    Leaves, stem, and bulbs are poisonous.

3. FALSE HELLEBORE

    Leaves, stem, and flowers are poisonous.

4. BANEBERRY

    White and red berries; both are poisonous.

5. JIMSON WEED

    The fruit is deadly.

6. FLY AMANITA

    Every part of the mushroom is poisonous.

7. DEADLY AMANITA

    Every part of the mushroom is poisonous.

8. POISON SUMAC

    Its white berries are deadly.

9. WHITE SNAKEROOT

    Leaves, flowers, and roots are poisonous.

FLY AMANITA   DEADLY AMANITA

10. POKEWEED

Leaves, flowers, and roots are poisonous.

Berndt Berglund
Author
Wilderness Survival

THE 10 BEST-TASTING
EDIBLE WILD PLANTS IN CANADA

1. LAMB'S-QUARTERS

Dip in boiling water, chop finely, and mix into a white sauce.

2. WATERCRESS

Wash, shred finely, and add to a green salad, or place between two pieces of buttered toast.

3. PURSLANE

Well washed, it is best eaten raw in a salad.

4. BLACK MUSTARD

A delightful green when picked early in spring while still small and added to other greens for a spring salad.

5. MILKWEED

Pick the flower clusters, dip in boiling water, and add to a cheese sauce.

6. DANDELION

Pick the young leaves, wash well, and shred finely for an excellent green salad base.

7. ROSE HIP

The fruit of the wild rose when picked in the fall, dried, and ground to a fine powder, then mixed with boiling water, makes a nourishing dessert soup. Serve cold with a dollop of whipped cream on top.

8. ARROWHEAD

Clean and boil as potatoes, or, peel and cut up for a potato salad.

9. WOOD SORREL

Add to a green salad. It will give it a sweet and sour taste.

10. STINGING NETTLE

Parboil, chop finely, serve with melted butter.

Berndt Berglund
Author
The Edible Wild

THE 10 BEST FISHING SPOTS IN CANADA

1. THE TUNULIK RIVER

High in the subarctic region of Quebec. At times big arctic char run into the Tunulik in such profusion that anglers' arms ache from landing and releasing so many fish!

2. THE MIRAMICHI RIVER

There are more productive rivers in which to catch that fabled fish, the Atlantic salmon, but the Miramichi is a classic. It is at once the lure, lore, and mystique of Atlantic salmon fishing. No one can truly say he has fished for Atlantic salmon until he has cast a fly on the Miramichi.

3. THE NORTH CHANNEL

Between Lake Huron's Manitoulin Island and the Ontario mainland. The rocky reefs and bars with gravelly shoals and deep drop-offs are ideal habitat for the bronze-backed smallmouth bass. And North Channel has some of the best bass fishing anywhere.

4. EAGLE LAKE

The Eagle has almost become synonymous with big muskellunge. I predict that a world-record musky will come out of Eagle Lake one day. (The musky is a hard fish to catch. And the truly big ones always get away.)

5. GOD'S LAKE

Big northern pike, succulent walleye, and lake trout are all found here, but it's the trophy brook trout that have made God's Lake a mecca to serious trout fishermen.

6. CAMPBELL RIVER

There are rivers with better fishing in British Columbia than the Campbell. In fact there are better rivers than the Campbell on Vancouver Island, where the Campbell flows. But there are no rivers with more charm. The Campbell is a fine salmon and steelhead stream. But the real joy in fishing it comes from fishing with the ghost of Roderick Haig-Brown, that master of enchanting and often poetic fishing prose, who made the river famous.

7. THE MOUNTAINS OF NORTH-CENTRAL BRITISH COLUMBIA.

For anglers who want to try a different kind of fishing trip, I would recommend a horseback trip with Lewis Clarke, the Fort St. James outfitter, into the mountains of north-central British Columbia. There you will get a chance to fish countless mountain streams for native rainbow trout and Dolly Vardens. But, equally important, you will get a chance to fish where few men have fished before. You will fish in country rich in wildlife and unparalleled scenery.

8. COLVILLE LAKE, NORTHWEST TERRITORIES

Trophy lake trout and sporting grayling are the main quarry, while the company of Will Bern Brown of Colville Lake Lodge is the frosting on the fishing cake.

9. QUEEN CHARLOTTE ISLANDS

For an angler who basically wants nothing more than to catch lots of fish, the rivers on the Queen Charlotte Islands with their fabulous steelhead runs are impossible to beat.

10. PRINCE EDWARD ISLAND

Not all of Canada's fishing is in streams, rivers, and lakes. We have thousands of miles of saltwater coastline with some outstanding saltwater fishing. My nod goes to Prince Edward Island and the giant bluefin tuna. The world record bluefin was taken here, a behemoth weighing 1,139 pounds. Bluefins of six to eight hundred pounds are boated so commonly they no longer excite anyone. As a result, P.E.I. has become as famous in international big-game fishing circles as the Indianapolis 500 is among automobile racing buffs. The main portion of the tuna fishing fleet is moored in the little community of North Lake.

Jerome Knap
Author
Fishing Secrets

THE 10 BEST HUNTING SPOTS IN CANADA

1. NASS RIVER

There is no question that the supreme thrill of big-game hunting must be a grizzly hunt, and one of the best places to bag a grizzly is in the wilderness at the headwaters of British Columbia's Nass River.

2. WILLMERE WILDERNESS

Canada's ultimate big-game trophy must be the bighorn sheep. Licences for bighorns are rationed with care so that no overhunting results; only mature rams with 4/5 curls in their horns can be taken.

Probably the best place to bag a trophy ram is in Alberta's Willmere wilderness where no motorized transport is allowed, and the best outfitter for the Willmere is Tom Vinson.

3. HEADWATERS OF THE ALBANY

Moose is Canada's most widely distributed big-game animal. It is found from the Yukon to Newfoundland, but the best moose hunting has to be with the Ojibway or Cree guides on the headwaters of the Albany.

The Indians are excellent moose callers on their birch-bark horns. If there is a lovesick moose within hearing distance, he'll respond. But will he come close enough for a shot? Some will slip in like ghosts but never show themselves. Only the cracking of the odd branch will warn the hunter.

The windswept coastlines of James and Hudson bays are staging areas for wildfowl on their southward migration in September.

Other bulls will roar in like locomotives, smashing down saplings as they come, but then they'll stop and snort to play a game of nerves. Every year more than one moose hunter gets "buck fever" — moose fever in this case — so badly that his hands shake too much to shoot.

4. JAMES AND HUDSON BAY COASTS

The Cree Indians put on other outstanding hunts for their "sports," and that is the goose hunt along the James and Hudson Bay coasts — in both Quebec and Ontario.

There are many hunting camps along the coast, but to reach them, hunters must fly in.

5. PRAIRIE POTHOLES OF SASKATCHEWAN

The prairie pothole country of Saskatchewan offers fine waterfowl hunting. In fact, bird hunters have long considered the rolling prairies of Saskatchewan to be a bird-hunting mecca.

Sharptail grouse and Hungarian partridge are amazingly abundant in some years. Ducks are plentiful as well. And there is some outstanding goose hunting in the stubble fields.

6. NEW BRUNSWICK'S SOUTHERN COUNTIES

A good hunting spot for the wingshooter is in New Brunswick, particularly the southern counties. The quarry here is woodcock and ruffed grouse.

New Brunswick has become so famous for its woodcock hunting that in October hunters from as far away as California and Texas come here to hunt this long-billed bird that has delighted the epicurean palate since the Middle Ages.

7. CRANE ISLAND

Another one of our great hunting spots is Ile aux Grues — Crane Island — just east of Quebec City. The island is one of the best places to hunt for snipe, the most difficult-to-hit game bird.

Teal, speedy and delicious little ducks, are also found there in great numbers. And, later, the greater snow geese stop on their southward migration from the arctic islands, where they nest.

8. UNGAVA BAY

A Quebec hunt that rates as one of the best is a hunt for bull caribou in the rolling tundra south of Ungava Bay.

The Quebec caribou story is an outstanding testimonial to modern game management. Caribou were an almost endangered species in Quebec about the time of World War I, and now they number some 170,000 and are increasing.

9. FORT CHIMO

The caribou hunt out of Fort Chimo is almost an outdoor adventure. The hunters' guides are Eskimos who, to a large extent, still live off the land. To hunt with them is an unforgettable experience.

10. QUEEN CHARLOTTE ISLANDS

The diminutive blacktail deer are so abundant here that they do not have enough browse to eat and are stunted.

Jerome Knap
Author
Where to Fish and Hunt in North America.

THE 10 MOST DANGEROUS ANIMALS IN CANADA

1. POLAR BEAR

Largest carnivore on earth. Not at all afraid of man.

2. GRIZZLY BEAR

Dangerous because of its unpredictability. Gradually losing its fear of man.

3. BLACK BEAR

Most dangerous when people get between female and her cubs; otherwise more afraid of us than we are of them.

4. PRAIRIE RATTLESNAKE

Poisonous bite, but will only bite if surprised.

5. MISSISSAUGA RATTLESNAKE

Range extends throughout cottage country and people tend to harass it, not knowing what it is. Poisonous venom.

6. COUGAR

Dangerous only if cornered

7. WOLVERINE

May attack if cornered; also may be rabid.

8. TIMBER WOLF

Often not dangerous unless wounded or rabid.

9. BISON

Because of its size do not tamper with a bull. It is big enough to do a lot of damage.

10. WALRUS

Rogue animals are dangerous to people in boats. Will attack with their tusks. If wounded, may turn on the hunter. Eskimos treat walruses with respect.

David Grainger
Author
Animals in Peril

The polar bear, the largest carnivore on earth, is not at all afraid of man and is by far the most dangerous animal in Canada.

THE 10 MOST FREQUENTED CANADIAN NATIONAL PARKS

	Number of Visitors
1. Banff National Park, Alberta	3,040,769
2. Kootenay National Park, British Columbia	2,265,016
3. Jasper National Park, Alberta	1,713,670
4. Prince Edward Island National Park, Prince Edward Island	1,394,705
5. Mount Revelstoke National Park, British Columbia	1,232,973
6. Glacier National Park, British Columbia	1,145,295
7. Yoho National Park, British Columbia	1,044,001
8. Riding Mountain National Park, Manitoba	965,427
9. Fundy National Park, New Brunswick	861,638
10. Cape Breton Highlands National Park, Nova Scotia	823,675

Department of Indian Affairs and Northern Development

THE 10 FAVOURITE BIRD-WATCHING SPOTS IN CANADA

1. LONG POINT ON LAKE ERIE

When the whistling swans are there; it's comforting to know that some huge wild birds still exist in thousands.

2. JOHNSTON LAKE, SOUTH OF MOOSE JAW

Because I can watch white pelicans all day long.

3. MILE 85 ON THE HAINES ROAD IN BRITISH COLUMBIA'S PANHANDLE

Where else can one see all three species of ptarmigan with chicks in an hour?

4. LESLIE SPIT, TORONTO

Because of the delightful sight of hundreds of ring-billed gulls going about their business of raising families as if in the wilderness, with the sky-line of the metropolis only a couple of miles away.

5. BIG PISKWANISH ON THE WEST COAST OF JAMES BAY

When the shorebirds are flying south, because here I once saw hundreds of migrating hudsonian godwits at a time when the species was thought to be verging on extinction.

6. ANYWHERE ALONG THE TORONTO WATERFRONT

In late winter because I love the music of oldsquaw ducks.

7. KLUANE LAKE, YUKON

Hawk owls, bohemian waxwings, Say's phoebes, timberline sparrows, rosy finches, Townsend's solitaires, red crossbills — and upland plover nesting in the spruce forest!

8. FORT ROSS, SOMERSET ISLAND (OR POLAR BEAR PARK IN ONTARIO FOR THAT MATTER)

Because there is nothing that can compare with the birdlife of an arctic summer.

9. A PRAIRIE SLOUGH WEST OF PORTAGE LA PRAIRIE

Because you're sure of seeing a slough of ducks.

10. ANYWHERE

That a great grey owl happens to turn up.

Terence M. Shortt
Artist/Author
Wild Birds of Canada and the Americas

THE 10 MOST ENDANGERED CANADIAN BIRDS

1. WHOOPING CRANE

This enormous white bird with its wild bugling cry once bred widely across the prairies of Canada and the United States. Shooting and the loss of habitat to farming reduced the population to 13 — now recovered to a tenuous one hundred.

2. BALD EAGLE

Eagles suffer from intrusion and disturbance during the nesting season and from the residues of toxic poisons in the flesh they eat. The coastal population in the West continues to flourish, but numbers in the East are much reduced, although apparently now stable.

3. PRAIRIE FALCON

The prairies of southern Alberta and Saskatachewan represent the northern limit of this crow-sized falcon's range. It is much affected by DDT and other herbicides, but at this moment does not appear to be in danger of extinction.

The Aleutian Canada Goose — one of the most endangered Canadian birds.

4. PEREGRINE FALCON

Perhaps the world's fastest-flying bird, the peregrine has disappeared as a breeding species from eastern North America. The small population in the eastern Arctic migrates to South America, and there is a stable non-migratory population in British Columbia and Alaska.

5. ALEUTIAN CANADA GOOSE

While not strictly a Canadian bird, this tiny goose breeds in the western Aleutians and migrates along the Pacific shores to California in winter. It was almost eliminated on its breeding islands by foxes introduced a hundred years ago, which have now been virtually eliminated. It is also much affected by shooting in California.

6. ESKIMO CURLEW

This small curlew was once so plentiful that wagonloads were shot on the Prairies during the northern migration each spring. It was also harassed on its wintering grounds in South America. The last sightings were one in Martha's Vineyard in 1972 and another near Moosonee, Ontario, in 1976. The possibility of recovery is remote.

7. HUDSONIAN GODWIT

Once thought to be extinct, this large shorebird's migration route was discovered in 1934 by Terence Shortt of Toronto. It breeds in the central Arctic and moves south along the western shore of Hudson Bay in late summer. Its condition appears to be secure.

8. PRAIRIE CHICKEN

The two species of prairie chicken, the greater and lesser, are in serious trouble. Their breeding grounds are constantly reduced by grazing and farming, and it is doubtful that enough habitat remains for them to survive.

9. KIRKLAND'S WARBLER

This blue and yellow warbler breeds in the jackpine forests of Michigan, but has been recorded in southern Ontario. Cowbirds now parasite the nests to such an extent that the population has dwindled to under 500 birds and continues to decline. Its future is in doubt.

10. IPSWICH SPARROW

Breeding only on Sable Island, ninety miles off the coast of Nova Scotia, this pale grey sparrow is at the mercy of the stability of its habitat. By late summer there are some ten to twelve thousand birds, but after a winter of foraging on the sand dunes of the eastern United States, only some 2,000 survive. Their survival depends on the protection from development of the shore areas where they winter.

John P. S. Mackenzie
Author
Birds in Peril

PREGNANCY PERIODS OF
10 CANADIAN ANIMALS

	Pregnancy Period (months)			Pregnancy Period (months)
1. HORSE	$11^7/_8$	6.	POLAR BEAR	$7^7/_8$
2. COW	$10^3/_4$	7.	BEAVER	$3^1/_2$
3. HUMAN BEING	9	8.	CAT	$2^1/_8$
4. REINDEER	$8^1/_8$	9.	DOG	$2^1/_8$
5. MOOSE	8	10.	FOX	$1^3/_4$

THE 10 MOST BEAUTIFUL
BIRDS IN CANADA

1. GREAT BLUE HERON

Stately bearing and classic, sculpturesque figuration make this, the tallest bird that most of us are likely to see in Canada, also one of our most comely.

2. AMERICAN KESTREL

Graceful flight and bright, tasteful colouring combined with abundance make this little falcon one of my favourites.

3. BLUE JAY

As colourful as any bird of the tropics. Because it is common we tend to overlook its beauty — familiarity breeds contempt. Too bad it hasn't a voice to match its plumage!

4. SNOWY OWL

The great arctic owl lends a touch of excitement to the wintry landscape. It is abroad in daylight and so is more readily seen and admired than other owls.

5. YELLOW-SHAFTED FLICKER

One must see the familiar flicker at close range to fully appreciate its refinement of colour and markings.

6. MOUNTAIN BLUEBIRD

Almost ethereal in the purity of its sky-blue feathers. Around prairie homes it has all the pretty ways and habits of the familiar red-breasted bluebird of the East.

7. RUFFED GROUSE

A truly magnificent bird with its huge fan tail and shining black ruffs. And it can be seen anywhere in Canada where there are woodlands.

8. PINTAIL

"Elegant" is the fitting adjective for this graceful, slender duck. Its colouring is modest but stylish. A bird of impeccable taste.

9. BOHEMIAN WAXWING

A bird of the northwest which we see mostly in winter. It is just a little more striking than the familiar cedar waxwing of the orchards and woodland edges. Both have an aristocratic bearing and sleek, well-groomed plumage.

10. ROSE-BREASTED GROSBEAK

With its plumage pied in rich black and snowy white, embellished by a flamboyant cravat and wing linings of exquisite carmine, the rose-breast is as handsome as any perching bird in the world.

Terence M. Shortt
Artist/Author
Wild Birds of Canada and the Americas

10 OF THE WORST PSYCHIATRIC PROBLEMS THAT COULD AFFECT YOUR DOG

1. ANXIETY SYNDROME

Means the dog is worried about almost anything and acts out his anxiety by biting or attacking people.

2. BARRIER FRUSTRATION

Occurs when the dog gets enraged because he cannot break his leash.

3. DOMINANCE FRUSTRATION

The dog thinks his master is not manly enough to protect the home, which can be upsetting, man being what the dog abandoned his pack for. Consequently the dog feels he must be boss and attacks anyone who comes into the home.

4. KENNEL SYNDROME

Results when the newborn puppy has been taken away from its mother too soon and spends its puppyhood in a kennel environment, deprived of canine or human love. The dog grows up unable to socialize with humans, is almost impossible to train, and is certain to become the neighbourhood tough.

5. SECRETARY OR LOVER SYNDROME

May develop when the master works late at the office or occasionally doesn't come home at all, and the dog gets cranky because he has not been fed and attended to.

6. NEW BABY SYNDROME

Occurs when the dog has long been the pampered one of the family and suddenly is in competition for attention. It can make him quite nasty.

7. NEW CAR SYNDROME

Much the same thing as the new baby syndrome.

8. POSTMAN SYNDROME

Caused by the uniform, the bag, the scent of mail, or the fact that the mailman regularly invades the dog's territory. Sooner or later the postman becomes a victim of the dog's fury.

9. PSYCHOSEXUAL MISORIENTATION

Arises when a puppy has been weaned traumatically and its maladjustment manifests itself in overeating, excessive scratching, or in a preoccupation with oral behaviour in general. That is, he bites.

10. SIBLING RIVALRY

Almost any change in a home situation that removes the dog from the limelight — a visiting aunt, a new husband, even guests for dinner — can bring out aggression in an insecure dog.

Iris Nowell
Author
The Dog Crisis

THE 10 MOST POPULAR BREEDS OF DOGS IN CANADA

1. German Shepherd
2. Doberman Pinscher
3. American Cocker Spaniel
4. Poodle
5. Labrador Retriever

6. Collie (rough)
7. Shetland Sheepdog
8. Irish Setter
9. Yorkshire Terrier
10. Pomeranian

Canadian Kennel Club

10 DISEASES YOU CAN GET FROM YOUR PET

1. RABIES

All the rabies horror stories are true. Once a human is bitten by a rabid animal, viral particles speed to the victim's central nervous system. Should the infection reach the brain before rabies vaccine has been administered, death occurs from acute encephalitis. Rabies can be transmitted to humans by pet dogs and cats, although in North America the fox, skunk, and bat are the more common vectors.

2. VISCERAL LARVA MIGRANS

Transmitted to humans by dogs infected with the common roundworm, *Toxocara canis,* which is shed in their feces, the route of transmission to humans is direct; that is, by ingesting the parasite in dogs' feces. Not as implausible as it may seem. Young children play where infected dogs have defecated and hands find their way into mouths. Once ingested, the larvae may remain inactive for months, even years, or the host may kill them off, but the danger is that larvae may attach to an organ and cause liver or kidney malfunction, bronchial disorders, or blindness.

3. CUTANEOUS LARVA MIGRANS

At least four different parasitic worms found in dogs' feces are capable of infecting man. The parasites penetrate the individual's skin and travel under it, producing a condition which resembles tightly condensed varicose veins. The disease occurs wherever fecal contamination is widespread and is contracted by walking, playing, or lying in places where infected dogs have defecated.

4. TOXOPLASMOSIS

Caused by a parasite shed in cats' feces that, similar to *Toxocara canis,* is ingested by humans who have touched infected feces and then put their hands in their mouths. Generally symptoms are minor and mimic flu or mononucleosis, but acute cases may result in blindness, brain damage, or heart failure. Toxoplasmosis is a serious risk for pregnant women, where the ingested organism may produce stillbirths, mental retardation, or blindness of the newborn.

5. LEPTOSPIROSIS

Spread to humans through infected dogs' or cats' urine. (Also transmitted by wildlife.) Large dogs are usually society's canine villains, but the small dog is the culprit here. With its short legs it waddles through infected puddles and transmits the leptospires to humans who romp with the dog, or puppies accidentally urinating on children can transmit it. Characterized by fever, headache, malaise, vomitting, and occasionally meningitis; fatality is 20 percent in patients with jaundice and kidney damage.

6. RINGWORM

The most common fungal disease in the world, ringworm is transmitted either from man to man (as in athlete's foot), from animals to man, or through soil transmission. The species transmitted from pet dogs (and cats), *Microsporum canis,* appears in circular scaling on the skin, frequently on the scalp, which can cause blindness. Although touching an infected pet results in human infection, even the dog's or cat's bedding, the carpet, or straw in the barn where pets sleep may contain spores that remain active for many months.

7. FLEAS

For centuries they have been a cursing, raging affliction of mankind. Fleas from dogs and cats may cause humans little clinical disease, although in persons with allergic reactions a fleabite may swell to the size of a hen's egg that suppurates and takes several weeks to heal. Since fleas are attracted to carbon dioxide, warmth, and movement — characteristics possessed by dog and man alike — fleas, although they prefer to ride around on a warm dog, will settle for a human when no dog is available.

8. ROCKY MOUNTAIN SPOTTED FEVER

Transmitted to man by a bite from the dog tick, *Dermacentor variabilis,* the disease manifests itself in fever, headaches, chills, and a rash that covers most of the body. It is effectively treated with antibiotics and usually results in no disability; if untreated the fatality rate is about 20 percent. The disease has shown a sharp increase in the past decade, notably in eastern North America.

9. CAT SCRATCH FEVER

As the name implies, this disease occurs from a scratch or bite from a cat and although symptons are commonly a painful sore at the bite area combined with fever, malaise, and swollen glands, in severe cases it may produce convulsions and encephalitis.

10. PSITTACOSIS (also called "parrot fever" or "ornithosis")

Fever, headaches, and coughs because of pneumonic involvement are the symptoms of this disease and may range from mild to acute; death is rare. Contracted by aerosol transmission from caged pet birds that may seem perfectly healthy, it is also a risk in places where pigeon or other bird droppings have accumulated in a confined space, for example around abandoned buildings, under train trestles and bridges.

Iris Nowell
Author
The Dog Crisis

THE 10 MOST POPULAR
BREEDS OF CATS IN CANADA

		Number of *Cats Registered*
1.	PERSIAN	1,334
2.	HIMALAYAN	569
3.	SIAMESE	214
4.	ABYSSINIAN	90
5.	BURMESE	66
6.	COLOUR-POINT SHORT HAIR	42
7.	SOMALI	25
8.	MANX	24
9.	EGYPTIAN MAU	17
10.	CHARTREUX	17

Canadian Cat Association

The Persian cat — the most popular breed in Canada.

THE 10 MOST ENDANGERED
ANIMALS IN CANADA

1. NORTHERN KIT FOX

Probably already extinct, although some may still exist in the Badlands of Alberta.

2. BLACK-FOOTED FERRET

Probably extinct. Has not been seen in Canada for five years. Impossible to breed in captivity.

3. VANCOUVER ISLAND MARMOT

One of two animals (the shrew is the other) found only in Canada. People are taking over its environment; no more than a hundred are left.

4. BLACK-TAILED PRAIRIE DOG

Victim of mass poisoning. Only two prairie-dog towns left on the Prairies.

5. NEWFOUNDLAND PINE MARTEN

Victim of human intrusion on its range by loggers. Still not protected.

The northern kit fox probably still exists in the Badlands of Alberta.

6. CALIFORNIA BIGHORN SHEEP

Suffered from overhunting and from livestock ranching which introduced disease. The most endangered of all bighorn sheep.

7. WOOD BISON

Getting into trouble because of overcrowding, disease, and possibly wolf predation. Found in Wood Buffalo National Park.

8. EASTERN COUGAR

Starting to get protection in the United States; not yet in Canada. Believed to be on the increase and with proper care may make a comeback.

9. NORTHERN SEA OTTER

Doing fairly well. Found from Vancouver Island north to Alaska. Others have been introduced to many areas.

10. ROOSEVELT ELK

Found only on Vancouver Island. It is suffering from pressure from man on its range.

David Grainger
Author
Animals in Peril

THE 9 MAJOR CAUSES OF
FOREST FIRES IN CANADA

	Percentage of Total Forest Fires	Number of Fires
1. Lightning	27.5	2,141
2. Recreation	20.6	1,600
3. Miscellaneous (known causes)	14.6	1,133
4. Settlement	9.4	732
5. Woods Operations	7.6	591
6. Railways	6.4	494
7. Incendiary	5.2	405
8. Unknown Causes	4.7	369
9. Other Industries	4.0	312
Total:	100.0	7,777

Statistics Canada

Lightning in Canada — the major cause of forest fires.

TRAVEL

THE 7 GREATEST ADVENTURES IN CANADA

1. SEVEN DAYS IN THE PETAWAWA RIVER BETWEEN LAKE TRAVER TO MacMANUS LAKE

In the early springtime, when the river roars like a lion, the water is bone-chillingly cold but the excitement in the rapids is magnificent.

2. THE HARICANAW RIVER, BY CANOE, FROM AMOS, QUEBEC, TO JAMES BAY IN 10 DAYS

The Haricanaw is historically important as it is the river that Radisson and Groseillier used to go west. It is a dirty river and not very interesting at the top because it runs through the northern Ontario and Quebec clay belt, but once one starts to descend to the Bay there are four days of solid rapids with areas of huge standing waves — not a river for amateurs.

3. THE SPANISH RIVER FROM BISCOTASING LAKE TO LAKE AGNEW, BY CANOE

Picturesque, with many rapids. It is a fine example of Canadian wilderness.

4. THE MADAWASKA RIVER FROM WHITNEY, ONTARIO, TO GRIFFITH, ONTARIO, BY CANOE

In the spring, a very exciting series of rapids and in the fall, with the colour, and the water of course much lower, a truly lovely four-day trip.

5. THE FRENCH RIVER, BY CANOE, FROM WOLSELEY BAY TO GEORGIAN BAY

With some famous rapids — Big Pine, Little Pine, the Blue Chute — but more than this, the history. If one follows the course laid out on topographical maps, this is listed as the voyageur channel; in fact, it is not the most westerly route and not the route taken by the voyageurs. The adventure involved here is finding the *real* voyageur route through the islands and many miles of the French River.

6. SAILING SQUARE-RIGGED SHIP — BRIGANTINE — FROM KILLARNEY, ONTARIO, THROUGH THREE OF THE GREAT LAKES TO TORONTO HARBOUR

In late fall, rolling and pitching in eight-foot quartering seas on Lake Erie and pulling up the hood of your raingear against the flying spray, waking at 4 a.m. to check the ship's position on the charts.

7. SCRAMBLING AND GLISSADING IN ROGERS' PASS

In June reading the diary of other climbers when staying in the historic 6,400-foot-high Hermit Hut; feeling awe at the realization of what Rogers and his men went through to find this pass among massive mountains such as the awesom Sir Donald.

J. T. M. Guest
Headmaster
Lakefield College School

The Banff Springs Hotel in Alberta — a superb summer resort in a natural setting.

THE 10 MOST POPULAR SUMMER RESORTS IN CANADA

1. BANFF AND LAKE LOUISE, Alberta

Superb hotels in the traditional style for longer stayers. Scenery, relaxation, sightseeing in a superb natural setting.

2. KELTIC LODGE, INGONISH, Nova Scotia

One of Canada's great hotels in every sense of the word, as well as the gateway to Cape Breton Highlands National Park and the Cabot Trail. Everyone from tour groups to families likes it.

3. PRINCE EDWARD ISLAND

Very broad but everything about the province is appealing as a resort — beaches, people, summer festival, cost.

4. HALIBURTON, Ontario

A playground for urban central Canadians. Cottages, lakes, peaceful countryside — just a few hours from Toronto and Ottawa. Accommodations from good to indifferent.

5. CHATEAU MONTEBELLO, Quebec

A hotel on a seventeenth-century seignorial estate in the foothills of the Laurentians, it has French food, culture, and atmosphere, with families, diplomats, and sportspeople as guests. One of the many great resorts of Quebec's Laurentian playground.

6. TORONTO, Ontario

Ontario Place, Yorkville, and the CNE — it is astoundingly popular with Americans and most other Canadians. Hotel packages and outdoor pools make it an urban playground.

7. ALGONQUIN HOTEL, St. Andrews-by-the-Sea, New Brunswick

Close to Saint John and its reversing falls, as well as to Fredericton and Moncton, this Tudor-style hotel is a long-time favourite with families and older persons. And just across the Bay of Fundy is Digby — see below.

8. OKANAGAN VALLEY, British Columbia

Summer retreat for the knowledgeable in Vancouver, Calgary, Edmonton. Less crowded but still majestic, compared to Banff/Lake Louise. The valley towns of Kelowna, Kamloops, and Penticton all have their own charm.

9. MUSKOKA, Ontario

Similar to Haliburton but a little more developed, more sophisticated, with larger resort hotels catering to groups.

10. DIGBY PINES RESORT, Nova Scotia

Heartland of the Annapolis Valley. Gateway to the Acadian country. Tranquil, accessible, Nova Scotia hospitality. Very popular with Halifax residents.

Hal Burns
Hal Burns Travel Ltd.

Gray Rocks Inn in St. Jovite, Quebec — one of the best tennis resorts in Canada.

THE 10 BEST TENNIS RESORTS IN CANADA

1. INN AND TENNIS CLUB AT MANITOU, Parry Sound, Ontario
2. GRAY ROCKS INN, St. Jovite, Quebec
3. THE PINES, Digby, Nova Scotia
4. CLEVELANDS HOUSE, Lake Rosseau, Minett, Ontario
5. JASPER PARK LODGE, Jasper, Alberta
6. ALGONQUIN HOTEL, St. Andrews-by-the-Sea, New Brunswick
7. MONT TREMBLANT LODGE, Mont Tremblant, Quebec
8. TYROLEAN VILLAGE RESORTS, Collingwood, Ontario
9. BANFF SPRINGS HOTEL, Banff, Alberta
10. LE CHATEAU MONTEBELLO, Montebello, Quebec

Nicholas Van Daalen
Author, *The International Tennis Guide*
and *The International Golf Guide*

129

Jasper Park Lodge in Alberta sports one of the most scenic public golf courses in Canada.

THE 10 BEST PUBLIC GOLF COURSES IN CANADA

1. GLEN ABBEY GOLF CLUB, 385 North Service Road W., Oakville, Ontario
   18 holes par 73 amateur   yardage 6,496 (front tees)
             par 72 professional yardage 7,226 (back tees)

2. THE GRAY ROCKS GOLF CLUB, Box 1000, St. Jovite, Quebec
   18 holes par 72   yardage 6,445

3. CAPE BRETON HIGHLANDS GOLF LINKS, Cape Breton Highlands National Park, Ingonish Beach, Nova Scotia
   18 holes par 72   yardage 6,475

4. JASPER PARK LODGE, Jasper Park, Alberta
   18 holes par 71   yardage 6,590

5. BANFF SPRINGS HOTEL, Banff, Alberta
   18 holes par 72   yardage 6,704

6. GREEN GABLES GOLF CLUB, Cavendish, Prince Edward Island
   18 holes par 72   yardage 6,410

7. MISSISSAUGA GOLF AND COUNTRY CLUB, 1725 Mississauga Road, Mississauga, Ontario
   18 holes par 72   yardage 6,853

8. MANOIR RICHELIEU GOLF CLUB, Murray Bay, Pointe au Pic, Quebec
18 holes   par 70   yardage 6,110

9. LE CHATEAU MONTEBELLO, Montebello, Quebec
18 holes   par 70   yardage 6,110

10. ALGONQUIN HOTEL, St. Andrews-by-the-Sea, New Brunswick
18 holes   par 71   yardage 6,314

Nicholas Van Daalen
Author
The International Golf Guide

THE 10 BEST PRIVATE GOLF COURSES IN CANADA

1. HAMILTON GOLF AND COUNTRY CLUB (founded in 1894), 232 Golf Links Road, Ancaster, Ontario

   27 holes   par 70   yardage 6,800 (back tees)

2. THE CAPILANO GOLF AND COUNTRY CLUB (founded in 1938), 420 Southborough Drive, West Vancouver, British Columbia

   18 holes   par 72   yardage 6,690

3. LONDON HUNT AND COUNTRY CLUB (founded in 1843), London, Ontario,

   18 holes   par 72   yardage 7,600

4. ROYAL COLWOOD GOLF AND COUNTRY CLUB (founded in 1914), 629 Goldstream Avenue, Victoria, British Columbia

   18 holes   par 70   yardage 6,789

5. ST. GEORGE'S GOLF AND COUNTRY CLUB (founded in 1929), 1668 Islington Avenue, Toronto, Ontario

   18 holes   par 71   yardage 6,797

6. THE ROYAL MONTREAL GOLF CLUB (founded in 1873), Bizard, Montreal

   18 holes   par 70   yardage 6,840

7. RIVERSIDE COUNTRY CLUB (founded in 1897), Rothesay, New Brunswick

   18 holes   par 71   yardage 5,960

8. ROSEDALE GOLF CLUB (founded in 1893), 1901 Mount Pleasant Road, Toronto, Ontario

   18 holes   par 70 men   yardage 6,355 (back tees)
              par 75 women   yardage 6,085 (front tees)

9. THE ROYAL QUEBEC GOLF CLUB (founded in 1935), Boischatel, Quebec

   18 holes   par 72   yardage 6,650

10. LAMBTON GOLF AND COUNTRY CLUB (founded in 1902), Scarlett Road, Toronto, Ontario

   18 holes   par 70   yardage 6,478 (back tees)

Nicholas Van Daalen
Author
The International Golf Guide

THE 10 MOST POPULAR CANADIAN FESTIVALS

	Number of Visitors
1. Canadian National Exhibition Toronto, Ontario	3,547,500
2. Calgary Exhibition and Stampede Calgary, Alberta	1,609,102
3. Pacific National Exhibition Vancouver, B.C.	1,279,626
4. Folklorama Winnipeg, Manitoba	1,000,000
5. Quebec Provincial Carnival Quebec, Quebec	553,000
6. Klondike Days Edmonton, Alberta	535,635
7. Regina Buffalo Days Exhibition Edmonton, Alberta	420,000
8. Festival du Voyageur Winnipeg, Manitoba	400,000
9. Royal Agricultural Winter Fair Toronto, Ontario	300,000
10. Red River Exhibition Red River, Manitoba	299,215

Canadian Government Office of Tourism

The Canadian National Exhibition boasts over three and a half million visitors during the summer months.

THE 10 MOST COMMON ACTIVITIES OF U.S. CITIZENS IN CANADA

1. Eating out in restaurants
2. Shopping
3. Individual sightseeing
4. Visiting historic sites or buildings
5. Visiting friends and relatives
6. Visiting museums, art galleries
7. Visiting night clubs
8. Swimming
9. Attending zoos and amusement parks
10. Going on day tours and trips

Canadian Government Office of Tourism

Vancouver, B.C. — probably Canada's most beautiful city.

THE 10 MOST BEAUTIFUL CITIES, TOWNS, AND VILLAGES IN CANADA

1. VANCOUVER, British Columbia

Dramatic views of mountains and sea; striking modern architecture.

2. NIAGARA-ON-THE-LAKE, Ontario

Classic Georgian houses in beautiful gardens; Shaw Festival. A sense of history in a gala summer atmosphere.

3. ROTHESAY, New Brunswick

Suburb of Saint John. Huge Victorian houses along winding river road. Old-fashioned gardens; old houses; old money.

4. BANFF, Alberta

Breathtaking mountain views; young people in a highly charged arts-crafts environment.

5. QUEBEC CITY, Quebec

Old World charm; atmosphere, food. Beautiful setting at the mouth of the St. Lawrence River.

6. ST. JOHN'S, Newfoundland

Picturesque harbour, narrow, winding streets, wooden Victorian houses, Wuthering Heights atmosphere.

7. TADOUSSAC, Quebec

Small fishing/tourist village where the Saguenay meets the St. Lawrence; the smell of the pine woods so typical of a northern summer.

8. CHESTER, Nova Scotia

White churches and white Cape Cod houses; sailboats, sunsets, views of islands.

9. SENNEVILLE, Quebec

Large, well-kept estates on the edge of the St. Lawrence, a suburb of Montreal.

10. KINGSTON, Ontario

Well-preserved pre-Confederation houses, leisurely academic atmosphere.

Nicholas Van Daalen
Author, *The International Tennis Guide*
and *The International Golf Guide*

THE 10 LARGEST AIRPORTS IN CANADA

	Number of Flights	Total Number Passengers
1. Toronto International	128,096	10,526,091
2. Montreal International	78,270	5,553,570
3. Vancouver International	58,944	4,938,877
4. Calgary International	44,197	2,592,956
5. Winnipeg International	37,051	1,971,663
6. Edmonton International	30,557	1,582,128
7. Ottawa International	33,225	1,576,905
8. Halifax International	24,261	1,302,348
9. Mirabel International	22,344	1,138,344
10. Edmonton Municipal	11,674	695,593

Statistics Canada

The Toronto International Airport — the largest in Canada.

Mourners and the five symbolic coffins for the 109 victims of the DC-8 air crash in Toronto on July 5, 1970.

THE 10 WORST CANADIAN
AIRLINE ACCIDENTS

	Airline	Date	Number of Dead
1. St. Therese, Quebec	Air Canada	November 29, 1963	118
2. Toronto, Ontario	Air Canada	July 5, 1970	109
3. St. Issondin, Quebec	Maritime Central Airlines (now EPA)	August 11, 1957	79
4. Tokyo, Japan	Canadian Pacific Airlines	March 4, 1966	64
5. Mt. Sclesse, British Columbia	Air Canada	December 9, 1956	62
6. Gustafsen Lake,* British Columbia	Canadian Pacific Airlines	July 8, 1965	52
7. Cranbrooke, British Columbia	Pacific Western Airlines	February 11, 1978	43
8. Newfoundland	Czechoslovakia Airlines	September 5, 1967	35
9. Honolulu, Hawaii	Canadian Pacific Airlines	February 22, 1962	27
10. Terrace, British Columbia	Northern Thunderbird Airlines	January 14, 1977	12

*This accident was the result of a bomb planted on the airplane.
All 52 passengers died.

Statistics Canada

THE 8 AGE GROUPS IN CANADA
WITH THE HIGHEST
PERCENTAGE OF AUTOMOBILE ACCIDENTS

Age Group	Number of Fatal Accidents	Number of Non-Fatal Accidents	Number of Accidents Involving Property Damage Only	Total	Percent
1. 25-34	1,828	54,865	190,529	247,222	22.2
2. 20-24	1,632	44,134	144,871	190,637	17.1
3. 35-44	1,022	32,104	113,482	146,608	13.2
4. 16-19	1,177	33,182	101,260	135,619	12.2
5. 45-54	797	24,789	87,049	112,635	10.1
6. 55-64	525	14,339	51,014	65,878	5.9
7. 65 and over	357	7,299	24,323	31,979	2.9
8. Under 16	45	1,094	1,540	2,679	0.2

Insurance Bureau of Canada

8
EATING AND DRINKING

10 GREAT CANADIAN
QUOTATIONS ON FOOD AND COOKING

1. Talk not to us of intellectual raptures; the mouth and stomach are the doors by which enter true delight.

   Viscount Milton and Dr. W.B. Cheadle, *English Travellers to Canada,* 1863

2. No finer compliment can be paid a cook than to eat freely and with relish of his cooking.

   Ralph Connor, *The Prospector,* 1904

3. There is nothing like feeding a man if you want to put him in a good humour.

   Francis W. Grey *The Curé of St. Phillippe,* 1899

4. Cooks...were always temperamental. If you flattered them they did better. If you didn't, they wilted. They were like women.

   Edward Meade, *Remember Me,* 1946

5. Substantial foods is like hugs, but fancies might come under the 'ead kisses.

   Mazo de la Roche, *Explorers of the Dawn,* 1922

6. It is fairly safe to say that the most fascinating subject in the country today is neither sex nor politics, religion nor women's hats — but eating.

   Sidney Katz, *Maclean's,* 1955

7. I remember once we tried to roast a beaver. I'm afraid we didn't much care for it!

   Pierre Berton and Janet Berton, *Canadian Food Guide,* 1966

8. In Quebec, as anywhere else, good food means good materials, lovingly prepared by someone who cares for the people who will eat it.

   Mme Jehane Benoit, *The Canadiana Cookbook,* 1970

9. Canadian cookery is not only an art, but a science as well. To cook economically is also an art — one that had to be practised by early settlers and lonely trappers in the wilderness, where no store-bought supplies could be obtained.

   Berndt Berglund and Clare E. Bolsby, *Wilderness Cooking,* 1973

10. If you don't like the price of cabbages...buy something else!

    Jean Chrétien, in a Montreal speech, July 1978

10 ITEMS OF ETIQUETTE CANADIANS SHOULD KNOW ABOUT TABLE MANNERS

1. A woman should never carve meat or fowl at the table.

2. Guests should not season food before tasting it, implying that it is not correctly seasoned.

3. When a chop is served with a paper frill, it is *not* an invitation to pick up the chop and eat it with your fingers.

4. The demi-tasse cup and saucer are for serving coffee after dinner in the living room. They should never be used when after-dinner coffee is served at the dining table.

5. Baked potatoes should be eaten from the skin. It is not correct to scoop out the entire potato, put aside the skin, and mash the contents all at once.

6. Butter or margarine should never be served at a formal dinner. At informal meals in the home, butter or margarine is served on a small plate or in a butter dish.

7. Grapes should be served at the table in a fresh fruit bowl at the conclusion of a meal. Bunches of grapes should be cut from the bowl. *Individual grapes should never be pulled off from the centrepiece or bowl.*

8. When at the table, napkins should not be taken from the table and unfolded until after grace is said. If no grace is said, the hostess's action should be followed.

9. The toothpick should never be used in public.

10. At the table, before lighting up, smokers should ask permission of other diners, including strangers. Smoking between courses is done but is not in good taste. At a banquet, diners may not smoke until after the toast to the Queen.

Claire Wallace
Author
Canadian Etiquette

THE 10 BEST RESTAURANTS IN CANADA

1. WINSTON'S, 104 Adelaide St. W., Toronto

Art Deco, Tiffany lamps, and more monied patrons per square foot than on Bay Street. Notwithstanding the opulence, one can, from time to time, receive an extraordinary dinner. The service is admirable, as is the wine cellar.

2. IL GIARDINO, 1382 Hornby St., Vancouver

Umberto Menghi owns three restaurants, of which this is the best. Expensive but tasteful. In addition to imported veal (from Montreal) and game, Umberto offers spectacular osso buco and a lemon-impregnated broiled chicken.

3. LE ST. AMABLE, 188 rue St. Amable, Montreal

The proprietor-owned-and-operated establishments are always the best and here one finds a large, large selection of entrées rendered in the classic fashion by a chef who understands the nuances of herbs and can produce a sauce worthy of the best in the land.

4. LHARDY'S, 634 Church St., Toronto

A relentless devotion to quality elevates Lhardy's and its companion establishment, Quenelles, to national recognition. While the name is Spanish, the cuisine is continental. The menu is limited, and changes with the seasons. The chef is part-owner, which is reassuring.

5. CHEZ BARDET, 591 rue Henri-Bourassa e., Montreal

The location is terrible, but everything else about André Bardet's establishment is of the highest order, including the many awards he has accumulated. Here is classic French cuisine; *haute cuisine* indeed. And a wine cellar of heroic proportions.

6. NAPOLEON, 79 Grenville St., Toronto

Christian Vinassac refreshes himself each August in France, then returns with new recipes which he himself renders with astonishing skill to a legion of faithful patrons. Quintessential French cuisine and a splendid cellar, cigars for the men, and flowers for the ladies.

7. THE RESTAURANT, Three Small Rooms, 22 St. Thomas St., Toronto

The Restaurant with its restrained service and inventive and unusual cuisine maintains its pre-eminent place as one of the very best in Canada.

8. L'ECHELLE DE JACOB, 27 Lucerne Blvd., Aylmer, Quebec

Ottawegians have discovered this gem in a renovated car barn, wherein the youthful proprietors lavish much care upon the cuisine, which is generally French rural. Charming decor and some adroit experimentation heighten the interest.

9. LA TRAIT DU ROI, 25½ rue de Notre Dame, Quebec City

More classic French cuisine in a beautifully decorated restaurant. The treat of kings is, apparently, excellent food and a wine cellar to match.

10. LE CHAMPLAIN, Chateau Frontenac, Quebec City

French and French Canadian cuisine, served in the grand manner, in what surely must be one of the handsomest hotels in the world; a spectacular restaurant in an equally spectacular setting.

Jeremy Brown
Author
Dining Out in Toronto

HORS D'OEUVRES

CREVETTES LINDI, SPÉCIALITÉ DE LA MAISON 5.00
Shrimps wrapped in fillet of Dover Sole, a Specialty of the House

COCKTAIL DE CREVETTES 4.25
Shrimp cocktail, chilled

CAVIAR FRAIS GARNI 11.00
Fresh Caviar Garnished

POIRE ALLIGATOR GARNIE DE CREVETTES 4.75
Avocado pear with Shrimps

**HUÎTRES FRAÎCHES SERVIES
SUR COQUILLE EN SAISON** 4.00
Fresh oysters, served in the shell (in season)

MOULES À L'ITALIENNE EN SAISON 4.25
Mussels with finely-chopped tomatoes, chives and oregano (in season)

COQUILLE ST-JACQUES 4.50
Scallops, mushrooms and cream sauce

SAUMON FRAIS À LA SUÉDOISE AVEC SAUCE DILL 4.75
Fresh salmon Swedish-style, with dill sauce

VOL AU VENT DE RIS DE VEAU 4.50
Sweetbreads in a patty shell with cream, madeira and calvados

POTAGES

CONSOMMÉ DU JOUR 1.50
Consommé of the Day

POTAGE DU JOUR 1.50
Soup of the Day

CRÈME CRESSONNIÈRE DE MON AMIE CARMEN 1.75
Cream of watercress Carmen

CRÈME VICHYSSOISE GLACÉE 2.00
Chilled cream of Vichyssoise

TORTUE CLAIRE THÉODORE AU SHERRY 2.50
Clear turtle soup with sherry Theodore

POTAGE TORTUE LADY CURZON 2.75
Turtle soup with curry and cream

SOUPE À L'OIGNON GRATINÉE 2.00
Onion soup au gratin

SALADES

SALADE SPÉCIALE WINSTON'S 2.25
Heart of romaine, endives, avocado and palm hearts

ENDIVES DE BELGIQUE AVEC VINAIGRETTE 2.25
Belgian endives with vinaigrette

SALADE ASCOT 2.00
Heart of romaine with fresh orange slices, oil and vinegar

Winston's Restaurant
104 Adelaide Street West, Toronto Telephone 363-1627

POISSONS

SOLE ANGLAISE POCHÉE "DARLING" 12.00
Poached whole Dover Sole "Darling" with cream sauce, lobster and brandy

FILET DE SOLE ANGLAISE BONNE FEMME 11.50
Fillet of Dover Sole Bonne Femme, with cream and mushrooms

SCAMPIS À LA WINSTON'S 11.00
Island scampis sautés with shallots and celery heads, simmered in
Port and garnished with braised lettuce served with Rice Pilaff

TRUITE À LA NOUVELLE ORLÉANS LE RUTH'S 11.50
Trout in pastry, stuffed with smoked salmon

TURBOT ANGELINA 11.50
Fresh turbot with mussels poached in white wine, fresh tomatoes,
saffron and glazed with sauce hollandaise

HOMARD SERVI AVEC BEURRE FONDU
Steamed lobster served with melted butter (Priced according to size)

ENTRÉES

**SUPRÊME DE VOLAILLE—
SPÉCIALITÉ DE LA MAISON** 10.25
Chicken suprême with shallots, pernod and calvados

CANETON DU LAC DE BROME MONTMORENCY 11.75
Brome Lake duckling with black cherries and cherry brandy

GIBIER SPÉCIAL DU JOUR 13.00
Chef's suggestion for the day "Game with wild rice"

FILET DE VEAU OSCAR 12.00
Fillet of veal with lobster, mushrooms, shallots and white wine

FILET DE VEAU 11.75
Veal with a thin slice of ham, cheese and blanched tomatoes

CARRÉ D'AGNEAU AUX AROMATES 11.50
Rack of lamb, served with Madeira Sauce,
glazed baby carrots and snow peas

ENTRECÔTE GRILLÉE 12.00
Grilled Sirloin Steak (12 oz)

FILET MIGNON AVEC SAUCE BÉARNAISE 12.50
Grilled filet mignon with béarnaise sauce

FILET DE BOEUF WELLINGTON 26.00
Fillet of beef wrapped in fine pastry, with périgorde sauce (for two)

CHÂTEAUBRIAND GARNI 26.00
Grilled, Bouquettiere of Vegetables double fillet of beef (for two)

FILET DE BOEUF FARCI AUX HUÎTRES 14.00
Filet mignon stuffed with fresh oysters

TOURNEDOS ROSSINI 13.50
Crown of Filet of Beef—on a crust—served with Foie Gras, and Truffles

Fresh in season vegetables (per person) 1.50

Coffee or Tea .75

The evening menu from Winston's in Toronto—Canada's best restaurant.

142

In Quebec, as anywhere else, good food means good materials,
lovingly prepared by someone who cares for the people who will eat it.

Mme Jehane Benoit
The Canadiana Cookbook

143

THE 10 BEST CANADIAN APHRODISIACS*

1. Wild Asparagus
2. Arctic Whale Blubber
3. Nova Scotia Lobster
4. West Coast Oysters
5. Niagara Peaches
6. Newfoundland Screech
7. Georgian Bay Sunfish
8. Manitoba Sturgeon Eggs (caviar)
9. Pure Buckwheat Prairie Honey
10. Black Pepper

*Although Gall Stones, Deer Antler Tips, and Prairie Oysters are not mentioned in the above list because of their scarce availability and extraordinary qualities, they are reputed to have strong aphrodisiac powers.

Exclusive to *The Canadian Book of Lists*

Nova Scotia lobster — reputed to be a powerful aphrodisiac.

THE 10 BEST CANADIAN RECIPES

1. WINSTON'S PÂTÉ

In his elegant restaurant, host John Arena serves this pâté with rye or toasted French bread every evening before dinner. It is delicious, but the trick is to find goose livers.

4	oz. goose livers	3	cloves garlic
1	lb. chicken livers	1	cup whipping cream
2	medium-sized onions, chopped		salt and pepper, to taste
1/2	oz. curry powder	1	oz. vintage port
1	teaspoon thyme	1	oz. cognac
3	whole bay leaves		

Sauté liver in frying pan and add all spices. Sauté onions and add to liver. Pass through mincer twice, then add cream, port, and cognac. Stir.

Pour into pan, place in double pan of water; and cook for one hour at 375°F. Chill and serve. Serves 8.

Winston's, Toronto

2. LOBSTER SOUP

The elderly lady who gave me this recipe said, "If you have been throwing the shells out after serving boiled or broiled lobster you have been throwing away one of the most delicious of all soups."

	shells of two lobsters	1	cup tomato juice
2	cups chicken stock or	1	bay leaf
2	chicken bouillon cubes		pinch of thyme
	dissolved in two cups		pinch of basil
	water		salt and pepper, to taste
1	cup dry white wine		

Crush the leftover shells lightly. You do not have to pound them. Place in a soup kettle and add all other ingredients. Simmer, covered, for one hour. Strain and store in refrigerator until needed. Serve hot or cold. Serves 4.

Marie Nightingale
Out of Old Nova Scotia Kitchens

3. JOE BATT'S ARM FISH CASSEROLE

This casserole got its curious name from Joe Batt who was a fisherman in Newfoundland and who used to prepare it on returning from a hard session on the Grand Banks. He preferred tinned goods to fresh — which is what made him eccentric in Newfoundland. The thing was that while

145

preparing this casserole he accidentally sliced his thumb into it, and by the time he reached the hospital, 50 miles away, word of mouth had expanded the thumb into an arm. The offending portion remained in the casserole, and those who tested it immediately proclaimed its excellence. Joe Batt's arm (i.e., thumb) was given the main credit. It's a real quickie meal.

1	package tomato vegetable soup	2	tins tuna
	handful of noodles	1	can shrimps
1	cup sour cream	1	cooked sausage (symbolic thumb)
	grated cheese		chili powder

Add 1½ cups boiling water to soup powder and let stand covered for 30 minutes. Boil noodles in salted water for seven minutes and drain. Put noodles in bottom of casserole dish. Put in layer of tuna fish. Add sausage and shrimps. Add sour cream to soup and chilli powder and pour over casserole. Put in remaining fish. Sprinkle grated cheese on top. Bake 30 minutes in 350°F. oven.

Peter Worthington and Ben Wicks
The Naked Gourmet

4. CHICKEN SUPRÊME

This recipe comes from Chez Bardet, one of Montreal's best-loved restaurants. Bon appétit!

4	boned chicken breasts	8	thin slices Emmenthal cheese
½	pt. 35% cream		
2	slices cooked ham	2	eggs
		1	oz. oil

Sprinkle chicken pieces lightly with flour, then dip them in a sauce made by beating eggs with a little oil, salt, and pepper. Place in a heated casserole dish to which you have added some oil; fry lightly, turning them over after several minutes. Transfer to a 350°F. oven for about 20 minutes, turning them once.

Add cream. Put half a slice of ham over each breast; top with cheese. Return to oven to melt cheese slightly. Remove chicken from oven and arrange on a serving plate. Boil down the cream until it has reached the desired thickness; season to taste and pour sauce over all.

Serve with creole rice and spinach.

André Bardet
Chez Bardet
Montreal

5. SPICED BEEF

A Christmas tradition among English Canadians.

1	8-lb. bottom round of beef, trimmed of all fat and bones

Marinade

1	oz. saltpeter	2	teaspoons ground allspice
2	tablespoons brown sugar	1	cup pickling salt
2	teaspoons ground cloves	2	tablespoons finely
2	teaspoons freshly grated nutmeg		crushed dry bay leaves

Cooking

1	tablespoon ground cloves	1	cup water
1	tablespoon ground allspice		piece of suet, 2 to 3 oz.

Place beef on a soft absorbent cloth large enough to wrap around meat completely. An old tea towel is ideal.

Combine dry ingredients for marinade. Pour over the beef and rub well into the surface. Wrap the beef in the cloth and place in a crock or glass bowl, cover, and refrigerate. Turn beef daily, kneading spices into beef, without removing cloth. The beef and spices form their own liquid. Leave for at least two weeks; three weeks is better.

To cook, rinse beef in cold water. Dry. Combine the one tablespoon cloves and the one tablespoon allspice and dust over the meat. Place in a roasting pan and add water. Slice the suet and spread over the top of the meat. Cover tightly and roast at 300°F. for three hours. Remove from the pan and, while still hot, pack beef into a bowl or crock. Cover with a plate and weigh down for 24 hours until cold and well pressed. Slice thinly.

Elizabeth Baird
Classic Canadian Cooking

6. GRAISSE DE RÔTI

An authentic Quebec daube. The famous graisse de rôti, which is served cold on toast, is made from the meat drippings. It is at its best cooked in an iron kettle.

4 to 5 lb. loin of pork			salt and pepper, to taste
2	garlic cloves	1	pork rind or pig's foot
1	teaspoon dry mustard	1	cup water
1	teaspoon savory		

Make four incisions in the loin and place half a garlic clove in each incision. Rub the meat all over with the dry mustard, letting most of it adhere to the fat. Sprinkle with savory, again letting most of it adhere to the fat.

147

Place the loin in the pan; add salt and pepper to taste. Cut the pork rind or pig's foot in several pieces and place them all around the meat. Add the water.

There are two ways you can now cook the roast:

- Place the pan over high heat and bring the whole to a boil. Cover and simmer over low heat for two hours, then uncover and cook over high heat until the liquid evaporates. Brown the fat part of the roast, then set the meat on a warm platter.
- Roast uncovered at 325°F. for 45 minutes per pound. When done, remove the meat to a warmed platter and place the pan over direct heat to make the gravy.

To make the gravy, in both methods, add one cup of water to the residue, then simmer for ten minutes, stirring and scraping the bottom of the pot all the time.

If you wish to have graisse de rôti instead of gravy, pass the pan juices through a fine sieve after scraping all the residue from the bottom of the pot. Refrigerate overnight.

Mme Jehane Benoit
The Canadiana Cookbook

7. CHEWY BROWNIES

The best I've ever tasted.

$^1/_2$	cup butter	1	cup walnuts
1	cup brown sugar	1	teaspoon vanilla
1	egg	$^1/_2$	cup flour
$^1/_2$	cup cocoa		pinch salt

Mix the ingredients in the order given and bake at 350°F. for 20 minutes in a greased cake pan. The brownies, cut in squares, will be soft and seem to be not finished — but that's the secret of their fudginess.

If you want the brownies even more chocolatey, use two squares of melted chocolate instead of cocoa.

Edna Staebler
Food that Really Schmecks

8. FIDDLEHEADS WITH CHEESE AND BLACK BUTTER

First, remove the loose brown coating by rubbing the fiddleheads between your hands.

24	fiddleheads	black butter
	Parmesan cheese	

In a three-quart saucepan place the fiddleheads with a little salt and enough water to cover, and boil for ten minutes. Remove from heat and drain thoroughly. On a long buttered dish sprinkled with grated Parmesan cheese, arrange fiddleheads in layers and sprinkle cheese between the layers.

When ready to serve, cover the cheese-sprinkled ferns copiously with black butter and glaze under the grill.

Black Butter

$^1/_2$	cup butter	chopped parsley

Put $^1/_2$ cup butter in a saucepan and cook until it is brown and begins to smoke. Add the chopped parsley and spread the mixture over the cheese-covered fiddleheads. Serves 4.

Berndt Berglund
The Edible Wild

9. MOLASSES AND OATMEAL BREAD

For those who have some Maritime-Scotch blood in their veins, and for those who wish they had, here is a recipe for molasses and oatmeal bread that succeeds even for the person who makes bread about once in four years. The recipe is my amalgamation of all the molasses-and-oatmeal-bread recipes I've read in the cookbooks of the Atlantic provinces — and it works.

1	cup Scotch-type oatmeal	3	tablespoons butter
2	cups boiling water	$^1/_2$	cup molasses
1	tablespoon or 1 envelope	3	teaspoons salt
	dried yeast poured on top	3	cups whole wheat flour
	of $^1/_2$ cup warm water,	$^1/_4$	cup wheat germ or plain
	flavoured with 1 teaspooon		flour
	ginger	2	cups all-purpose flour

Let the yeast sit in the water for about ten minutes. Make sure all particles are dissolved; if not, mix well. Pour boiling water over oatmeal while yeast is sitting.

Let the water and the oatmeal cool slightly, and then add yeast, molasses, salt, and butter, blending well. Now add three cups of whole wheat flour and $^1/_4$ cup wheat germ, beating hard. (Use a large bowl and a wooden spoon.) Add two cups of plain flour.

149

It will now be impossible to beat further; kneading time has come round. You must knead for about 15 minutes on a floured board, pressing down with the palms of your hands and turning over the dough so that it will get smooth and elastic. It is hard work, so if there is a willing child around give him or her a piece of the dough to knead; it will do it, as well as your child, no harm. When you think you've had enough, form the dough into a big ball, put it in a greased bowl, and brush the top of the dough with soft butter. Let it rise in a warm place for about 1¹/₂ to two hours. (I open my oven door flat, turn on the oven to 150°F., or warm, put the bowl of rising dough on the door and let the warm air from the oven waft over it.)

After the dough has doubled in bulk, punch it down, divide it into two parts, and put the two loaves into greased loaf pans. If it is now midnight, and you don't feel like waking the rest of the household at 4 o'clock in the morning for a taste of hot homemade bread, place the pans containing the dough in the refrigerator with weights on top of the dough (cans of soup or something like that), and go to sleep. The next morning, or whenever, take the pans out of the refrigerator and allow the loaves to rise a second time for about two hours the same way as before.

Bake at 375°F. for 40 minutes. The loaves should be ready if the crust sounds hollow when you tap it. It is a very crusty loaf with a slightly sweet flavour. Eat some of it immediately. This bread also keeps well (and freezes beautifully).

Sondra Gotlieb
The Gourmet's Canada

10. ROYAL CANADIAN COFFEE

The textures and tastes are fit for the gods.

8	oz. very hot coffee	1	oz. rye whisky
¹/₂	tablespoon granulated sugar	1	tablespoon whipped cream
1	oz. maple liqueur		

Wet rim of glass (or mug) with maple liqueur. Dip rim into sugar. Pour sugar and maple liqueur into glass. Pour in boiling coffee. Add whisky and top with whipped cream.

Note: Optionally, the amount of coffee and alcohol can be reduced to six oz. and ¹/₂ oz. each of maple liqueur and rye whisky. Rim of glass or mug can be caramelized over a flame at the table, after being coated with sugar.

For larger groups, caramelization can be done ahead of time, by cooking sugar to a light caramel and dipping glasses' or mugs' rims into it. Care should be exercised with delicate glasses, as caramelized sugar is very hot.

Chef Tony Roldan
Harbour Castle Hilton
Toronto

10 TYPICALLY CANADIAN EPICURIAN DELIGHTS

1. NEWFOUNDLAND DOG
Very good eating and there's plenty for everyone. Salt and smoke meat with juniper berries, raspberry branches, and Indian Tea.

2. BOILED PORCUPINE
Burn off quills, then wash, boil, and eat.

3. BAKED SKUNK
Clean thoroughly, then skin and bake with salt and pepper. Ensure that specimen is dead.

4. RABBIT À LA MODE
Soak sliced rabbit in vinegar and water for two days. Add salt and pepper and dredge in flour. Cook rabbit in melted fat and vinegar water until tender. Remove rabbit and add flour and ice cream to broth to make gravy. Serve only to your closest friends

5. WILLOW TIPS CEREAL
Pick fresh green willow buds in early spring. Add milk and sugar and eat.

6. FRIED WHALE MEAT
Acquire a medium to large whale, preferably over two-and-a-half tons. Cut up into small, bacon-size pieces and fry with onions in grease. Invite the neighbourhood.

7. BOILED LYNX
Cut into small pieces and boil until tender.

8. BOILED REINDEER TONGUES
Place reindeer tongues in boiling water and cook until ready. If you hear Bambi-like voices coming from inside the pot, tongues are not ready.

9. BAKED SEAL FLIPPERS
Ingredients: onions, baking soda, fat, Worcestershire Sauce, water, and seal flippers. Bake at 350°F. until reasonably tender. If, after three hours the flippers are not tender, your butcher has cheated you.

10. MUSKRAT TAILS
Dip into boiling water and pull off fur. Boil or bake — it does not matter; the end result is still the same.

David Ondaatje
Exclusive to *The Canadian Book of Lists*

5 REASONS WHY MOST CANADIANS OVEREAT

1. As children, their mothers use them as guinea pigs for their cooking.
2. To avoid sex.
3. Because they believe big is best...this goes for bellies and beer.
4. They don't know what to do with their time.
5. Because doctors advise against it.

David Scott-Atkinson
Public Relations Executive
and Canadian Trend Observer

THE 10 CANADIAN FOODS WITH FEWER THAN 10 CALORIES PER SERVING

1. Club soda
2. Coffee (black)
3. Tea (clear)
4. Sauerkraut juice
5. Watercress
6. Zucchini (baked)
7. Dill pickle
8. Asparagus
9. Raw lettuce
10. Spinach

Dr. Zak Sabry
Nutritionist
Former Head of Nutrition Canada

THE 7 BEST DIETS
CANADIANS SHOULD FOLLOW

1. *The Prudent Diet*, published by David White, Port Washington, N.Y.

2. *New York Department of Health Diet*, published by the Department of Health, New York.

3. *Weight Watchers Diet*, published by Weight Watchers, Inc., New York.

4. *Diet Workshop Diet*, published by the Diet Workshop, available from local branches.

5. *AMA: the Healthy Way to Weigh Less Diet*, published by the American Medical Association, Chicago.

6. *Ladies' Home Journal Diet*, Macmillan, New York.

7. *Antonetti's Computer Diet*, Evans, New York.

Ruth Fremes and Dr. Zak Sabry
Nutrition Experts, Authors
NutriScore

THE 7 WORST DIETS
CANADIANS FOLLOW

1. *Dr. Linn's Last Chance Diet*, Bantam, New York.

2. *Dr. Atkins' Diet Revolution*, David McKay, New York.

3. *Dr. Atkins' Super Energy Diet*, David McKay, New York.

4. *The Zero Calorie Diet* (fasting), published in various magazines.

5. *Dr. Stillman's Inches-Off Diet*, Prentice Hall, Englewood Cliffs, New Jersey.

6. *The Drinking Man's Diet*, Cameron, San Francisco.

7. *Zen Macrobiotic Diet*, Ignoramus Press, Los Angeles.

Ruth Fremes and Dr. Zak Sabry
Nutrition Experts, Authors
NutriScore

THE 10 CANADIAN PROVINCES THAT SPEND THE MOST MONEY IN RESTAURANTS

		($ '000)
1.	ONTARIO	722,196
2.	QUEBEC	635,382
3.	BRITISH COLUMBIA*	203,989
4.	ALBERTA	159,160
5.	MANITOBA	100,382
6.	SASKATCHEWAN	58,547
7.	NOVA SCOTIA	41,027
8.	NEW BRUNSWICK	36,549
9.	NEWFOUNDLAND	18,505
10.	PRINCE EDWARD ISLAND	4,763

*Includes Yukon and Northwest Territories

Statistics Canada

THE 10 MOST POPULAR MAIN DISHES CONSUMED BY CANADIANS AT HOME

1. Fried chicken

2. Roast beef (including stews made from left-over roasts)

3. Baked ham

4. Spaghetti with meat sauce, then meat balls

5. Meat loaf

6. Fish (various, including canned)

7. Pork chops

8. Pot roasts and other less expensive cuts of beef

9. Macaroni with cheese, and other forms of pasta

10. Steak

Jeremy Brown
Exclusive to *The Canadian Book of Lists*

THE 10 MOST POPULAR
SOFT DRINKS CONSUMED IN CANADA

1. Coca-Cola
2. Pepsi-Cola
3. Seven-Up
4. Diet Cola
5. Ginger Ale

6. Orange
7. Root Beer
8. Fruit-flavoured diet drinks
9. Mountain Dew
10. Cream Soda

Jeremy Brown
Author
Dining Out in Toronto

THE 10 MOST POPULAR
CANADIAN DRINKS

1. Water
2. Milk
3. Coffee
4. Tea
5. Orange Juice (frozen imported)

6. Coca-Cola
7. Beer (domestic)
8. Wine (imported)
9. Canadian Rye Whisky
10. Wine (domestic)

Jeremy Brown
Author
Dining Out in Toronto

9
ENTERTAINMENT

10 CANADIANS WHO HAVE WON ACADEMY AWARDS, EITHER IN AMERICAN OR CANADIAN FILMS

1. MARY PICKFORD

Best actress, *Coquette,* 1928-29, Special Academy Award in 1975: "In recognition of her unique contributions to the film industry and the development of film as an artistic medium."

2. NORMA SHEARER

Best Actress, *The Divorcee,* 1929-30.

3. MARIE DRESSLER

Best Actress, *Min and Bill,* 1930-31.

4. MACK SENNETT

Special Academy Award in 1937 "for his lasting contribution to the comedy technique of the screen."

5. DEANNA DURBBIN

Special Academy Award in 1938 (with Mickey Rooney) "for their significant contribution in bringing to the screen the spirit and personification of youth, and as juvenile players setting a high standard of ability and achievement."

6. LOUIS B. MAYER

Special Academy Award in 1950 "for distinguished service to the motion picture industry."

7. CHRISTOPHER CHAPMAN

Best Documentary, 1967, *A Place to Stand.*

8. F.R. CRAWLEY

Best Documentary (feature length) 1975, *The Man who Skied Down Everest.*

9. CO HOEDEMAN

Best Animated Short, 1977, *The Sand Castle* (NFB).

Canadian actress Mary Pickford won an Academy Award in 1975.

10. BEVERLY SHAFFER

Best Live Action Short, 1977, *I'll Find a Way* (with Yuki Yoshida).

*ALSO

A Special Academy Award to the National Film Board in 1941 "for distinctive achievement" with *Churchill's Island* and a special Academy Award to Warner Brothers for "producing *The Jazz Singer*, the pioneer talking picture which has revolutionized the industry."

Gerald Pratley
Director
Ontario Film Institute

THE 10 BIGGEST-GROSSING
CANADIAN MOVIES (ENGLISH) *

1.	The Apprenticeship of Duddy Kravitz	$1,800,000
2.	Black Christmas	$1,800,000
3.	Why Shoot the Teacher	$1,400,000
4.	Shivers	$1,065,170
5.	Shadow of the Hawk	$1,020,000
6.	Death Weekend	$964,716
7.	Rabid	$900,000
8.	Lies My Father Told Me	$875,000
9.	Paperback Hero	$700,000
10.	Recommendation for Mercy	$640,000

*Domestic Gross Only

Sid Adilman
Entertainment Columnist
The Toronto Star

THE 10 BIGGEST-GROSSING
CANADIAN MOVIES (FRENCH) *

1.	Deux femmes en or	$2,500,000
2.	l'Initiation	$1,883,000
3.	Valerie	$1,684,000
4.	Bingo	$1,500,000
5.	Il était une fois dans l'est	$1,000,000
6.	J'ai mon voyage	$1,000,000
7.	Les Beau Dimanches	$1,000,000
8.	Tiens tois bien après les oreilles à Papa	$900,000

9. l'Aventure d'une jeune veuve $800,000

10. Les Malles $750,000

*Domestic gross only.

Sid Adilman
Entertainment Columnist
The Toronto Star

THE 10 BEST CANADIAN FILMS *

1. BRETHREN

Dennis Zahoruk's understanding, natural, and well-acted study of a small-town Ontario family which comes together on the death of the father to discover themselves and reveal their traits, traumas, and weaknesses.

2. GOIN' DOWN THE ROAD

Don Shebib's simple, classic film from William Fruet's screenplay of two uneducated and unemployed Maritimers and their desperate search for happiness in Toronto. Beautifully played by Paul Bradley and Douglas McGrath.

3. ISABEL

Paul Almond's somewhat murky film set in Quebec about a young girl's vivid imaginings in a gloomy family home is nevertheless unforgettable and oddly moving because of Genevieve Bujold's intense performance.

4. MON ONCLE ANTOINE (My Uncle Antoine)

Claude Jutra's almost perfect film about Nephew Benoit and his growing awareness of life in his uncle's village shop. A finely recreated glimpse of yesteryear, written by Clement Perron.

5. THE ONLY THING YOU KNOW

Clarke Mackey's only full-length film, largely improvised in a way both entirely natural and believable, about a lost and lonely girl betrayed by her first love.

6. OUTRAGEOUS

A lively, humorous, and engaging film about the shabby life of a transvestite homosexual and a mentally unbalanced girl to whom he brings a touch of sanity.

*In alphabetical order.

Goin' Down the Road, *beautifully played by Paul Bradley and Douglas McGrath, is one of the best Canadian films ever made.*

7. REJEANNE PADOVANI

Deny Arcand's harsh and unrelenting exposé of political and industrial corruption in Quebec; we know it happens everywhere, but no one else has had the courage to film it.

8. THE ROWDYMAN

Gordon Pinsent's appealing, rougish, romantic remembrance of his younger days in Newfoundland. Robust and lively and filled with the windy, salty sea air of Newfoundland.

9. SKIPTRACER

Zale Dalen's remarkable study of a debt collector's lonely life in Vancouver and how he comes to hate himself and his work. Convincingly played by David Peterson in a sure and knowing treatment of the subject.

10. LE TEMPS D'UNE CHASSE (Once Upon a Hunt)

Francis Mankiewicz's controlled and sensitive portrait of a trio of French-speaking Montrealers who escape their family responsibilities for a weekend of hunting and womanizing, and of their eventual tragedy.

Gerald Pratley
Director
Ontario Film Institute

THE 10 WORST CANADIAN FILMS

1. BLACK CHRISTMAS
A shoddy thriller which doesn't work, pitifully attempting to look American, unconvincing, contrived, and repellant.

2. CHILD UNDER A LEAF
A foolish and juvenile attempt to give a scatty romanticism to a painfully boring adulterous affair.

3. THE CLOWN MURDERS
Confused and bewildering crime melodrama, in which a practical joke turns into an act of revenge — no one is quite sure why.

4. DEATH WEEKEND
A deliberate bloodbath of unreasoned and calculated sex and violence, the tragedy of which is that the system forced the talented William Fruet to make it in order to work.

5. L'EAU CHAUDE, L'EAU FRETTE (Hot Water, Cold Water)
Common and vulgar comedy about assorted inhabitants of a rowdy rooming house in Montreal; unfunny, unfit, and lacking any sense of truth.

6. THE RAINBOW BOYS
A comedy-drama which fails to appeal to any audience, young or old, and loses its way among some magnificent B.C. scenery.

7. SHIVERS (The Parasite Murders)
This could have been a worthy horror film; instead, it became a revolting piece of cheap sensationalism.

8. SLIPSTREAM
A pseudo-philosophical ramble on the Prairies, as a disc jockey attempts to come to grips with life and ambition.

9. RITUALS
Another calculated journey into violence in vaguely American territory for no clearly defined reason.

10. WOLFPEN PRINCIPLE
A dense, dark, and terribly tedious piece of symbolism about man and nature.

Gerald Pratley
Director
Ontario Film Institute

THE 10 BEST CANADIAN MOVIE MAKERS *

1. Michel Brault, cameraman-director-producer
2. Donald Brittain, producer-director
3. Gilles Carle, director
4. Tom Daly, producer
5. Claude Jutra, director
6. Allan King, producer-director
6. Richard Leiterman, cameraman
8. Norman MacLaren, animator
9. Peter Pearson, director
10. Eric Till, director

*In alphabetical order.

Sid Adilman
Entertainment Columnist
The Toronto Star

6 WAYS TO FEND OFF EAGER MOVIE PUBLICISTS IN CANADA

1. "Charlie, I'm absolutely *lost for words!* Thank you, and good night."
2. "Charlie, believe me, this is one they'll *all* be talking about!"
3. "Charlie,my wife couldn't get here tonight. Just wait till I tell her what she *missed!*"
4. "Charlie, what we've just seen is more than just another motion picture. It's an *experience!*"
5. "Charlie, I don't mind telling you I've *never* encountered anything to compare with it!"
6. "Charlie, by God *you've* done *it again!*"

Clyde Gilmour
Movie Critic, Broadcaster

10 MEMORABLE MOMENTS
AND LASTING ACCOMPLISHMENTS
IN AND OUT OF CANADIAN MOVIES

1. Peter Pearson's first fiction film, *The Best Damn Fiddler from Calabogie to Kaladar,* with screenplay by Joan Finnegan, with Kate Reid and Chris Wiggins as the indomitable parents, and Margot Kidder as the daughter who thinks there must be a better way to live.

2. The Canadian Film Awards presentation ceremony in 1968, the first time under the revised system, where both Norman McLaren *(Pas de Deux)* and Christopher Chapman *(A Place to Stand)* received standing ovations.

3. Stuart Gillard's perfect performance as the young reporter in *Why Rock the Boat* which brought so accurately to life the young man described in William Weintraub's novel.

4. The classic simplicity, honesty, and lasting appeal of *Drylanders,* the National Film Board's first excursion into feature films. Directed by Don Haldane.

5. The body of work by Allan King, with its experimental documentary methods culminating in his beautiful, dramatic *Who Has Seen the Wind.*

6. The liveliness, humour, frankness, and sense of place of almost all French-language Canadian films.

7. The work of Larry Kent, which created an authentic Canadian feeling in the cinema during the difficult days of the early sixties with *Bitter Ash, Sweet Substitute*, and *When Tomorrow Dies.*

8. The beautiful, vigorous, and vivid photography of Jean-Claude Labrecque, which has graced and enlivened many of the most important films made in Quebec since the early sixties.

9. John Grierson's first return to Canada on the occasion of the National Film Board's 25th Anniversary in 1964.

10. A collective compliment to all Canadian actors and actresses in all Canadian films.

Gerald Pratley
Director
Ontario Film Institute

French Canadian Genevieve Bujold may be the best Canadian actress today.

THE 10 BEST CANADIAN ACTRESSES *

1. Genevieve Bujold
2. Jackie Burroughs
3. Denise Filliatraut
4. Barbara Hamilton
5. Martha Henry

6. Frances Hyland
7. Micheline Lanctot
8. Jane Mallett
9. Monique Mercure
10. Kate Reid

*In alphabetical order

Sid Adilman
Entertainment Columnist
The Toronto Star

John Colicos — renowned internationally as one of the finest Canadian actors.

THE 10 BEST CANADIAN ACTORS *

1. John Colicos
2. Jean Duceppe
3. Jean Gascon
4. Bruno Gerussi
5. William Hutt

6. Jean Lapointe
7. Gordon Pinsent
8. Christopher Plummer
9. Douglas Rain
10. Jean Louis Roux

*In alphabetical order.

Sid Adilman
Entertainment Columnist
The Toronto Star

10 INTERNATIONALLY FAMOUS MOVIES WITH MAJOR CANADIAN CONTENT

1. THE GODFATHER
   Produced by Al Ruddy.

2. THE IPCRESS FILE
   Directed by Sidney Furie.

3. JAMES BOND MOVIES
   Most of them co-produced by Cubby Broccoli.

4. AIRPORT
   Written by Arthur Hailey, from his book of the same name. Directed by Arthur Hiller.

5. IN THE HEAT OF THE NIGHT
   Directed by Norman Jewison.

6. THE CHARGE OF THE LIGHT BRIGADE
   The star was Christopher Plummer.

7. KLUTE
   Donald Sutherland co-starred with Jane Fonda.

8. LOVE STORY
   Arthur Hiller scored again as director.

9. GEORGY GIRL
   Directed by Sylvio Narrizano.

10. F.I.S.T.
    Directed by Norman Jewison.

Bill Marshall,
Producer
Outrageous

10 WAYS TO FINANCE A CANADIAN MOTION PICTURE *

1. TAX SHELTER FINANCING
   The Canadian Income Tax Act provides an incentive to an investor purchasing an ownership interest of a "certified feature production" by permitting him to deduct from his income from all sources 100 percent of the purchase price.

*Usually a combination is necessary to raise all the required money.

2. A NEGATIVE PICK-UP DEAL WITH A MAJOR U.S. DISTRIB-UTOR

In this arrangement a distributor such as Warner Bros., Paramount, or Universal agrees to advance to the producer at the time of delivery of the completed picture a sum of money against the producer's share of distribution receipts. The agreement with the distributor is then discounted with a bank to provide the money to make the film.

3. PRE-SALE OF THE PICTURE TO A CANADIAN AND A U.S. TELEVISION NETWORK

These agreements usually call for a minimum of two runs with an option for successive runs, commencing 28 months after first theatrical release of the picture. The sale moneys are then used to make the film.

4. PRE-SALE OF CANADIAN AND U.S. TELEVISION SYNDICA-TION RIGHTS

These agreements call for television exhibition of the picture over local stations subsequent to its network play. The producer can expect to receive from such a sale somewhere between one-third to one-half of the amount the network pays.

5. PRE-SALE OF PAY-TELEVISION RIGHTS

The major company involved in pay-television in the United States is Home Box Office, a division of Time-Life Television. The agreement usually calls for exhibition of the film on pay-television during the period approximately 9-18 months after first theatrical release.

6. PRE-SALE TO INFLIGHT TELEVISION

Self-explanatory.

7. ADVANCE FROM FOREIGN TERRITORIES

These agreements are usually made at one of the important annual film festivals (Cannes, for example) through a producer's sales representative either before or during principal photography of the picture.

8. CO-PRODUCTION AGREEMENT WITH PRODUCERS FROM OTHER TERRITORIES

These agreements are usually made in accordance with the formal treaties entered into between Canada and the United Kingdom, France, Italy, Germany, and Israel.

9. INVESTMENT BY THE CANADIAN FILM DEVELOPMENT CORPORATION

The Corporation has always had a general policy of investing a maximum of $200,000 in any motion picture. However, this amount has been exceeded in particular cases in the past. Latterly the Corporation has been willing to enter into bridge-financing arrangements with producers covering the pre-production period, that is, until the final budgeted financing is in place.

10. INVESTMENT BY A CANADIAN THEATRE CHAIN (FAM-
    OUS PLAYERS OR ODEON THEATRES)
    Neither corporation has put any money into films in recent months
because they have been waiting for the government's policy on the imposition
of quotas and levies on exhibitors to be clarified. But they have invested in
the past and no doubt will do so again sometime in the future.

Garth H. Drabinsky
Lawyer, Movie Producer

THE 10 ALL-TIME BEST
TELEVISION PROGRAMS EVER
PRODUCED IN CANADA

1. THE TENTH DECADE, CBC, produced by Cameron Graham

2. THIS HOUR HAS SEVEN DAYS, CBC, produced by Douglas Leiterman
   and Patrick Watson

3. CONNECTIONS, CBC, produced by Martyn Burke and Bill Macadam

4. JACK KANE'S MUSIC MAKERS, CBC, produced by Norman Sedawie

5. AIR OF DEATH, CBC, produced by Larry Gosnell

6. QUENTIN DURGENS, M.P., produced by Ronald Weyman and David
   Gardiner

7. HOCKEY NIGHT IN CANADA, CBC/CTV, produced by Ralph
   Mellanby

8. CTV INQUIRY: FAILING STRATEGY, produced by Jack McGaw

9. NATIONAL DREAM, CBC, produced by Jim Murray

10. JALNA, CBC, produced by John Trent

Jack Miller
Television Critic
The Toronto Star

10 FAVOURITE CANADIAN PLAYS

1. THE FIRST FALLS ON MONDAY

By Arthur Murphy of Halifax. Murphy makes real drama out of history.

2. A TOUCH OF GOD IN THE GOLDEN AGE

By John Palmer of Toronto. Too much of a good thing as it stands, the play has almost the only second act worth a damn written by a Canadian up to that point.

3. LISTEN TO THE WIND

By James Reaney of London, Ontario. A lovely, Bronté-ish theatrical evening without the filigree and over-ornamentation that make the Donnelly circle so inaccessible.

4. CREEPS

By David Freeman of Montreal. Probably for personal reasons (I had polio as a child and had to teach myself to walk over the objections of the experts). I admire this story of independence attained.

5. THREE DEAD SISTERS

By Glen Bodyan of Winnipeg. This riotously funny scatalogical put-on has never been produced. I don't know why.

6. SAME TIME NEXT YEAR

By Bernard Slade formerly of Toronto and now of Los Angeles. A fine commercial comedy, and would there were thirty more!

7. ZASTROZZI

By George Walker of Toronto. Controlled, economical, practically twelve-tone.

8. ME?

By Martin Kinch of Toronto. A great statement of the artist's schizophrenic need for order and chaos, involvement and distance. Very Toronto, very Canadian.

9. ON THE JOB

By David Fenario of Montreal. In which the agitprop characters keep throwing off their ideological masks and letting us see the people underneath.

10. LEAVING HOME

By David French of Toronto. Derivative but the start of an important career.

Tom Hendry
Playwright

THE 10 GREATEST CANADIAN THEATRICAL ACHIEVEMENTS

1. Establishment of Canada Council in 1957

2. The Charlottetown Festival, launched in 1965

3. Le Théâtre du Nouveau Monde, begun in 1951

4. The Manitoba Theatre Centre, started in 1958

5. Ed Mirvish's purchase of the Royal Alexandra Theatre, saving it from certain demolition in 1963

6. Creation of The National Ballet of Canada in 1951

7. The Shaw Festival, begun by the late Brian Doherty in 1962

8. The Stratford Festival, the brainchild of Tom Patterson, in 1953

9. Michel Tremblay's 11-play cycle about east-end Montreal starting with *Les Belles-Soeurs,* which premiered in 1968

10. The Young People's Theatre Centre, founded by Susan Rubes in 1977

Sid Adilman
Entertainment Columnist
The Toronto Star

THE 10 GREATEST CANADIAN OPERA SINGERS

1. EMMA ALBANI (1847-1930)

Our first operatic superstar was born Marie-Louise Emma Cecile Lajeunesses in Chambly, Quebec, before turning soprano, Italianizing her name, repeatedly serenading Queen Victoria, and eventually being made a Dame by George V.

2. EDWARD JOHNSON (1881-1959)

From Guelph, he called himself Edoardo di Giovanni as a budding tenor in Italy but came back to North America to star at the Metropolitan Opera and eventually (1935-1950) became its general manager.

3. RAOUL JOBIN (1906-   )

Made his debut in Paris in 1930 and became one of the most sought-after tenors in the French operatic repertory before returning to Montreal in 1957 to teach singing.

170

4. GEORGE LONDON (1920-   )

Left Montreal as a child, studied in Los Angeles, and became one of the leading bass-baritones of his day, as famous for his acting as his singing.

5. LEOPOLD SIMONEAU (c. 1920-   )

Another Montrealer, Simoneau was known not only for his French roles but as one of the greatest Mozart tenors of his generation.

6. PIERRETTE ALARIE (1921-   )

Mrs. Leopold Simoneau offstage, Alarie often sang opposite her husband in the French and Mozart repertory.

7. JON VICKERS (1926-   )

Perhaps the greatest tenor Canada has ever produced, Vickers is our reigning operatic superstar and the answer to a Wagnerite's prayer.

8. LOUIS QUILICO (1926-   )

Yet another Montrealer, Quilico has sung an enormous repertory on stages as far afield as Moscow's Bolshoi and New York's Metropolitan in the course of becoming our leading baritone.

9. MAUREEN FORRESTER (1931-   )

Not only Canada's but probably the world's greatest contralto, Forrester devotes more time to concerts than opera but has turned green at The Met (Erda in *Das Rheingold*) and even flown a broom on television (the Witch in *Hansel and Gretel*).

10. TERESA STRATAS (1938-   )

Born Anastasia Stratakis in Toronto, Stratas has sung on nearly all the world's major stages following her victory in the 1959 Metropolitan Opera auditions.

William Littler
Music Critic
The Toronto Star

THE 10 BEST SYMPHONY ORCHESTRAS IN CANADA

1. The Toronto Symphony

2. The Montreal Symphony Orchestra

3. The Vancouver Symphony Orchestra

4. The Winnipeg Symphony Orchestra

5. The Hamilton Philharmonic

6. The Quebec Symphony Orchestra

171

7. The Atlantic Symphony Orchestra

8. The Edmonton Symphony Orchestra

9. The Calgary Philharmonic Orchestra

10. The London Symphony Orchestra

*The National Arts Centre Orchestra, a classical orchestra of 46 players
rather than a full-sized modern symphony orchestra, belongs in a class
by itself. It produces the most refined orchestral playing heard
in Canada.

William Littler
Music Critic
The Toronto Star

THE 10 MOST FREQUENTED
CANADIAN THEATRE FESTIVALS

	Attendance Figures 1977
1. Rainbow Stage, Manitoba	779,234
2. Stratford Festival, Ontario	504,000
3. Festival Ottawa, Ontario	228,798
4. Shaw Festival, Ontario	137,844
5. Charlottetown Festival of the Arts, Prince Edward Island	68,090
6. Banff Festival of the Arts, Alberta	30,000
7. Festival Lennoxville, Quebec	23,000
8. Guelph Spring Festival, Ontario	12,113
9. Canadian Mime Theatre, Ontario	10,000
10. Kipawa Showboat Company, Nova Scotia	3,000

Canadian Government Office of Tourism

Maureen Forrester — one of the best Canadian opera singers of all time.

THE 15 BEST CANADIAN PERFORMERS *

1. Dave Broadfoot
2. Jean Carignan
3. Maureen Forrester
4. Glenn Gould
5. Don Harron
6. Pauline Julien
7. Karen Kain
8. Monique Leyrac

9. Gordon Lightfoot
10. Anne Murray
11. Oscar Peterson
12. The Travellers
13. Jon Vickers
14. Gilles Vigneault
15. Johnny Wayne and Frank Shuster

*In alphabetical order.

Sid Adilman
Entertainment Columnist
The Toronto Star

Dave Broadfoot — a fascinating Canadian performer.

THE 10 MOST SOUGHT-AFTER BROADCAST PERFORMERS IN CANADA

1. Pierre Berton
2. Dave Broadfoot
3. Fred Davis
4. Don Harron
5. Tommy Hunter

6. Betty Kennedy
7. Anne Murray
8. Gordon Pinsent
9. Gordon Sinclair
10. Charles Templeton

Jerry Lodge
Talent Agent

Gordon Pinsent is probably the most sought after broadcast performer in Canada.

Canadian Oscar Peterson may be the greatest living jazz pianist in the world today.

10 BEST CANADIAN JAZZ MUSICIANS OF ALL TIME

1. MAYNARD FERGUSON, trumpet

He specializes in high-note flights — some of his solos are detected only by cocker spaniels — but when he falls into a more subdued mood, he can etch a nice melodic line.

2. OSCAR PETERSON, piano

Some say he's the best pianist in the jazz business, the logical successor to Art Tatum. Whatever his ranking, he plays with scintillating technique and enormous energy.

3. MOE KAUFFMAN, alto saxophone and flute

Look behind the occasional gimmicks — electrified horns, blowing two altos at once, jazzing the classics and rocking the jazz — and you'll find a musician with a delicious imagination and a gift for direct communication.

4. ED BICKERT, guitar

He's the great melodist of the guitar, a player with a gossamer touch, an unshakable sense of rhythm, and an unending source of invention.

5. TRUMP DAVIDSON, trumpet, vocals

A mainstream player until his death in 1978, he brought an original sense of phrasing and tasteful rambunctiousness to Canadian jazz.

6. ROB McCONNELL, valve trombone

He's a vivid player and adroit arranger, but maybe his most essential contribution comes as the leader and chief inspiration of the swooping, powerful big band known as the Boss Brass.

7. DON THOMPSON, bass, piano vibraharp

He also writes haunting songs — viz "A Country Place" — and as a studio engineer, he has masterminded some gorgeous jazz albums, many of which feature his own exquisite playing.

8. PHIL NIMMONS, clarinet and leader

His big bands, showcasing his own ambitious and successful compositions, have offered listeners some of the most valuable of all-Canadian large-group jazz.

9. SONNY GREENWICH, guitar

He's a daring and adventurous soloist who has expanded the guitar's possibilities into some fairly far-out territory.

10. GUIDO BASSO, flugelhorn and trumpet

He has a personal, sometimes quirky, often romantic, consistently enthralling way of blowing his horn, and his talent for improvisation seems to know no identifiable bounds.

Jack Batten
Author, Columnist

THE 10 MOST POPULAR PLAYS OR MUSICAL COMEDIES TO PLAY CANADA IN THE LAST 15 YEARS

1. ANNIE
2. A CHORUS LINE
3. HAIR
4. OH COWARD!
5. TRIBUTE
6. JACQUES BREL IS ALIVE AND WELL AND LIVING IN PARIS
7. SOUND OF MUSIC
8. HEDDA GABLER
9. SPRING THAW '67
10. FIDDLER ON THE ROOF

Gino Empry
Public Relations and
Personal Management Services

THE 10 LONGEST-RUNNING CANADIAN SHOWS OR CANADIAN ENGAGEMENTS OF IMPORTED SHOWS

1. Anne of Green Gables
2. Belinda
3. Godspell
4. Hair
5. Jacques Brel is Alive and Well and Living in Paris
6. My Fur Lady
7. Suddenly This Summer
8. Spring Thaw
9. Sweet Reason
10. You're a Good Man, Charlie Brown

Sid Adilman
Entertainment Columnist
The Toronto Star

THE 10 CANADIAN SONGS MOST SUNG BY CANADIANS IN THE EARLY PART OF THE TWENTIETH CENTURY

1. When You and I Were Young, Maggie
   Written by George Washington Johnson, 1864

2. Darktown Strutters' Ball
   Written by Shelton Brooks, 1917

3. Some of These Days
   Written by Shelton Brooks, 1910

4. Peg o' My Heart
   Written by Alfred Bryan, 1913

5. The World is Waiting for the Sunrise
   Written by Lockeridge-Sights, 1919

6. Sweethearts on Parade
   Written by Carmen Lombardo, 1928

7. I'll Never Smile Again
   Written by Ruth Lowe, 1939

8. When My Baby Smiles at Me
   Written by Bill Munro, 1920

9. Beer Barrel Polka
   Written by Vejvoda, 1938

10. Alouette
    Traditional French Canadian folksong

THE 10 CANADIAN SONGS
MOST SUNG BY CANADIANS
LATER IN THE TWENTIETH CENTURY

1. There's a Bluebird on Your Windowsill
   Written by Elizabeth Clarke, 1948

2. Far Away Places
   Written by Kramer -Whitney, 1948

3. My Heart Cries for You
   Written by Percy Faith, 1952

4. Walk Hand in Hand with Me
   Written by Johnny Cowell

5. Four Strong Winds
   Written by Ian and Sylvia Tyson, 1966

6. Aquarius
   Written by Galt McDermott, 1966

7. If You Could Read My Mind
   Written by Gordon Lightfoot, 1969

8. Snowbird
   Written by Gene MacLellan, 1970

9. Spinning Wheel
   Written by David Clayton Thomas, 1973

10. My Way
    Written by Paul Anka, 1974

THE 10 TOP-SELLING COUNTRY RECORDS IN THE PAST 15 YEARS WRITTEN AND/OR PERFORMED BY CANADIANS

1. Four Strong Winds
   Performed by Bobby Bare, written by Ian Tyson.

2. Snowbird
   Sung by Anne Murray, written by Gene MacLellan.

3. Paper Rosie
   Sung by Gene Watson, written by Dallas Harms.

4. Someone Loves You Honey
   Sung by Charley Pride, written by Don Devaney.

5. Someday Soon
   Sung by Judy Collins, written by Ian Tyson.

6. Summer Wages
   Written and sung by Ian Tyson.

7. Canadian Pacific
   Sung by George Hamilton IV, written by Ray Griff.

8. Wreck of the Edmund Fitzgerald
   Written and sung by Gordon Lightfoot.

9. The French Song
   Performed by Lucille Starr, written by Pease and Vincent.

10. Farmer's Song
    Written and sung by Murray McLaughlin.

CFGM Radio
Richmond Hill, Ontario

"Snowbird" sung by Anne Murray, and written by Gene MacLellan, was one of the 10 top-selling country records in the last 15 years.

THE 10 BEST MALE AND FEMALE CANADIAN VOCALISTS

1. Dan Hill
2. Gordon Lightfoot
3. Anne Murray
4. Murray McLaughlin
5. Bruce Cockburn

6. Patsy Gallant
7. René Simard
8. David Clayton Thomas
9. Joni Mitchell
10. Burton Cummings

Ron Scribner
President
Music Shoppe Agency

Popular Gordon Lightfoot is still the best Canadian folk singer.

THE 10 MOST POPULAR
CANADIAN COUNTRY ENTERTAINERS
IN THE LAST 15 YEARS

1. Carroll Baker

2. Hank Snow

3. Tommy Hunter

4. Ronnie Prophet

5. Ian Tyson

6. Gordon Lightfoot

7. Anne Murray

8. Good Brothers

9. Carlton Showband

10. Stompin' Tom Connors

CFGM Radio
Richmond Hill, Ontario

8 FAVOURITE POPULAR SONGS
WRITTEN BY CANADIANS

1. UNTIL IT'S TIME FOR YOU TO GO
   Buffy Saint Marie

2. A MILLION MORE
   Robbie MacNeill

3. JUST BIDIN' MY TIME
   Gene MacLellan

4. BOTH SIDES NOW
   Joni Mitchell

5. DIRTY OLD MAN
   Bob Ruzicka

6. GOOD MORNING STARSHINE
   James Rado and Jerome Ragni

7. CANADIAN SUNSET
   Norman Gimbel and Eddie Heywood

8. EARLY MORNING RAIN
   Gordon Lightfoot

Anne Murray
International Singing Star

6 MORE GREAT SONGS
WRITTEN BY CANADIANS

1. Come to Me, Sweet Marie
   Written by Cy Warman, 1893

2. K-K-K-Katy, Beautiful Katy
   Written by Geoffrey O'Hara, 1882

3. In the Shade of the Old Apple Tree
   Written by Harry H. Williams, 1905

4. Mademoiselle from Armentières
   Written by Gitz Ingraham Rice, 1910

5. It's a Long Way to Tipperary
   Written by Harry H. Williams, 1912

6. There'll Always Be an England
   Written by Gordon V. Thompson, 1939

184

THE 10 BEST CANADIAN ROCK GROUPS

1. Rush
2. Heart
3. Max Webster
4. Chilliwack
5. Good Brothers

6. Prism
7. Trooper
8. Bachman-Turner Overdrive
9. April Wine
10. The Hometown Band

Ron Scribner
President
Music Shoppe Agency

10
ART AND THE
ARTS

10 GREAT CANADIAN
QUOTATIONS ON ART AND ARTISTS

1. To be sincere is one of the first requisites of good art, even of good taste.

   Clara Bernhardt, *The Poet's Function,* 1939

2. For a Puritan a life devoted to one of the arts is a life misused: the aesthetic life is not a form of the good life.

   E. K. Brown, *The Problem of Canadian Literature,* 1943

3. Art lies in understanding some part of the dark forces and bringing them under the direction of reason.

   Robertson Davies, *A Voice from the Attic,* 1960

4. Art...begins with the world we construct, not with the world we see...

   Northrop Frye, *The Educated Imagination,* 1963

5. Man in Canadian art is rarely in command of his environment or ever at home in it.

   Elizabeth Kilbourn, *The Centennial Art Show,* 1968

6. Art generalizes while science itemizes.

   Peter McArthur, *To Be Taken with Salt,* 1903

7. Today there is no lack of energy and good will where most of the arts in Canada are concerned; what's needed now is more discrimination; and that's not an easy quality to sustain in this small country.

   Robert Weaver, *Monkeys on Our Backs,* 1959

8. I always suspect an artist who is successful before he is dead.

   John Murray Gibbon, *Pagan Love,* 1922

9. An artist has to take life as he finds it. Life by itself is formless wherever it is. Art must give it form.

   Hugh MacLennan, *Two Solitudes,* 1945

10. Time uses the man of action, but the artist uses time.

    Robert Weaver, *The Canada Council,* 1957

"Lake Superior" by Lawren Harris — the founding member of the Group of Seven.

THE 7 ORIGINAL MEMBERS OF THE GROUP OF SEVEN*

1. Lawren Harris (1885-1970)

2. J.E.H. Macdonald (1873-1932)

3. Frank Carmichael (1890-1945)

4. Frank Johnston (1888-1949)

5. Arthur Lismer (1885-1969)

6. Fred Varley (1881-1969)

7. A. Y. Jackson (1882-1974)

*Tom Thomson, who died tragically and mysteriously in a boating accident in 1917, was not an original member of the famous Group of Seven painters, although, had he lived, the group almost certainly would have been called the Group of Eight when they had their first major exhibition in 1920.

THE 10 MOST IMPORTANT
NINETEENTH-CENTURY CANADIAN PAINTERS

1. Cornelius Kreighoff (1815-1872)

2. Paul Kane (1810-1871)

3. William Raphael (1833-1914)

4 Lucius R. O'Brien (1832-1899)

5. Frederick Arthur Verner (1836-1928)

6. Robert Harris (1849-1919)

7. Paul Peel (1860-1892)

8. Marc-Aurèle de Foy Suzor-Côté (1869-1937)

9. Homer Watson (1855-1936)

10. Ozias Leduc (1864-1955)

Geoffrey P. Joyner
Director
Sotheby Parke Bernet (Canada) Limited

"Portage Past the Rapids" by Cornelius Kreighoff, the most important nineteenth-century Canadian painter.

"Hunter Awaiting Seal at Breathing Hole" by William Kurelek, one of the most important twentieth century Canadian painters.

THE 12 MOST IMPORTANT
TWENTIETH-CENTURY CANADIAN PAINTERS

1. Paul-Emile Borduas (1905-1960)

2. James Wilson Morrice (1865-1924)

3. Clarence Gagnon (1881-1942)

4. Maurice Cullen (1866-1934)

5. Miller Brittain (1912-1968)

6. Robert Wakeham Pilot (1897-1967)

7. Emily Carr (1871-1945)

8. David Milne (1882-1953)

9. Alex Colville (1920-   )

10. Jean-Paul Riopelle (1923-   )

11. A. J. Casson (1898-   )

12. William Kurelek (1927-1977)

Geoffrey P. Joyner
Director
Sotheby Parke Bernet (Canada) Limited

189

THE 10 MOST EROTIC
CANADIAN WORKS OF ART

1. THE SECHELT IMAGE (*c.* 500 B. C.) — Centennial Museum, Vancouver.

   One of the prehistoric stone sculptures found in southern British Columbia, supposedly demonstrating the lifting of a boulder as a feat of male strength, this powerful image of strength grips a phallus but has a vulva as well — the first bisexual figure in Canadian art.

2. PORTRAIT OF A NEGRO SLAVE (1786), François Beaucourt — McCord Museum, McGill University, Montreal.

   In a delicate metaphor, the Negro slave's right breast is contrasted to the fruit she holds on a plate — the first instance of pictorial (partial) nudity in Canadian art.

3. A VENETIAN BATHER (1899), Paul Peel — The National Gallery of Canada, Ottawa.

   Paul Peel was the first artist in Canadian art to adequately reveal the beauty of differently textured surfaces (flesh, lace, velvet, fur) and the first to paint the full nude, although always adolescent. There is a certain quality of ambiguity in the work — the torso could, at first glance, be that of a boy, although on closer inspection, it is seen as female.

4. BATHING WOMAN, CAPRI (1890), William Blair Bruce — The National Gallery of Canada, Ottawa.

   Bruce was one of the first Canadian artists to paint women fully nude in a wash of sunlight and water, albeit sketch size. Later he developed this idea into his monumental mural, *La Joie des Néréides* (The National Gallery of Canada) where numerous nude nymphs, many with red hair, disport themselves in the sea.

5. ILLUSTRATION FOR A POEM BY LEONARD COHEN FROM THE LIMITED EDITION OF *LOVE WHERE THE NIGHTS ARE LONG* (1962) by Irving Layton and Harold Town, Harold Town — Artist's Collection.

   This is the first work published in Canada of oral sex.

6. TWO FIGURE SERIES VII (1963), Graham Coughtry — Collection of Mr. and Mrs. Morton H. Rapp, Toronto.

   Graham Coughtry is the first artist in Canada to paint and exhibit pictures of intercourse or active sexuality, sometimes interpreted as anguished struggles. From intention to realization, his subject was the erotic. Even the way of painting the canvas with its drips, splashings, and heavy impasto had a sexual connotation for the artist ("It's like having flesh").

7. LISTENING TO THE STONES (1966), Dennis Burton — Art Bank, Ottawa.

Burton is the first artist in Canada to develop an obsession with garter belts which led to full-scale study of female genitalia; he also displayed a marked interest in voyeurism (as in this work).

8. UNTITLED (1971), Robert Markle — The Robert McLaughlin Gallery, Oshawa.

Markle was the first artist in Canada to use prostitutes and chorus girls as the subject matter of his work; his figures running, falling, or suspended in air provide their own unique and erotic note to the scene.

9. YANKEE GO HOME (1973-74), John Boyle — Artist's Collection.

Group sex and fellatio appear!

10. CELEBRATION LANDSCAPE #7 (1976), Joyce Hall — Mendel Art Gallery, Saskatoon.

One of the first women artists in Canada to depict male genitalia, giant-size.

Joan Murray
Director
The Robert McLaughlin Gallery
Oshawa, Ontario

THE 10 MOST VALUABLE PAINTINGS IN CANADIAN PUBLIC COLLECTIONS

1. Cornelius Krieghoff, *Merrymaking*, 1860 (Beaverbrook Art Gallery, Fredericton), was purchased in 1958 for $25,000 and is presently worth $500,000.

2. Tom Thomson, *The Jack Pine*, 1916-1917 (National Gallery of Canada, Ottawa), is only one of several superb canvasses by this forerunner of the Group of Seven, any one of which would be worth $450,000 today.

3. James Wilson Morrice, *The Ferry, Quebec, circa* 1909 (National Gallery of Canada, Ottawa), is the most significant Canadian subject by an artist who spent a great portion of his life outside Canada. Current Value: $200,000.

4. James Edward Hervey Macdonald, *The Solemn Land,* 1921 (National Gallery of Canada, Ottawa), is one of a number of large canvasses by this Group of Seven member worth $175,000.

5. Lawren Stewart Harris, *Isolation Peak, circa* 1930 (Hart House Collection, University of Toronto), is one of this artist's most important works and well worth $150,000.

6. Frederick Horsman Varley, *Stormy Weather, Georgian Bay, circa* 1920 (National Gallery of Canada, Ottawa), painted about the time of the Group of Seven was formed and with a current value of $150,000.

7. Emily Carr, *Tanoo, Q.C.I.,* 1913 (Province of British Columbia, B.C. Archives, Victoria). In this painting she is at her best and also largest. Value: $125,000.

8. Clarence Alphonse Gagnon, *Horse Racing in Winter, Quebec, circa* 1925 (Art Gallery of Ontario, Toronto), is one of the most colourful and interesting, although not quite as valuable at $125,000.

9. Paul Kane, *Indian Encampment on Lake Huron, circa* 1845-50 (Art Gallery of Ontario, Toronto) represents another nineteenth-century artist whose picture would be worth $100,000 today.

10. Jean-Paul Riopelle,*Pavane,* 1954 (National Gallery of Canada, Ottawa), is probably the highest-priced contemporary Canadian artist whose work is internationally accepted. Current value: $80,000.

Geoffrey P. Joyner
Director
Sotheby Parke Bernet (Canada) Limited

THE 10 GREATEST CANADIAN BIRD ARTISTS *

1. ROBERT BATEMAN

"Andrew Wyeth, plus a bird." World class, with fine mastery of detail, colour, light, and composition embellished by first-hand experience.

2. ALAN BROOK

The Canadian master of the first half of the twentieth century whose marvellous birds suffered woefully from rotten reproduction. Had he been American (sad to say) his fame would have been universal.

3. ALBERT HOCHBAUM

His love of waterfowl, and his sense of kinship with the wind, water, and weeds of their world are palpable.

4. GARY LOW

A relative newcomer whose super-realism and dramatic sense of layout easily raise him above the average.

5. J. FENWICK LANSDOWNE

A superlative technician who is at his very best when he can control his obsession for detail. His freer work is wonderful.

*In alphabetical order.

Terence Michael Shortt is probably the most skillful and most knowledgeable bird artist in the world today.

6. THOREAU MACDONALD

"A fond observer" who can infuse a painting with an almost Gothic sense of drama. His use of colour and his layouts are exceptional.

7. GEORGE McLEAN

An astonishing freedom of design which combines the essences of art and nature. Good graphic tension from a master draftsman.

8. ERNEST THOMPSON SETON

If only he had not been straight-jacketed by the page layout demands of his publishers! An exquisitely talented observer and a master of pen, pencil, brush, and palette.

9. ANGUS SHORTT

An academic might think he's good; a sportsman *knows* he's good. Only years of first-hand observation, plus good training, can produce waterfowl paintings of this calibre.

10. TERENCE MICHAEL SHORTT

The Dean. In my estimation, the most skillful and most knowledgeable bird artist in the world today. Uncanny sense of life, movement, and individual personality. The professional whose guidance and friendship are appreciated by other professionals.

David Lank,
Conservationist and Nature Writer
President, Antiquarian Press Limited

193

THE 10 GREATEST WILDLIFE ANIMAL ARTISTS *

1. ROBERT BATEMAN

His canvasses are conceived of as art with superb animals, then integrated into the overall design.

2. PETER BUERSCHAPER

Canada's leading painter of fish in their underwater setting is now expanding into new areas.

3. MARTIN GLEN LOATES

Extraordinary ability to use watercolours transparently; he understands the breaking of fur as well the delicacy of a moth's wing.

4. GEORGE McLEAN

Unafraid to confront nature as it really is. A real heavyweight.

5. ANKER ODUM

Known for his unparalleled portraits of bugs, but equally deserving for all sides of wildlife. His control is as outstanding as his versatility.

6. CARL RUNGIUS

A German/American whose greatest work was of the large Canadian western fauna. After his "photographic" phase, he mastered impressionistic overlays of colour. One of the true artists in history.

7. ERNEST THOMPSON SETON

The truth of his field sketches was translated into the most powerful interpretations of everything from weasels to wolves. The *wild* in the *wilderness* was tangible.

8. CLARENCE TELLENIUS

His understanding of animals is matched by his understanding of paint. Unafraid to reflect true colour. Few are his equal as an artist.

9. ROBERT PHINNEY

Who is to bird sculpture what Michelangelo was to church ceiling painters. Perhaps the greatest in history.

10. THE CANADIAN ESKIMO

Collectively, whose genius flourished despite not having had words either for "art" or "artist" until the coming of the white man.

*In alphabetical order.

David Lank
Conservationist and Nature Writer
President, Antiquarian Press Limited

"La Communiante" by James Wilson Morrice was sold at Sotheby's in Toronto for $98,000 — the highest price ever paid for Canadian art at an auction.

THE 10 HIGHEST BIDS FOR CANADIAN ART MADE AT AUCTIONS

1. $98,000.

James Wilson Morrice, *La Communicante,* oil on canvas; 83.2 x 107.9 cms, purchased by a Quebec dealer at Sotheby Parke Bernet's May 1978 auction.

2. $58,000.

For a group of 18 sketches by Clarence Gagnon, based on the novel *Maria Chapdelaine.* Sold in Toronto, May 1977.

3. $48,000.

Lawren Stewart Harris, *In the Ward, 1918,* oil on canvas, 29 x 35 inches, sold at Maynard's in Vancouver on October 11, 1972.

4. $45,000.

At Sotheby's in Toronto in October 1974 for a large canvas of *Lake Superior* by Lawren Stewart Harris. From the well-known John A. MacAulay Collection, Winnipeg.

5. $41,000.

A record auction price for a canvas by Cornelius Krieghoff depicting a *Portage Past the Rapids* (oil on canvas, 46.3 x 60.6 cms). Sold by Sotheby's in May 1978.

6. $36,000.

Franklin Carmichael, *Evening, North Shore, Lake Superior,* oil on canvas, 76.3 x 90 cms. An auction record for this Group of Seven artist.

7. $36,000.

Tied with the Carmichael above, for a work by Emily Carr, also an auction record. Sold at Sotheby's, May 1978.

8. $32,000.

Arthur Lismer, *North Shore, Lake Superior,* oil on canvas, 100 x 125 cms. Sold at Sotheby's in May 1975.

9. $31,000.

Another Group of Seven canvas. J.E.H. Macdonald's *Rapid in the North* sold at Sotheby's in May 1975.

10. $26,000.

F.H. Varley's *Arctic Seas* sold in May 1975 in Toronto seems to confirm healthy auction prices for almost any good-quality painting by the Group of Seven.

Geoffrey P. Joyner
Director
Sotheby Parke Bernet (Canada) Limited

THE 11 WORST CRITICS IN CANADIAN ART HISTORY

1. PAUL DUVAL

Real name Norman Droy....In some ways I admire Duval...living by his wits he is able to get by on so little. However, his writing is like the stuffing coming out of the furniture in a tenth-rate hotel...it's just grubby upholstery on the chair of vanity publishing.

2. DENNIS REID

Not a good read. He snouts out platitudes like a pig after truffles and then marinates them in the tepid water of concepts that would seem dull even if you were getting a thousand dollars a word to read the stuff...a creche course in puerile writing.

3. JARED SABLE

Fleeing from a career in cement-block-making he managed to mix words together in a manner that convinced everyone that he was back working at his original trade.

4. ANDREW HUDSON

A pimp for Greenberg cant, his writing is as predictable as string and instantly breaks at any attempt to tie original art into a logical explanation...his drawing confirms the belief that he is utterly without talent.

5. KEN CARPENTER

Another prisoner chained to Clement Greenberg's critical gut wagon ...Carpenter stumbles over the pebbles in the dust of his own confusion convinced that art can be cut to fit critical theory...he builds with rubber nails.

6. BARRY LORD

An avowed enemy of the free and open society...and naturally a hearty glutton at the public trough...Lord is so lacking in wit that as a Marxist-Maoist agitator, he had the temerity to complain that some reproductions of Tom Thomson's work were too red.

7. GEORGES BOGARDI

A nouveau nothing so far behind what is really going on that he is in danger of a head-on collision when it comes back. His writing has as much chance of penetrating Canadian culture as a moth the nose of a jet.

8. BARRIE HALE

Secretly lusting after a sports-writing career...he sees art as a matter of box scores...unfortunately, having spent so much time in the Isaacs Gallery locker room...he missed all the real games.

9. JOYCE ZEMANS

Dusty, fly-specked nonsense from a fixture academic who will never come within hailing distance of an original thought...fascinated by footnotes...she is not even a bunion on the small toe of Canadian art.

10. THE LATE AUGUSTUS BRIDLE

Incomphrensible master and founding father of the gibberish school of art reporting....he became a favourite target for *New Yorker* magazine send-ups.

11. ARNOLD ROCKMAN

Having failed at using criticism as a springboard for a career as an artist, he paddled his tiny talent into the safe harbour of academia.

Harold Town
Artist, Author

Harold Town, controversial artist and columnist, is outspoken about Canadian art critics.

THE 10 MOST USEFUL REFERENCE
BOOKS ON CANADIAN ART

1. J. RUSSELL HARPER, *Painting in Canada, A History*

    Still the most complete source; contains numerous illustrations.

2. R.H. HUBBARD, *The National Gallery of Canada Catalogue: Vol. III.*

    Provides an excellent alphabetical listing of all major Canadian artists, although it is somewhat out-of-date. Originally available for $5, it now sells for about $300 a copy.

3. SOTHEBY & CO. (Canada) LTD., *Canadian Art at Auction, 1968-1975*

    Presents an alphabetical guide of artists whose works cover almost three centuries of art in Canada. Only book to provide prices.

4. R.H. HUBBARD and J.R. OSTIGUY, *Three Hundred Years of Canadian Art*

    An excellent pictorial survey.

5. PAUL DUVAL, *Canadian Watercolour Painting*

    The only comprehensive book covering this medium, it has become a collector's item in its own right.

6. J. RUSSELL HARPER, *Early Painters and Engravers in Canada*

    An invaluable biographical dictionary containing many hard-to-find references to Canadian artists born before Confederation.

7. DENNIS REID, *A Concise History of Canadian Painting*

    An authoritative handbook for the general reader.

8. DENNIS REID, *The Group of Seven*

    The definitive work.

9. CHARLES P. DE VOLPI

    Has compiled about a dozen volumes, each providing a profusely illustrated record of provinces, regions, or cities of Canada. A visual as well as a documentary delight.

10. ALL CATALOGUES AND HANDBOOKS

    Issued by major public galleries listing permanent collections, these works range from small soft-cover catalogues to lavishly produced reference lists.

Geoffrey P. Joyner
Director
Sotheby Parke Bernet (Canada) Limited

THE 9 GREATEST PRINTS BY CANADA'S 9 BEST PRINTMAKERS

1. DAVID MILNE: *BARNS* (1931)

Exquisite colour drypoint, a process Milne invented and first tried with a washing-machine wringer in 1925, the epitome of rural Ontario. It might have been had for $5 up to 1945 or so. Today, one would have little change from $3,000.

2. HAROLD TOWN: *SEA BURST* (1958)

Rich, sensuous, multi-form, *Sea Burst* is one superb example among many hundreds of "single autographic prints" that Town created between 1953-1958. With virtuosity and flamboyant invention, Town worked variations in colour lithography into the richest single lode of print images ever produced in this country or any other. The National Gallery declined to purchase it for $75, at a time when Town's prints were sweeping up international prizes.

3. YVES GAUCHER: *HOMAGE TO WEBERN* (1964)

Technical innovation, as with Milne and Town, was the midwife of this suite of three sparse, austere, and provoking prints. Made with laminated paper, both a male and a female plate, plus black and grey inking, they mark a turning point in Gaucher's work that led directly to the lithographs *Transitions* and to the great series of grey paintings between 1967-71.

4. CHRISTOPHER PRATT: *BREAKWATER* (1976)

The masterful control of the silkscreen medium hides behind Pratt's forceful Newfoundland images, yet he is essentially an abstract artist deeply concerned with the processes of making universal images. This golden-sectioned, simple design, so serene and yet so charged with energy, was based on a drawing by his ten-year-old son Ned.

5. KENOJUAK: *THE ENCHANTED OWL* (1963)

The original edition of this unforgetable stone cut was in two versions: black/green and the bitter-lemon/black/red. It has been reproduced countless times, including on one of Canada's great stamps. Seventy-five dollars invested in one print in 1963 would net more than $15,000 today.

6. CHARLES GAGNON: *MILLERTON* (1975)

This blueprint print and a suite of eight silkscreens (1969) are the only prints so far by this painter, composer, sculptor, filmmaker, photographer, designer, but his genius shines through everything he touches.

7. JAIN BAXTER: *FIVE VINEGAR BOTTLES* (1965)

The first Xerox print in Canada (of small plastic vinegar pouches) and one of many traditional prints and imaginative imprints by which Baxter, as the N.E. Thing Co., has altered the definitions of print technology.

8. W. J. PHILLIPS: *KARLUKWEES*

A master of the wood-block print, Phillips tended to saccharine renditions seldom tuned to his subjects. This print, of an Indian village in a gentle evening snowfall, matched technique and subject perfectly and produced his one and only indisputable masterpiece.

9. GREG CURNOE: *HOCKEY STICKS*

As Canadian as maple syrup, this print is the inked transfer, with all the history of breaks, repairs, and torn tape, of the feet of four hockey sticks. An obvious simple idea that hasn't occurred often enough.

David Silcox
Author, Cultural Affairs Officer
Metropolitan Toronto

THE 10 EARLIEST PRINTED VIEWS OF CANADA

1. THE DESCELIERS MAPPEMONDE, 1546

Graphically shows natives, European explorers, and native fauna, and covers the area from Labrador to Florida.

2. THE HARLEIAN MAPPEMONDE, 1536

Illustrates exploration and hunting in Canada.

3. THE DESCELIERS PLANISPHERE, 1550

Shows very descriptive and decorative details, including a small drawing of the Indian town of Hochelaga, a European talking to Indians in sign language, and a group of hunters shooting ostriches.

4. THE PLAN OF HOCHELAGA, 1556

Published by Ramusio; this engraving is generally considered to be the first picture of Canada.

5. THE RESIDENCE AT QUEBEC, 1608

By Samuel de Champlain (16 scenes).

6. NIAGARA FALLS, 1698

By Louis Hennepin.

7. NIAGARA FALLS, 1711

By Herman Moll.

8. THE ST. LAWRENCE RIVER, 1760

Six prints done after sketches by Captain Hervey Smith, A.D.C. to General Wolfe. Published in 1760 by Thomas Jefferys, London.

9. THE SCENOGRAPHIA AMERICANA, 1760

A collection of 28 line-engraved views of North American cities, including Canadian cities.

10. QUEBEC VIEWS, 1759

Twelve line engravings by Richard Shortt.

F. St. George Spendlove
Author
The Face of Early Canada

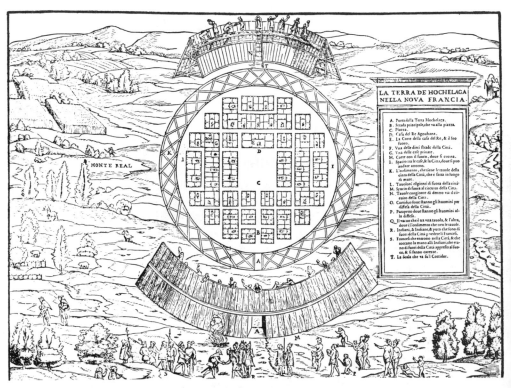

The Plan of Hochelaga, 1556. Published by Ramusio, this engraving is generally considered to be the first picture of Canada.

THE 10 MOST CELEBRATED
CANADIAN ESKIMO PRINTMAKERS

1. Davidialuk Amittu, E9-824,*Povunguituk

2. Luke Anguhadluq, Baker Lake

3. Tivi Etook, George River

4. Kananginak, E7-1168, Cape Dorset

5. Kenojuak, E7-1035, Cape Dorset

6. Kiakshuk, E7-1057, Cape Dorset

7. Lucy, E7-1068, Cape Dorset

8. Parr, E7-1022, Cape Dorset

9. Pitseolak, E7-982, Cape Dorset

10. Pudlo, E7-899, Cape Dorset

*From 1941-70 an assigned disc was used by Eskimos as identification and was also used on their carvings since they had no last names. These numbers were recorded on small fibre discs which they wore around their necks.

David Mitchell
Hudson's Bay Company

THE 12 MOST CELEBRATED
CANADIAN ESKIMO CARVERS

1. Akeeaktashook (1898-1954), Port Harrison

2. Karoo Ashevak (1940-1974), E4-196,*Spence Bay

3. Axangayuk (1937-   ), E7-289, Cape Dorset

4. Henry Evaluardjuk (1923-   ), E5-846, Frobisher Bay

5. Johnny Inukpuk (1911-   ), E9-904, Port Harrison

6. Kiawak (1933-   ), E7-1103, Cape Dorset

*From 1941-70 an assigned disc was used by Eskimos as identification and was also used on their carvings since they had no last names. These numbers were recorded on small fibre discs which they wore around their necks.

7. Vital Arnasungnark Makpa (1922-   ), E2-120, Baker Lake

8. Manno (1923-   ) E7-887, Cape Dorset

9. Oshooweetook 'B' (1923-   ), E7-1154, Cape Dorset

10. Saila Pauta (1916-   ), E -990, Cape Dorset

11. Joe Talirunili (1899-1976), E9-818, Povungnituk

12. John Tiktak (1916-   ), E1-266, Rankin Inlet

David Mitchell
Hudson's Bay Company

THE 10 MOST INTERESTING PEOPLE TO CARICATURE

1. PIERRE TRUDEAU

Interesting to draw because of his balding head, arching eyebrows, almond-shaped eyes, high cheekbones, buck teeth, flattened nose, and wild hair—not to mention strange manner of dress!

2. RENÉ LÉVESQUE

The cigarette is vital, along with the white stringy hair. Also the clothes, which resemble an unmade bed.

3. JOE CLARK

A real challenge! Why? Because it's very difficult getting a resemblance when you can't draw a chin on the caricature.

4. JOHN DIEFENBAKER

Once the bulging eyes and rooster-like hair are drawn, the rest is easy. Folds of sagging folds of sagging jowls.

5. WILLIAM DAVIS

A nice round, nothing kind of face, a scoop of hair, squinting eyes, and a big cigar...easy to draw on Monday mornings.

6. DAVID CROMBIE

Extremely difficult. Keeping him in proportion to the things around him generally means drawing him in miniature. A brush is required.

7. ROBERT STANFIELD

Saddled with the banana trademark from day one makes this gentleman a cinch to draw. Nothing more is required.

The Right Honourable Pierre Elliott Trudeau — an interesting person to caricature.

8. MARC LALONDE

This man has so much facial character that generally a very realistic drawing is required with just slight unexaggeration.

9. JEAN CHRÉTIEN

The sagging eyes can sometimes be difficult but the really hard part is drawing a front view with the mouth in profile on the left cheek. Harder still a left profile with a full view of the mouth on the cheek. Harder even still a right profile...you can't see the mouth.

10. JOHN Q. PUBLIC

Balding, unshaven, ragged clothes, bare feet, and patched, pathetic, very close to the heart, real nice guy. Easy to draw from any angle, particularly being dumped on!

Andrew Donato
Cartoonist
The Toronto Sun

THE 10 LARGEST ART GALLERIES IN CANADA*

	Operating Expenditure
1. Art Gallery of Ontario	$4,579,049
2. The National Gallery (Ont.)	3,828,500
3. Musée des Beaux Arts (Que.)	1,675,732
4. The Winnipeg Art Gallery (Man.)	1,673,440
5. The Vancouver Art Gallery (B.C.)	992,866
6. Parc des Champs de Bataille Musée (Que.)	794,500
7. The Edmonton Art Gallery (Alta.)	592,459
8. The McMichael Canadian Collection (Ont.)	556,500
9. Musée d'Art Contemporain (Que.)	454,100
10. The Saskatoon Gallery (Sask.)	438,565

*By 1976 operating expenditure

Statistics Canada
Museums, Art Galleries,
and Related Institutions

THE 10 LARGEST MUSEUMS IN CANADA*

		Operating Expenditure
1.	Royal Ontario Museum	$7,405,121
2.	The National Museum of Man (Ont.)	7,269,005
3.	Ontario Science Centre	6,076,217
4.	Biosystematic Research Institute (Ont.)	3,913,800
5.	British Columbia Provincial Museum	3,487,058
6.	National Museum of Natural Sciences (Ont.)	3,033,300
7.	Glenbow-Alberta Institute (Alta.)	2,880,515
8.	The National Museum of Science and Technology (Ont.)	1,839,502
9.	Manitoba Museum of Man and Nature	1,773,562
10.	Provincial Museum of Alberta	1,647,701

*By 1976 operating expenditure

Statistics Canada
Museums, Art Galleries,
and Related Institutions

THE 10 SYMPHONY AND OPERA COMPANIES WITH THE BIGGEST GROSSES AND AUDIENCES IN CANADA

		Revenue	*Audience*
1.	Toronto Symphony	$3,502,050	412,000
2.	Montreal Symphony	3,338,992	282,081
3.	Canadian Opera Company	3,182,888	99,315
4.	Vancouver Symphony	2,574,486	294,386
5.	Winnipeg Symphony	1,274,564	200,000
6.	Hamilton Philharmonic	1,152,632	146,931
7.	Vancouver Opera	1,102,405	68,425
8.	Edmonton Symphony	1,043,409	166,157
9.	Orchestre Symphonique de Quebec	1,028,326	77,832
10.	Calgary Philharmonic	897,781	83,000

Arnold Edinborough, Author, Publisher
Compiled by the Staff of the
Council for Business and the Arts in Canada

THE 10 THEATRE AND BALLET COMPANIES WITH THE BIGGEST GROSSES AND AUDIENCES IN CANADA

		Revenue	Audience
1.	Stratford Festival	$5,437,000	504,963
2.	National Ballet of Canada	4,045,000	328,344
3.	Royal Winnipeg Ballet	2,076,062	263,387
4.	Les Grands Ballets Canadiens	1,920,471	126,263
5.	Théâtre du Nouveau Monde	1,836,885	275,746
6.	Shaw Festival	1,625,724	137,800
7.	Citadel Theatre	1,340,447	224,153
8.	Manitoba Theatre Centre	1,296,971	145,335
9.	Toronto Arts Productions	1,287,202	115,696
10.	The Playhouse Theatre	979,359	72,500

Arnold Edinborough, Author, Publisher
Compiled by the Staff of the
Council for Business and the Arts
in Canada

11
COMMUNICATIONS

10 GREAT CANADIAN QUOTATIONS ON WRITERS AND WRITING

1. Canadian writers are hungry writers!

   Hugh MacLennan, *The Story of a Novel*, 1960

2. Most Canadian writers belong to a single social group identifiable with a university-based Establishment.

   Robert L. McDougall, *The Dodo and the Cruising Auk*, 1963

3. Nobody is more embittered than a neglected writer.

   Mordecai Richler, *The Uncertain World*, 1969

4. For the great bulk of Canadian writers the environments of childhood and of "the struggle for a living" are uniform in kind; professional, relatively well-to-do, "genteel," above all, academic.

   Robert L. McDougall, *The Dodo and the Cruising Auk*, 1963

5. To the state and the politicians the writer is simply not important.

   Morley Callaghan, *Solzhenitsyn,* 1970

6. There are two kinds of writers: the one who tries to see the world out of his own eyes, and the other one, the commercial writer, who tries to see the world out of the eyes of others.

   Nathan Cohen, *Heroes of the Richler View*, 1958

7. The vice of the literary mind is excessive subtlety, just as that of the theatrical mind is trivial profusion.

   Robertson Davies, *A Voice from the Attic*, 1960

8. A writer is, by definition almost, a man sensitive to influences; he may reject them or accept them, search for them or flee from them, but he cannot be neutral or unfeeling about all of them.

   Roderick Haig-Brown, *The Writer in Isolation*, 1959

9. Many writers have the courage to show us the hairshirt they are wearing, but only the greatest will display the raw and itchy skin it conceals.

   Irving Layton, *Some Observations and Aphorisms*, 1968

10. No writer in his senses writes solely to make money. If money is what he wants most, he needs his head examined if he becomes a writer.

    Hugh MacLennan, *The Story of a Novel*, 1960

The discovery of oil at Leduc, Alberta, in 1947 is one of the 10 greatest Canadian news events.

THE 10 GREATEST
CANADIAN NEWS EVENTS

1. The pact between Georges Etienne Cartier and John A. Macdonald which made Confederation...if only temporarily...a viable prospect. It also started Canada with a Prime Minister named John Macdonald and a Premier of Ontario also named John Macdonald. Obviously not the same man.

2. The sinking of the *Empress of Ireland* in the Gulf of St. Lawrence in 1914.

3. The Halifax Explosion of 1917.

4. The birth of the Dionne Quintuplets on May 28, 1934.

5. The building of the Canadian National Railway, finished in 1885.

6. The day in July 1929 when Mackenzie King and his Cabinet resigned en masse so that there was no Prime Minister and no government for 24

hours, at which point Lord Byng summoned Arthur Meighen. Mr. Meighen was twice Prime Minister of Canada but was never elected to that office.

7. The day in 1919 when a group of Ontario farmers were democratically elected to govern Ontario but elected neither a lawyer nor did they have a leader, hence no Premier. The Attorney General must be a lawyer, so they persuaded W.E. Raney of Toronto to take that post. He won the seat of Wellington North and became Attorney General. There being no leader, Ernest Drury, a Crown Hill farmer and secretary of the United Farmers, was chosen. He was so poor he could not afford a Toronto hotel or boarding house, so he lived with a relative.

8. The discovery of oil at Leduc, Alberta, in 1947.

9. The disbanding of the Fraser Highlanders in Quebec after the victory over France. This left Quebec with many Anglos, of name, who became solid French Canadians through absorption. Examples: Robert Burns of the Lévesque Cabinet; Claude Ryan, leader of the Libertal Party; Daniel Johnson, former Premier.

10. The Frank Rock Slide in Alberta on April 29, 1903, which buried an entire village under rock. A hundred dead were never recovered.

Gordon Sinclair
Author, Broadcaster

THE 10 BEST LIVING
JOURNALISTS IN CANADA

1. Barbara Frum
   CBC Radio, *As It Happens*

2. Alexander Ross
   Editor, *Canadian Business*

3. Dennis Harvey
   CBC, Assistant General Manager

4. Robert Fulford
   Editor, *Saturday Night* Magazine

5. Trent Frayne
   Sports Columnist, *Toronto Sun*

6. Walter Stewart
   Maclean's Magazine

7. John Fraser
   China correspondent, *Globe and Mail*

8. Harry Bruce
   Freelance Writer, *The Canadian*

9. George Bain
   Ottawa Columnist, *Toronto Star*

10. Peter C. Newman
    Editor, *Maclean's* Magazine

Shirley Sharzer
Assistant Dean
Journalism School
University of Western Ontario

Toronto Life *is reputed to be the best magazine sold in Canada today.*

THE 10 BEST MAGAZINES
SOLD IN CANADA

1. *Toronto Life*

2. *Harrowsmith*

3. *Toronto Calendar,*

   Montreal Calendar,

   and *Vancouver Calendar*

4. *Weekend Magazine*

5. *Chatelaine*

6. *The New Yorker*

7. *Sports Illustrated*

8. *Reader's Digest*

9. *Stimulus*

10. *Canadian Business*

Terry O'Malley
President
Vickers & Benson (advertising agency)

THE 10 BEST NEWSPAPERS
SOLD IN CANADA

1. *The Winnipeg Tribune*
2. *The Fredericton Gleaner*
3. *The Globe and Mail*
4. *Le Devoir*
5. *The Stratford Beacon-Herald*

6. *The St. Catharines Standard*
7. *The Mississauga Times*
8. *The Toronto Star*
9. *The Vancouver Sun*
10. *The New York Times*

Terry O'Malley
President
Vickers & Benson (advertising agency)

THE 10 PROVINCES
WITH THE GREATEST NUMBER
OF DAILY NEWSPAPERS

	Number of Daily Newspapers	*Circulation*
1. ONTARIO	48	2,200,000
2. BRITISH COLUMBIA	19	1,655,000
3. QUEBEC	14	1,333,000
4. ALBERTA	8	445,000
5. MANITOBA	7	255,000
6. NOVA SCOTIA	6	165,000
7. NEW BRUNSWICK	6	136,000
8. SASKATCHEWAN	4	128,000
9. NEWFOUNDLAND	3	64,000
10. PRINCE EDWARD ISLAND	3	33,000

Statistics Canada

Robert Morley, the famous British comedian, reading the Toronto Sun — *the sixth largest newspaper publisher in Canada.*

THE 6 LARGEST NEWSPAPER PUBLISHERS IN CANADA

	Gross Sales ($ millions)	Net Profits ($ millions)	Number of Employees
1. Southam Press Limited	312.6	25.1	7,203
2. Thomson Newspapers Ltd.	257.9	47.3	7,000
3. Torstar Corporation	220.9	12.1	3,600
4. F.P. Publications Limited**			
5. Quebecor Inc.	104.4	3.4	1,800
6. The Toronto Sun Publishing Corporation	23.5	1.5	590

*Based on 1977 financial information.

**F.P. is a private company and therefore financial information is not available. However, it is believed that on a gross revenue basis, F.P. would be the fourth-largest newspaper publishing company in Canada.

H. A. Arrell
Analyst
Gardiner Watson Limited

The defence of Newfoundland's annual seal hunt might well be the best run annual public relations program in Canada.

CANADA'S 10 GREATEST PUBLIC RELATIONS PROGRAMS

1. Defense of Newfoundland's annual seal hunt.

2. The St. Lawrence Seaway — Hydro's flooding of the towns and relocation of the people.

3. Canada's Centennial.

4. Expo '67.

5. Launch of Wintario Lottery.

6. "Canada at the Crossroad." Key city tour by Cabinet Minister Bryce Mackasey to interpret "unity" to business leaders.

7. The national nurse's strike.

8. Big Brothers' campaign.

9. The establishment of the Cancer Society.

10. The launching of the CN Tower.

David Scott-Atkinson
Public Relations Executive and
Canadian Trend Observer

THE 7 LARGEST BROADCASTING
COMPANIES IN CANADA*

	Gross Sales ($ millions)	Net Profits ($ millions) (Loss)	Number of Employees
1. Canadian Broadcasting Corporation	513.0**	(275.0)	11,500
2. Maclean-Hunter Limited	198.3	9.7 .	4,000
3. Baton Broadcasting Incorporated	65.7	7.7	467
4. Selkirk Holdings Limited	55.6	5.8	1,036
5. Télé-Métropole Inc.	39.4	5.8	639
6. Chum Limited	37.8	3.0	
7. Standard Broadcasting Corporation Limited	36.6	4.7	530

*Based on 1977 financial information.
**Including appropriation from Federal Government of $415.9 million.

H. A. Arrell
Analyst
Gardiner Watson Limited

THE 10 MOST EMBARRASSING
BLOOPERS IN CANADIAN RADIO

1. A prominent Toronto news commentator, reporting on a severe heat wave, is said to have told his audience that the temperature rose so high that "several women in the downtown area collapsed from heat prostitution."

2. An announcer in London, Ontario, given a supermarket spot to read, had this line to contend with: "For the best in bread..." It came out: "For the breast in bed...."

3. And though it's been denied many times, there are still those who will swear they heard a harried CBC announcer give a rushed station break as, "This is the Canadian Broadcorping Castration."

4. Joe Forster of CHIN, Toronto, tells of the time early in his career when he was reporting news. This was when the late Colonel Sam McLaughlin of General Motors fame had just returned to his home in Oshawa after undergoing an operation for a bowel obstruction. Joe wrapped up his story with, "Colonel McLaughlin was treated at a Toronto hospital for a bowel movement."

5. John Henderson of CKWW, Windsor, tells about an announcer who was talking about the French Grand Prix. He pronounced the last word to rhyme with sticks!

6. Paula Mitchell of CKOC, Hamilton, reports that a young newscaster, alone in the newsroom, was hit with a story from Africa reporting that the President of a small nation had been assassinated. The rookie didn't know how to pronounce the President's name. So, after informing his audience that the leader of a small African nation had been assassinated, he said, "The President's name is being withheld pending notification of next of kin."

7. And, speaking of rookies, there was the excited one who, when informed just before air-time that a major figure in his station's area had suddenly died, bulletined the fact, closing with the information that "...he was 78 degrees."

8. We shall be kind and not mention the announcer or the station on which a shocked audience heard an unintended transposition in the coverage of a tournament at the London Hunt and Country Club.

9. Anne Arsenault, the TV personality, will never forget the time she read a story about a Sudbury controversy involving the big INCO complex. "Now," she read, "news from the International Nipple Company...."

10. Who could forget the lady who gave social advice after a man wrote her with this problem: "How," he wanted to know, "do you handle the scene at a cocktail party where you are holding a drink in one hand and perhaps some peanuts in the other and your host introduces you to someone?" "What is correct," said the lady, "is to hold your drink in one hand, your nuts in the other, and bow your head courteously."

Phil Stone
Radio Arts
Humber College

12
LITERATURE

10 GREAT CANADIAN QUOTATIONS ON CANADIAN LITERATURE

1. The Canadian literateur must depend solely on himself and nature. He is almost without the exhilaration of lively and frequent literary intercourse.

   W. E. Collins, *Natural Landscape*

2. Though politically we have achieved nationhood, emotionally we are still colonials — the sooner we outgrow this childish attitude, the sooner will our literature come of age.

   Mary Elizabeth Colman, *A Poet Speaks to the Critics*, 1938

3. Our French fellow-countrymen are much more firmly united than the English colonists; though their literature is more French than Canadian, and their bond of union is more religious than literary or political.

   E. W. Dewart, Introduction to *Selections from Canadian Poets*, 1864

4. The first qualification of the student of Canadian literature is a thick skin. He must be incapable of being bored.

   Kildare Dobbs, *Miss Crotchett's Muse*, 1958

5. The literature of this country begins in rotten romanticism.

   Louis Dudek, *The Two Traditions*, 1962

6. A good deal is being said about Canadian literature, and most of it takes the form of question and answer as to whether a Canadian literature exists.

   Archibald Lampman, *Two Canadian Poets*, 1891

7. Until recently, Canada enjoyed the unenviable distinction of being the only civilized country in the world where the study of its own literature was not made compulsory in the schools and colleges.

   Lorne Pierce, Foreword to *An Outline of Canadian Literature*, 1927

8. The way ahead in the academic waters of Canadian lit is clearly charted. You find yourself a dead and obscure writer and stake a claim to his revival.

   Mordecai Richler, *Wally Sylvester's Canadiana*, 1960

9. Canadian literature, when it has not been neglected entirely, has been contemptuously dismissed or extravagantly praised.

   A. J. M. Smith, Introduction to *The Book of Canadian Prose*, 1965

10. When our poets can free themselves from the omnipresence of two powerful and conflicting voices... we shall see the advent of a strong and indigenous Canadian literature.

W. P. Wilgar, *Poetry and the Divided Mind in Canada*, 1944

THE 10 BEST CANADIAN BOOKS

1. MORLEY CALLAGHAN'S STORIES (1959), by Morley Callaghan, $1.25 paper

2. THE EMPIRE OF THE ST. LAWRENCE (1956), by Donald Creighton, $8.95 cloth, $5.50 paper

3. ANATOMY OF CRITICISM: FOUR ESSAYS (1957), by Northrop Frye, $3.25 paper

4. LAMENT FOR A NATION (1965), by George P. Grant, $4.50 cloth, $1.50 paper

5. THE FUR TRADE IN CANADA: AN INTRODUCTION TO CANADIAN ECONOMIC HISTORY (1930), by Harold Adams Innis, $12.50 cloth, $2.75 paper

6. THE STONE ANGEL (1964), by Margaret Laurence, $7.50 cloth, $2.50 paper

7. SUNSHINE SKETCHES OF A LITTLE TOWN (1912), by Stephen Leacock, $7.50 cloth, $1.50 paper

8. THE GUTENBERG GALAXY: THE MAKING OF TYPOGRAPHICAL MAN (1962), by Marshall McLuhan, $10.00 cloth, $1.50 paper

9. COLLECTED POEMS (2nd edition, 1958), by E.J. Pratt, $9.95 cloth

10. ST. URBAIN'S HORSEMAN: A NOVEL (1971), by Mordecai Richler, $7.95 cloth

Robert Fulford
David Godfrey
Abraham Rotstein
for *Read Canadian*

THE 10 BEST CANADIAN CHILDREN'S BOOKS

1. BONNIE McSMITHERS, YOU'RE DRIVING ME DITHERS by Sue Alderson

    A picture book for young children which is full of fun and vitality.

2. MARY OF MILE 18 by Anne Blades

    A sharp focus for children on one kind of Canadian life.

3. THE LOON'S NECKLACE by Elizabeth Cleaver

    Listed under the illustrator because it is the collage pictures which give the book its meaning.

4. FROZEN FIRE by James Houston

    This fast-paced story about two boys' life-and-death struggle in the frozen north is a good read for anyone.

5. A PRAIRIE BOY'S WINTER by William Kurelek

    A stunning portrayal of life on the Prairies.

6. ALLIGATOR PIE by Dennis Lee

    Dennis Lee has succeeded in four short years in making his poetry part of the everyday speech of children across the country.

7. LISTEN FOR THE SINGING by Jean Little

    In this story of a partly sighted girl entering high school, Jean Little has captured the atmosphere of the old Toronto.

8. GOOD-BYE MOMMA by Tom Moore

    A moving story of a boy's response to his mother's death and the problems of growing up in a Newfoundland outport community.

9. UNDERGROUND TO CANADA by Barbara Smucker

    A believable account of the dangerous adventures of two girls who escape from pre-Civil War U.S.A. to freedom in St. Catharines.

10. THE SANDWICH by Ian Wallace

    Good taste triumphs over one's conformity in an interestingly designed book.

Judy Sarick
The Children's Book Store
Toronto

10 GREAT CANADIAN QUOTATIONS ON BOOKS

1. To know a good book is to know a good man.

   Bliss Carman, *The Friendship of Art*, 1904

2. You may stop a man's mouth by crammin' a book down his throat, but you won't convince him.

   T. C. Haliburton, *Sam Slick*, 1853

3. A good book has no ending.

   R. D. Cumming, *Skookum Chuck Fables*, 1915

4. We shall find nothing in books which has no existence in ourselves.

   Robertson Davies, *A Voice from the Attic*, 1960

5. Books, like men, are better understood when we know the mental environment from which they have risen.

   William H. New, Introduction to *Odysseus Ever Returning*, 1969

6. The more a book is publicly attacked the better it sells.

   Milton Wilson, *Callaghan's Caviare*, 1962

7. Books are selves;
   They should be made to feel like folks at home —
   And not like strangers, stacked there on those shelves.

   Robert Norwood, *Bill Boram*, 1921

8. A book arises as much in the mind of the reader as in that of the writer; and the writer's art consists above all in creating response....

   F. P. Grove, *In Search of Myself*, 1940

9. There are still a few of us booklovers around despite the awful warnings of Marshall McLuhan with his TV era and his pending farewell to Gutenberg.

   Frank Davies, *Typescript into Book*, 1958

10. I love old books
    Frayed from the searching
    Of truth-hungry fingers....

    Wilson MacDonald, *I Love Old Things*

THE 10 BEST
CANADIAN NOVELS*

1. THE STONE ANGEL by Margaret Laurence

2. FIFTH BUSINESS by Robertson Davies

3. AS FOR ME AND MY HOUSE by Sinclair Ross

4. THE MOUNTAIN AND THE VALLEY by Ernest Buckler

5. THE TIN FLUTE by Gabrielle Roy

6. THE APPRENTICESHIP OF DUDDY KRAVITZ by Mordecai Richler

7. THE DOUBLE HOOK by Sheila Watson

8. THE WATCH THAT ENDS THE NIGHT by Hugh MacLennan

9. WHO HAS SEEN THE WIND by W.O. Mitchell

10. THE DIVINERS by Margaret Laurence

*3-day nationwide poll of authors, academics, and critics at conference in Calgary, 1977.

Canadian Book Publishers Association

THE 10 MOST ENJOYABLE
CANADIAN BOOKS

1. COMING THROUGH SLAUGHTER by Michael Ondaatje

2. THE STONE ANGEL by Margaret Laurence

3. SURFACING by Margaret Atwood

4. IN AN IRON GLOVE by Claire Martin

5. AS FOR ME AND MY HOUSE by Sinclair Ross

6. THE BOOK OF EVE by Constance Beresford-Howe

7. THE WARS by Timothy Findley

8. TEMPTATION OF BIG BEAR by Rudy Wiebe

9. MAD SHADOWS by Marie-Claire Blais

10. THE TIN FLUTE by Gabrielle Roy

Beth Appeldoorn
Longhouse Book Shop Ltd.

10 GOOD DETECTIVE/ MYSTERY/CRIME BOOKS BY 10 CANADIAN WRITERS

1. AN AFRICAN MILLIONAIRE (1897) by Grant Allen

Short stories featuring Colonel Clay, con man, thief, and master of disguise, a forerunner for Raffles. Clay's exploits still appear in anthologies. Grant Allen lived and wrote in England, but was born near Kingston, Ontario. He also shocked the Victorian world with a sexy novel, *The Woman Who Did*. She did, indeed.

2. THE ADVENTURES OF JIMMY DALE (1917) by Frank L. Packard

Jimmy Dale, equally lawless, was a gentleman-safecracker, a witty clubman by day, who robbed by night to right injustices. The series of Dale books, better known for their sales volume than their literary merit, continued until 1935. The author, born in Montreal and educated at McGill, was of American parentage and did all his writing in the United States.

3. THE MAN WHO COULDN'T SLEEP: BEING A RELATION OF THE DIVERS STRANGE ADVENTURES WHICH BEFELL ONE WITTER KERFOOT WHEN, SORELY TROUBLED WITH SLEEPLESSNESS, HE VENTURED FORTH AT MIDNIGHT ALONG THE HIGHWAYS AND BYWAYS OF MANHATTAN (1919) by Arthur Stringer

Short detective stories. Stringer was born in Chatham, Ontario, and became Vice-President of the University of Toronto. This freakishly titled book and its successor, *The Diamond Thieves,* are possibly Canada's only contributions to the Golden Age of the detective story.

4. WALL OF EYES (1943) by Margaret Millar

The first of two detective novels Margaret Millar wrote featuring Inspector Sands of the Toronto Police Department. Millar, originally Margaret Sturm of Kitchener, Ontario, has produced many other, more professionally written books since she and her husband Kenneth Millar (Ross Macdonald) moved to California after the War, but *Wall of Eyes* is one of her distinctively Canadian works. (Regretfully, Macdonald himself has been omitted since, although he lived for many of his early years in Ontario, he was born in California.)

5. THE WEIRD WORLD OF WES BEATTIE (1963)
by John Norman Harris

Erupting from a new talent, this exuberant Toronto-based mystery novel was oddball enough to capture much of the spirit of the period. The mystery is solved by a bright, newly graduated lawyer, helped by freaky friends. The equally youthful author, who had cashed in his life insurance to launch his literary career, died the next year. God knows how different the Canadian genre would have been had he lived.

6. LET'S KILL UNCLE (1964) by Rohan O'Grady

An enchanting combination of crime chiller and fairy story, set on an island off the coast of British Columbia. Suave Uncle is trying to murder two captivatingly awful brats, and since the island's Mountie thinks they're lying, they plot Uncle's destruction. Rohan O'Grady lives in West Vancouver, and has written other macabre delights.

7. SIN SNIPER (1970) by Hugh Garner

Mass panic in Toronto's Cabbagetown in its pre-chic era (Garner's established stamping ground), set off by an unknown sniper. This was novelist Garner's first detective story featuring the rough-tongued, hard-bitten Inspector Walter McDumont. McDumont has made further popular appearances, although showing increasing disenchantment with his changing city.

8. IF YOU WANT TO SEE YOUR WIFE AGAIN (1972)
by John Craig

The star of a successful TV soaper is kidnapped by other members of the series team after she resigns to marry a Toronto department store tycoon; tycoon becomes victim of hilarious sequence of botched extortion demands. Craig is a Torontonian who varies crime fiction with children's books.

9. YET SHE MUST DIE (1973) by Sara Woods

Among the best of the two dozen or so detective stories featuring English barrister Antony Maitland that bestselling author Sara Woods has had published since 1962. Based on Wallace murder sensation about 40 years earlier, Yorkshire-born Sara Woods lived and wrote in Halifax from 1957 until 1977; her home is now in London, Ontario — but the action in her mysteries (frequent book club selections) rarely strays far from London, England.

10. DEATH IS A DRUM BEATING FOREVER (1977)
by John Wyllie

One of the series of unusual detective novels (five, so far) written by Canadian-born John Wyllie, featuring a big, calm, black, Montreal-trained physician, Dr. Quarshie, who has returned to organize health services in his unidentified African nation but constantly becomes involved in solving assassinations, poisonings, and other wrongdoings, usually with political implications. Always a nice blend of tribal lore, primitive guile, and earthy humour, told with clear-eyed but sympathetic understanding.

Derrick Murdoch
Author
The Agatha Christie Mystery

5 GOOD SPY STORIES BY
5 CANADIAN WRITERS

1. MILO (1969) by Shaun Herron

Irish-born author Shaun Herron was a newspaperman in Winnipeg when he wrote his first novel featuring Milo, the tired, embittered CIA agent, but its action was mainly set in rural Quebec. Bounding unexpectedly from caricature to sombre reality, and from parody to parable, the novel's freshness and literary graces give a promise Herron's later Irish-based Milo novels fulfil.

2. KOSYGIN IS COMING (1974) by Tom Ardies

A fast, mildly bawdy and frequently violent comedy-thriller set in Vancouver, in which an unpredictably impetuous plainclothes RCMP corporal on an obscure security detail is swept out of his depths and becomes uncertain which side he is helping when the USSR president makes his state visit to Canada. Author Tom Ardies, whose home is in Penticton, B.C., has also written several successful Washington-based extravaganzas but, to date, this is his only all-Canadian venture.

3. AGENCY (1974) by Paul Gottlieb

Written when Hungarian-born Paul Gottlieb was a director of a Montreal ad agency, this unusual black comedy thriller is about another agency presumably in New York, used as the cover for an unscrupulous foreign power whose nefarious plans include advertising campaigns achieving destruction by corruption. The book's central character and other employees who suspect the plot are in danger of more direct treatment.

4. BLUEPRINT (1977) by Philippe van Rjndt

Who is Iron Mask, the high level spy at Soviet espionage headquarters who is leaking top secrets to West Germany? To discover his identity, Captain Roy of the GRU allows himself to be accepted in Bonn as a defector, with surprising consequences. The novel set many people wondering equally about the identity of the pseudonymously named young European-born author, who arrived in Canada a few years before with a seemingly vast knowledge of international espionage networks. This was his second book; both are intricately plotted and written in a vein of deadly seriousness.

5. TO CATCH A SPY (1978) by Chris Scott

Another defector novel but written in a dryly observant, often witty manner by a Yorkshire-born Canadian who frankly claims no first-hand knowledge of espionage but has a competent grasp of its literary possibilities. The plot concerns a latter-day Kim Philby and speculates whether Philby — or his fictional avatar — could really have been a triple agent.

Derrick Murdoch
Author
The Agatha Christie Mystery

10 EXCLUSIVELY CANADIAN WORDS

1. COVIVANT

(kō-vē-VAWNT or kō-vē-VONGH) noun.

A person who is living with, but not married to, a member of the opposite sex. "Mother and Dad I'd like you to meet Debbie, my covivant." (Latin: *co* — together; *vivere* — to live)

Coined by Shirley Yamada, Toronto, who says, "This word is even bilingual. What more could you want?"

2. DEK

(dĕk) noun.

A group of ten, to replace the non-metric *dozen*. (Greek: *deka* - ten)

Coined by John Rutherford, Scarborough, Ontario, who says, "A dollar a dek has a nice ring, and *twenty* would become a *double-dekker*."

3. FUZZTACHE

(FŬZ-stăsh) noun.

A moustache on a young man before he starts to shave. (Peach *fuzz* + mous*tache*)

Coined by Mario Bartoletti, Sunderland, Ontario.

4. LUPPER

(LŬP-ĕr) noun.

A mid-afternoon meal in place of *l*unch and s*upper*.

"Now that I'm on a diet, I'm down to only two meals a day — brunch and lupper."

Coined by Rob Marsh and Dave Wallace, Toronto.

5. POLEQUATOR

(PŌl-ĕ-kwā-tŏr) noun.

The 45° latitude line, mid-way between the Equator and the North or South Pole. The Polequator passes through or touches four Canadian provinces: Ontario, Quebec, New Brunswick, and Nova Scotia. It could become our newest tourist attraction.

(Pole + Equator)

Coined by Bill Sherk, Toronto.

6. PWELGAS

(PWĔL-găs) noun.

Acronym for the Seven Deadly Sins of *p*ride, *w*rath, *e*nvy, *l*ust, *g*luttony, *a*varice, and *s*loth.

The perfect word for a church service running overtime: "...and lead us not into pwelgas..."

Coined by Bill Sherk, Toronto.

7. RIGGAFRUTCH

(RĬG-ă-frŭch) expletive.

A perfectly clean swear word with a therapeutic value equal to or greater than any four-letter word yet invented.

(Born out of spontaneous verbal combustion — "Riggafrutch!" — in the middle of a music rehearsal.)

Coined by Bob Krueger, Toronto.

8. SESQUILINGUAL

(sĕs-kwĭ-LĬNG-gwăl) adjective.

Knowing one language and part of another.

"I'm not bilingual. I'm sesquilingual!"

(Latin: *sesqui* — one-and-a-half; *lingua* — tongue)

Coined by Bill Sherk, Toronto.

9. SESQUIPHONIC

(sĕs-kwĭ-FŎN-ĭk) adjective.

Having a sound followed by an echo.

Disc jockey broadcasting from an echo chamber: "Folks, this program is coming to you in sesquiphonic sound!"

(Latin: *sesqui* — one-and-a-half; Greek: *phone* — sound)

Coined by John Calvin, Toronto.

10. SPŎRK

(spŏrk) noun.

A spoon with fork prongs at the tip. Available in plastic at fried chicken outlets.

(*sp*oon + f*ork*)

Coined by Desmond Ottley, Mississauga, Ontario.

Bill Sherk
Author
Brave New Words, a forthcoming
dictionary of words coined by Canadians.

THE 10 MOST COMMON WORDS
USED BY CANADIANS

1. The
2. And
3. Of
4. A
5. To

6. In
7. Is
8. You
9. That
10. It

Exclusive to *The Canadian Book of Lists*

THE 10 LARGEST BOOK
PUBLISHING COMPANIES IN CANADA

	Estimated 1978 Sales
1. Harlequin Enterprises Ltd.	$90,000,000
2. McGraw-Hill Ryerson Ltd.	22,000,000
3. Gage Educational Publishing Ltd.	12,500,000
4. McClelland & Stewart Ltd.	11,500,000
5. Prentice-Hall of Canada Ltd.	9,500,000
6. The Macmillan Company of Canada Ltd.	9,000,000
7. Holt, Rinehart and Winston of Canada Ltd.	8,500,000
8. Thomas Nelson & Sons (Canada) Ltd.	7,000,000
9. Doubleday Canada Ltd.	6,500,000
10. Ginn and Company	6,000,000

Ron Besse
President and Chief Executive Officer
Gage Educational Publishing Ltd.

THE 10 WORST SWEAR WORDS IN THE CANADIAN LANGUAGE

1. __ __ __ __

2. __ __ __ __

3. __ __ __ __ __ __ __ __ (French)

4. __ __ __   __ __ __ __

5. __ __ __

6. __ __ __ __ __ __ __

7. __ __ __ __ __   __ __ __ __ __ __

8. __ __   __ __   __ __ __ __

9. __ __ __ __

10. __ __ __ __ __

Exclusive to *The Canadian Book of Lists*

13
PRIVATE AND CONFIDENTIAL

10 GREAT CANADIAN QUOTATIONS ON SEX

1. Erotic books feed a part of that fantasy life without which man cannot exist.

   Robertson Davies, *A Voice From the Attic*, 1960

2. Unconsummated relationships depress outsiders perhaps more than anybody.

   Alice Munro, *The Peace of Utrecht*, 1968

3. Pornography is another intellectual mode which serves as a substitute for feeling.

   Miriam Waddington, *All Nature into Motion*, 1969

4. Canadians move slowly, but when they are aroused they move with remarkable speed. Our way of life is puritanism touched by orgy.

   Claude T. Bissell, *The Strength of the Univeristy*, 1968

5. Sexual indulgence should only occur about once in a week or ten days, and this of course applies only to those who enjoy a fair degree of health. But it is a hygienic and physiological fact that those who indulge only once a month receive a far greater degree of the intensity of enjoyment than those who indulge their passions more frequently. Much pleasure is lost by excesses where much might be gained by temperance, giving vent to the organs for the accumulation of vervous force.

   B. G. Jefferies and J. L. Nichols, *Light on Dark Corners*, 1894

6. Chinese marxists are like Quebec collegians. On questions of religion and sex they lose their sang-froid.

   Pierre Elliott Trudeau and Jacques Herbert, *Two Innocents in Red China*, 1968

7. Sex is the only luxury available to the ordinary man. Whether the ordinary woman also considers it a luxury is perhaps open to question.

   John H. Redekop, *The Star-Spangled Beaver*, 1971

8. There are only two subjects that appeal nowadays to the general public, murder and sex; and, for people of culture, sex-murder.

   Stephen Leacock, *Frenzied Fiction*, 1938

9. If you drive modesty out of the world, you will go a long way toward driving out sexual morality also.

Charles F. Paul, *Saturday Night*, 1914

10. Orgasms really have very little to do with making love, and men who require their women to respond with *petit mal* seizures that can be picked up on the Richter scale are not making love but asking for reassurance.

Merle Shain, *Some Men Are More Perfect than Others*, 1973

11 IMPORTANT WAYS THAT WOMEN CAN PLEASE MEN

1. By marrying them.

2. By divorcing them.

3. By not trying to be one.

4. Not expecting them to get romantic (a) when you are wearing your favourite housedress (b) when they are watching their favourite TV program (c) under any circumstances after ten years of marriage.

5. By refraining from pointing out that you would have been much better off with Jack — even if it's true.

6. Eliminating *sotto voce* nightly readings of Erica Jong's account of the younger man's enthusiasm for oral sex *every* day of the month.

7. Giving him the joy of the unexpected gift paid for by your own American Express card or, preferably, Daddy's Trust Fund.

8. By not wearing your brains on your sleeve, especially in a sleeveless dress.

9. By not leafing through *The Joy of Lesbian Sex* after a particularly tender marital interlude.

10. By appearing to be dumber than he, which, let's be frank, is not all that difficult.

11. By taking no for an answer.

Barbara Amiel
Author
By Persons Unknown

THE 10 BEST CANADIAN LOVERS

1. TRUCK DRIVERS
Tough, demanding, masculine, free-wheeling. The modern day *courier-du-bois*.

2. DOCTORS
Integrated, decisive, dedicated, inquisitive.

3. BUSINESSMEN
Aggressive, light-hearted, ambitious, always willing to make a deal!

4. TEACHERS
Talkative and indecisive but extremely active and attentive.

5. POETS
Gentle but intense.

6. PILOTS
Enigmatic, fluctuating, driving, and determined.

7. LUMBERJACKS
Strong, willing, and willful — can service enormous demands.

8. OILMEN
Dark, mysterious, resourceful, and penetrating.

9. ENGINEERS
Loving and creative. Excellent hands.

10. FRENCH CANADIANS
Unreliable and emotional — but poetic and sophisticated. Ambitious explorers.

Jacqueline Cloutier
Exclusive to *The Canadian Book of Lists*

THE 5 WORST CANADIAN LOVERS

1. POLITICIANS

    Enormous potential. Seldom deliver promises.

2. LAWYERS

    Fussy, particular, and detailed. Quick.

3. ACCOUNTANTS

    Tender and affectionate — but too security-conscious. Precise.

4. BANKERS

    Dedicated but generally incapable.

5. ACTUARIES

    Clean, meticulous, and moody. Not very expressive or ambitious.

Jacqueline Cloutier
Exclusive to *The Canadian Book of Lists*

Politicians are among the 5 worst Canadian lovers. They have enormous potential, but seldom deliver promises.

10 GREAT CANADIAN
QUOTATIONS ON LOVE

1. Love is both the source of life and the law of living.

   John W. Bilsland, *Vision of Clarity*, 1960

2. People who are in love are nearly always unobservant. Their eyes and ears seem to be dulled.

   Janey Canuck, *Open Trails*

3. The measure of a man's power to help his brother is the measure of the love in the heart of him, and of the faith that he has that at last the good will win.

   Ralph Connor, *Black Rock*, 1898

4. Short love is sweetest, and most love curdles if you keep it.

   Robertson Davies, *A Jig for the Gypsy*, 1954

5. Isn't it better to wear the love of one man than the admiration of half a dozen?

   Sara Jeannette Duncan, *The Imperialist*, 1904

6. Woman must depend on man for fame. Her only immortality is love.

   John Hunter-Duvar, *The Enamorado*, 1879

7. In love-making, as in war, there is no substitute for victory.

   Irving Layton, *Some Observations and Aphorisms*, 1968

8. Love is a gentle plant. You cannot force its growth.

   Stephen Leacock, *Nonsense Novels*, 1911

9. In comparison with a loving human being, everything else is worthless.

   Hugh MacLennan, *Each Man's Son*, 1951

10. Love is so scarce in this world that we ought to prize it, however lowly the source from which it glows.

    Susanna Moodie, *Old Woodruff and His Three Wives*, 1847

14
SPORTS

10 GREAT CANADIAN
QUOTATIONS ON SPORTS

1. Hit 'em where they ain't.

   Willie Keeler, Canadian-born Baltimore Oriole, 1907

2. Hockey is the Canadian metaphor, the rink a symbol of this country's vast stretches of waves and wilderness, its extremes of climate, the player a symbol of our national struggle to civilize such a land.

   Bruce Kidd, *The Death of Hockey*, 1972

3. A sportsman is a man who, every now and then, simply has to get out and kill something.

   Stephen Leacock, *What's a Sport?*, 1941

4. Supervised and progressive physical education is an essential part of an educational system.

   R. Tait McKenzie, 1926

5. What a vast difference between the free and easy contests of the 1880s and the highly commercialized sport of today.

   Lon Marsh, *Rattlesnake Hunt to Hockey*, 1934

6. Sport is one area where no participant is worried about another's race, religion, or wealth; and where the only concern is "have you come to play?"

   Henry Roxborough, *One Hundred — Not Out*, 1966

7. If the time comes that Canada needs defenders, she will draw them from the ranks of rowers, boxers, lacrosse, and hockey players.

   John Shaw, Mayor of Toronto, 1904

8. Ski racing is an intense pressure sport. You need intelligence to ski. A dummy has never succeeded in competitive skiing—there are just too many mental problems to cope with out on the hills.

   Nancy Greene, *Autobiography*, 1968

9. There is nothing complicated about learning to play hockey so well that you can enjoy playing it, and it will teach you to be a good winner and gracious loser.... qualities you will carry all through your life.

   Gordie Howe, *Hockey Here's Howe*, 1963

10. The difference between the amateur and the professional is that the amateur fights to hurt and the professional fights to win.

   Stephen Mezei, *The Canadian Theatre Preview*, 1942

Gordie Howe, author of Hockey Here's Howe, *states: "There is nothing complicated about learning to play hockey so well that you can enjoy playing it, and it will teach you to be a good winner and gracious loser . . . qualities you will carry all through your life."*

Swimming is the most popular sport in Canada.

THE 10 MOST POPULAR
SPORTS IN CANADA

	Number of *Canadians over 14* *Participating*
1. SWIMMING	32%
2. ICE SKATING	17%
3. TENNIS	13%
4. GOLF	11%
5. ICE HOCKEY	8.4%
6. CROSS-COUNTRY SKIING	8%
7. ALPINE/DOWNHILL SKIING	7%
8. CURLING	5%
9. ALLEY BOWLING	4%
10. BASEBALL/SOFTBALL	2%

Statistics Canada

Most Canadians would like to learn to play tennis.

10 SPORTS CANADIANS WOULD MOST LIKE TO START

1. Tennis
2. Swimming
3. Alpine (Downhill) Skiing
4. Cross-Country Skiing
5. Alley Bowling
6. Golf
7. Ice Hockey
8. Recreational Skating
9. Curling
10. Gymnastics

Statistics Canada

THE 10 MOST INTERESTING FACTS ABOUT SPORTS IN CANADA

1. The first games of golf in Canada were played immediately after the siege of Quebec in 1759 by Highland officers of General Wolfe's army.

2. Houdini — the world's greatest magician — died in Montreal in 1926 when a McGill University student hit him, testing his boast that he could take a blow in his stomach from any man. He had just eaten a full meal.

Houdini died in Montreal in 1926 from a fatal stomach blow delivered by a McGill University student. He had just eaten a full meal.

3. On Christmas Day 1885 in Kingston, Ontario, members of the Royal Canadian Rifles took their field hockey sticks and a lacrosse ball to the ice. This was the founding of ice hockey.

4. The Toronto Argonauts did not originally start out as a football club but rather as a rowing club.

5. The longest N.H.L. hockey game was played on March 24, 1936, between Montreal and Detroit. Overtime went 116 minutes and 30 seconds. Detroit won to end a game that had lasted almost six hours.

6. In 1925 the Hamilton Tigers of the N.H.L. were suspended and fined. The team went on strike because they felt they had played more games than they had been paid for. The team's manager retaliated by selling them to New York.

7. Twenty dollars in the toe of a shoe, a stove for one wife, and a coat for a second, were prizes awarded during the 1930's and 1940's for the winners of the Grey Cup.

8. Joshua Slocum, a native of Nova Scotia, sailed around the world alone in three years and two months. He was one of the first to do so. He should, however, take an extra bow for bravery as he couldn't swim.

9. The 1962 Grey Cup final was played over two days, as a thick bed of fog with nine and a half minutes remaining caused the officials to postpone the rest of the game until the next day.

10. From 1915 to 1940 the Edmonton Grads reigned supreme in world basketball. During that time they played 522 games, winning 502 and tying the rest. During these years the team never lost a game. No other team in the history of Canadian sports has ever matched their performance.

THE 10 GREATEST CANADIAN OLYMPIC HEROES

1. GEORGE ORTON

A University of Toronto middle-distance runner who won 121 races, including many Canadian and United States championships; in 1900 at Paris Games he became the first Canadian-born athlete to win an Olympic title.

2. ROBERT KERR

Outstanding sprinter who, after winning all Canadian honours, won the bronze medal in the 100 yards event and the gold in the 220 yards race at the 1908 Olympiad in London. Later coached and managed national teams.

3. GEORGE GOULDING

First competed as a distance runner then became a walker; established many world records and, in 1912, at the Stockholm Olympiad, was the winner of the 10,000 metres event.

4. GEORGE HODGSON

A Montreal swimmer who represented Canada in the 400 and 1,500 metres swims at Stockholm in 1912, winning both races and setting records which lasted many years.

5. PERCY WILLIAMS

A fleet-footed Vancouver schoolboy who represented Canada at the Amsterdam Olympiad in 1928. He won the gold medal in the 100 metres event and repeated in the 200 metres, even though competing against fresh opposition. In 1930 he won the British Commonwealth title, despite a leg injury which shortened his career.

6. ETHEL CATHERWOOD

Termed the "Saskatoon Lily"; famed for both beauty and talent; won the women's high jump at the 1928 Amsterdam Olympiad and enabled Canadian girls' team to win international honours.

7. GERALD OULETTE

An expert rifleman; won small-bore Prone event at 1956 Melbourne Olympiad with perfect 600 score; in later years won many more honours, including Bisley competitions.

8. FANNY ROSENFELD

A versatile woman athlete who competed successfully in a variety of sports; won the silver medal in the 100 metres race at 1928 Amsterdam Olympiad and was a member of the gold-winning 400 metres relay team; named outstanding female Canadian athlete of first fifty years.

9. PHILIP EDWARDS

McGill University student who represented Canada in three successive Olympiads — 1928-32-36 — winning five medals; respected for both ability and sportsmanship.

10. THREE-MAN EQUESTRIAN TEAM

Tom Gayford, Jim Elder, Jim Day — won the prestigious Grand Prix Equestrian Jumping Competition which was the final event in the 1968 Mexican Olympiad and was televised around the world.

Henry Roxborough
Author
Great Days in Canadian Sport

Percy Williams won 2 gold medals in the 1928 Amsterdam Olympics.

10 GREAT CANADIAN SPORTS ACHIEVERS

1. ZORRA TUG-OF-WAR TEAM

In late 1880s when "tugging" was a big-time sport, five Zorra Township (near Woodstock) farmers formed a team which, in 1893, when all members were over forty years old, out-pulled all other national champions at the Chicago World's Fair to become the world's best.

2. SAM HUGHES

In the 1870s, this outstanding all-round athlete was Ontario's one-mile champion runner, an expert marksman, and hailed as "the best lacrosse player in the world"; during World War I he became Canada's Minister of National Defence and was knighted.

3. HARRY GILL

Born in Orillia, Ontario; in 1900 in New York he won the all-round American track and field championship with a point total unbroken for several years; he later became the University of Pennsylvania coach and was noted as both an author of many books and a manufacturer of sports goods; also coached schoolboys in Ontario camps.

4. WALTER KNOX

Born in Coldwater, Ontario; in early 1900s won many Canadian track and field championships; tied world record in 100-yard race in San Francisco; won North American all-around title in Toronto and world honours in England; later coached Canadian National teams; in 1950 named "Canada's outstanding track and field athlete during half-century."

5. THOMAS LONGBOAT

An Onondaga Indian who early showed prowess in distance running; in 1906 after winning Canadian races and while still in his teens he won the notable Boston Marathon in record time; he later turned professional and won matched races against world's best marathoners.

6. TOMMY BURNS

Born Noah Brusso in Hanover, Ontario; starred in amateur lacrosse, hockey, and speed skating; then, despite a small frame, pursued a boxing career until he became world's heavyweight boxing champion; after being defeated in 1908, he still continued fighting; later became a religious leader.

7. GEORGE LYON

In early youth was famed in curling, cricket, baseball, and tennis; later turned to golf and in 1904, when 46 years old, he won the Olympic gold medal at St. Louis Olympiad where he defeated both the American and British title holders; he continued winning Canadian golf honours until they became monotonous.

8. W. J. (TORCHY) PEDEN

In the years when six-day bicycle racing was at its peak, this Vancouver athlete was a featured competitor and frequent winner; also held world-record for one-mile paced even; was hailed as "King of the Cyclists."

9. MARLENE STEWART (later MARLENE STREIT)

Although small in stature and weighing little more than 100 pounds, this young Fonthill, Ontario, golfer won national titles in Canada, England, and United States even while a teenager; has continued her excellent performance for many years.

10. DOUGLAS HEPBURN

A Vancouver athlete who was crippled from birth yet chose to become a weightlifter; despite early ridicule he continued to develop strength and skill until, in 1949, he won the United States National Open title; in 1950, in Stockholm, Sweden, he became recognized as "world champion weightlifter"; later he turned to professional wrestling and became a featured performer.

Henry Roxborough
Author
Great Days in Canadian Sport

Tom Longboat, an Onondaga Indian, may be one of the greatest Canadian marathon runners ever.

THE 10 GREATEST CANADIAN ATHLETES IN WINTER SPORTS

1. LOUIS RUBENSTEIN

In 1890, after winning many figure-skating honours in Canada and the United States, he won the world's title in St. Petersburg, Russia; later he travelled widely in Canada and became a prominent organizer in cycling, bowling, athletics, and other sports; also served many years as a Montreal alderman.

2. JACK McCULLOCH

An all-round Winnipeg speedskater; after winning national titles, he became world-champion in 1897; he later turned to manufacturing the first tube skates which bore his name.

3. FRED ROBSON

A Toronto-born speedskater who established many world's records in distances from 50 yards to one mile; also jumped hurdles and barrels as attractions at skating meets.

4. CHARLES GORMAN

A New Brunswick speedskater who, in the 1920s, won many national and American honours and made new records which were unbroken through several years.

5. LELA BROOKS

A member of a notable speedskating family who also won every available Canadian, American, and world female title, Lela Brooks won her first championship when only 14 and continued until, in 1925, in a meet in Chicago, she defeated 200 other competitors to be awarded world honours.

Anne Heggtveit won a gold medal in the women's slalom at the 1960 Winter Olympic Games.

6. BARBARA ANN SCOTT

An Ottawa figure-skater. In 1948, in a brief space of five weeks, she won three crowns when she captured the first places in European, Olympic, and world competitions and was hailed "Queen of the Blades."

7. ANNE HEGGTVEIT

After winning top honours in European women's skiing in 1959, the young Ottawa girl won the gold medal in a field of 41 entrants in the women's slalom event in the 1960 Olympic Games held at Squaw Valley in the United States.

8. DONALD JACKSON

Oshawa-born figure-skater. When only 19 he won the men's Canadian and North American figure skating titles; three years later he won the world's championship held in Prague; then turned professional and was featured in ice-shows.

9. BARBARA WAGNER and PAUL ROBERT

In 1955, in a period of sixteen days, the couple won the Canadian, North American, and world's titles in figure-skating pairs competition; during three more years they repeated these honours and in the 1960 Olympic Games they captured the gold medals.

10. NANCY GREENE

Sensational British Columbia skier who won the first world skiing competition in 1967; in 1968 she repeated the honour and also won the gold and a silver medal in the Olympic Games. In both years she was voted "Canada's outstanding female athlete."

Henry Roxborough
Author
Great Days in Canadian Sport

THE 10 GREATEST CANADIAN ATHLETES IN AQUATIC SPORTS

1. EDWARD (THE BOY IN BLUE) HANLAN

Won the world's professional sculling championship in 1876 and retained the title for seven years; competed in Canada, United States, England, and Australia; won over 300 consecutive races; is honoured by statue in Toronto's C.N.E. grounds.

2. JACOB (JAKE) GAUDAUR

At 38 years of age succeeded Hanlan as world-champion sculler and held the title for five years until defeated by a sculler twelve years younger; father of a son who was also a great athlete and is currently Commissioner of Canadian Football League.

3. ST. JOHN FOUR (also known as PARIS CREW)

A famed New Brunswick crew comprised of four watermen — Fulton, Ross, Price, and Hutton; in 1867, in Paris, they defeated all international four-oared crews and attracted world-wide attention; they continued racing until 1871.

4. LOUIS (LOU) SCHOLES

Toronto-born son of John F. and brother of Jack, both of whom were world champions in athletics and boxing. Lou, after winning sculling titles in Canada and United States, won the notable Diamond Sculls in 1904 in England; recognized as world's outstanding amateur sculler; later became Ontario's Sports Commissioner.

5. GEORGE (THE CATALINA KID) YOUNG

When only 17 years old, competed against 103 starters in a marathon swim of 25 miles from Catalina Island to California mainland; not only was he the only entrant to finish but he earned the $25,000 prize.

6. JOSEPH (BIG JOE) WRIGHT

One of Canada's greatest all-round athletes who excelled in boxing,

Edward (The Boy in Blue) Hanlon won the world's professional sculling championship in 1876 and retained the title for 7 years.

wrestling, baseball, and football but preferred rowing, a sport in which he won many international honours in both personal performance and coaching; later voted Canada's greatest oarsman of first half-century!

7. UNIVERSITY OF BRITISH COLUMBIA CREW

In 1956, this four-man crew, all university students coached by noted Frank Read, represented Canada at the 1956 Olympics; even though hurriedly assembled and trained, they defeated all other international entrants in heat, semi-final, and final to win the gold medal.

8. MARILYN BELL

In 1954, when only 16 years old, after swimming nearly forty miles through more than 21 hours, she crossed Lake Ontario from Youngstown, Ohio, to Toronto; one year later she was the youngest swimmer to ever cross the English Channel; in 1956, when only eighteen she conquered difficult Juan de Fuca Strait.

9. ELAINE TANNER

A versatile Vancouver swimmer. When only sixteen, at the British Commonwealth Games in Jamaica, she won four gold and three silver medals; in 1967 she continued winning and also set two new world records; in 1968 at the Mexico Olympics, while still a teenager, she won two silver and one bronze medal. In 1966 she was voted "Canada's athlete of the year."

10. CINDY NICHOLAS

World's leading female distance swimmer; first woman to ever swim English Channel both ways; her time beat all records by ten hours; in 1977 she was voted "Canada's female athlete of the year."

Henry Roxborough
Author
Great Days in Canadian Sport

THE 10 TOP RINKS IN CANADIAN CURLING HISTORY

1. ERNIE RICHARDSON, Regina

There's not much doubt that Ernie and his brother Sam and cousins Wes and Arnold qualify for the number one spot. They are the only team to have ever won four Canadian and world titles, but, more than that, they had a bearing, a class, a stature all their own.

2. KEN WATSON, Winnipeg

If Watson had won four Briers, he would likely have been ranked number one. He was the first of the three-time Brier winners, and it was Ken Watson who helped to popularize the game across the entire country. His sense of strategy, his sliding delivery, and, in later years, his efforts to help establish the World Championship put him into this spot, uncontested.

3. MATT BALDWIN, Edmonton

There is a real toss-up for third spot between Baldwin and his fellow Albertan, Ron Northcott. Both are three-time winners of the Brier, and both helped revolutionize the strategy of the game. But I pick Matt for the number three spot because he was one of the most colourful curlers ever to play in Canada. And for that reason alone he deserves to be ranked slightly ahead of Northcott.

4. RON NORTHCOTT, Calgary

The first three-time winner of the Canadian Championship to become a three-time world champion when he won the Scotch Cup in 1966, and the Air Canada Silver Broom in its first two years, 1968 and 1969. "The Owl" had one of the greatest front ends in curling history with Fred Story at lead and Bernie Sparkes at second. He used three different thirds for his three titles and all excelled under his direction.

5. HOWARD (PAPPY) WOOD, Winnipeg

Although I never saw the great Pappy Wood in action until his later years, his career is the stuff of which curling legends are made. One of my favourite stories concerns his Brier victory of 1940. In that year, his son, Howard Jr., phoned him to tell him that they needed somebody to skip an entry in the mammoth Manitoba bonspiel. (Pappy had already made the Guinness Book of Records for the number of years that he had curled consecutively in the Manitoba bonspiel. At last count it was somehwere around 67 — or is it 77? — consecutive competitions.) At any rate, he entered at the last moment with a pickup rink and proceeded to go through the bonspiel undefeated. He then went on to the Brier which he won with a record of nine straight victories. According to my Manitoba friends, he rates in the top five.

6. DON DUGUID, Winnipeg

Dugie first curled in the Brier in 1957 and won his first Canadian title as a third with Terry Braunstein in 1965. But he came into his own as a fearless skip when he led his Manitoba team of Bryan Wood, Jim Pettapiece, and Rod Hunter to Brier and world titles in 1970 and 1971. His record of 17 straight wins in Silver Broom play still stands.

7. HEC GERVAIS, Edmonton

The great battles of the late fifties and early sixties were between Ernie Richardson of Regina and Hec Gervais of Edmonton. "The Friendly Giant" was a colourful figure, always good for an outstanding game, no matter where or when. Not only was he able to break the Richardson skein of wins in 1961 (and go on to win world acclaim), he came back in 1974 to win the Brier again, even though he was unable to follow that up with a second World Championship.

8. AB GOWANLOCK, Dauphin, Manitoba

I name Gowanlock and Billy Walsh (ninth choice) on the basis of their reputation, their double Brier titles, and the esteem they command from older curlers. Gowanlock first won in 1938 against a tough field and then came back 15 years later to gain his second Brier win in 1953.

9. BILLY WALSH, Winnipeg

Being a loyal Ontarian, I'd have to figure that anybody who could beat the great Alfie Phillips Sr. of Ontario had to be an outstanding curler. Walsh managed that feat in a Brier playoff (the only Brier playoff that went to an extra end) in 1956 in Moncton. He won his first Brier in 1952. An outstanding curler by all accounts.

10. TERRY BRAUNSTEIN, Winnipeg, and GARNETT CAMP-BELL, Avonlea, Manitoba

Garnett (at the time of writing) is the all-time winner of the award of most appearances in a Brier (10) and even though he is eligible for seniors competitions now, is still rated as one of the outstanding curlers in the entire land. The family victory (with brothers Lloyd, Glenn, and Don) in 1955 provided Saskatchewan with its first Canadian championship and heralded the start of a new era in Saskatchewan curling.

Braunstein first made the Brier in 1958 when he took his schoolboy rink from Winnipeg to Victoria and forced Matt Baldwin to a playoff before Baldwin won the Brier. That was enough to convince Canadian curling that school rinks should be limited to school competition. But Terry came back with a magnificent display of curling in Saskatoon in 1965 to win the Canadian crown. Recently Terry has been active in the Association of Competitive Curlers and has helped put a great deal back into the game. For all of these reasons he deserves the tie with the famous Campbell clan rink of Saskatchewan.

Doug Maxwell
Television Broadcaster

CANADA'S 10 BEST BRIDGE PLAYERS *

1. GERALD CHARNEY

A member of the Canadian Open Team at the World Bridge Olympiads in 1968 (Deauville) and 1972 (Miami), with Canada earning a bronze medal in each of these Olympiads. Although partnered with Bill Crissey in the Olympiads, Charney has also played in various invitational events in Europe and in special matches, partnered with Sammy Kehela, with good results. Charney has won several regional titles in American Contract Bridge League competitions. A fine natural bidder.

2. BILL CRISSEY

Partnered Charney at the 1968 and 1972 Olympiads and winner of several ACBL regional titles. Recognized as an action player who makes things happen and is tough to play against.

*Listed alphabetically.
These are the foremost players in Canada from
1960 (the year of the first World Bridge Olympiad) to 1978.

3. BRUCE ELLIOTT

Represented Canada at the 1960 and 1968 World Olympiads. Several national and regional titles including consecutive Spingold victories in 1964 and 1965.

4. SAM GOLD

Represented Canada at the 1964 World Bridge Olympiad (New York, fourth-place finish). Several regional titles. Inventor of several duplicate movements and, although not active in tournament competitions over the past several years, responsible for the development of many of Montreal's fine young bridge players.

5. BRUCE GOWDY

Represented Canada in the 1960, 1972, and 1976 Olympiads, a Spingold winner in 1949, a member of the Canadian National Open Team Champions in five consecutive years (1949 - 1953 inclusive), and winner of other regional and trial events.

6. SAMMY KEHELA

Represented Canada in all five World Bridge Olympiads held thus far, winner of many national and regional championships, and recognized for many years as one of the world's finest players.

7. ERIC KOKISH

Second-place finisher in the 1978 World Pair Tournament, a Spingold winner, with several regional victories. Fine scientific bidding theorist.

8. ERIC MURRAY

Represented Canada in all five World Bridge Olympiads. Represented North America in World Championship Zonal Competitions — in 1962 with Charles Coon, in 1966 with Sammy Kehela, and in 1967 with Kehela again. Co-inventor the Drury Convention. Winner of numerous national and regional titles and also ranks, with Kehela, as one of the world's greatest players.

9. PETER NAGY

Partnered Eric Kokish in second-place finish at the 1978 World Pair Tournament. Excellent card play technique and, although a relative newcomer, recognized as having great potential. Captained Women's Team at 1972 World Bridge Olympiad.

10. PERCY SHEARDOWN

Represented Canada in 1960 and 1968 World Bridge Olympiads. Holder of numerous national and regional titles, usually in partnership with Bruce Elliott (see above). Sheardown made enormous contributions to the development of Ontario bridge players and, although no longer very active in tournament competition, is still one of the world's best on card play and defense.

Al Lando
Non-Playing Captain
Three Canadian Bridge Olympiads

THE 10 MOST EXCITING
CANADIAN RIVERS FOR CANOEISTS

1. BACK RIVER, Northwest Territories

For its raw challenge of white water and polar winds, and its Barren Lands' sweep and colour.

2. CHURCHILL RIVER, Saskatchewan and Manitoba

For its varied friendly beauty and atmosphere of history as an early highway in exploration and fur trade.

3. COPPERMINE RIVER, Northwest Territories

For lonely grandeur and sense of high adventure; its rapids and wildlife.

4. DUMOINE RIVER, Quebec

For its continuous, adventurous rapids, runnable even when the leaves have turned.

5. FRASER RIVER, British Columbia

For its menacing canyons and wild rapids, many of them forbidden to undecked canoes.

6. FRENCH RIVER, Ontario

For rocky, pine-clad beauty, rich in early history of passing explorers, missionaries, and fur brigades.

7. LIARD RIVER, British Columbia and Yukon Territory

For its scenery as it punches through the mountains; the dreadful challenge of its foaming gorges.

8. SOUTH NAHANNI RIVER, Northwest Territories

For its special splendour of cathedral canyons, awesome beauty, and abundant wildlife.

9. PETAWAWA RIVER, Ontario

For its springtime joys of running white water through sunny pre-Cambrian wilderness.

10. UP THE RAT RIVER AND DOWN THE PORCUPINE RIVER, Northwest Territories and Yukon Territory

For the satisfaction of crossing over the continent's spine by one's own stamina, and for the stark beauty of its mountain pass north of the tree-line — the waterway from the Mackenzie Delta to Alaska.

Eric Morse
Dean of Canadian whitewater canoeists

THE 10 BEST CANADIAN FOOTBALL TEAMS IN CFL HISTORY

1. TORONTO ARGONAUTS, 1950 Grey Cup Champions

The Argonauts defeated the Winnipeg Blue Bombers by a score of 13-0. This Toronto team was voted as the best of the half-century.

2. CALGARY STAMPEDERS, 1948 Grey Cup Champions

The Stampeders defeated the Ottawa Rough Riders 12-7 in the championship game to go the year without a loss.

3. EDMONTON ESKIMOS, 1956 Grey Cup Champions

The Eskimos defeated the Montreal Alouettes 50-27 in the highest-scoring game in Grey Cup history. This was the third of three successive Eskimo Grey Cup Teams. The Alouettes were the losers in all three instances.

4. WINNIPEG BLUE BOMBERS, 1961 Grey Cup Champions

The Blue Bombers defeated the Hamilton Tiger-Cats 21-14 in overtime, and won the Grey Cup in four out of the five years from 1958-1962.

5. OTTAWA ROUGH RIDERS, 1969 Grey Cup Champions

The Ottawa Rough Riders defeated the Saskatchewan Roughriders 29-11. Ottawa took the Grey Cup four times in nine years, with the 1969 team being the most powerful.

6. TORONTO ARGONAUTS, 1945 Grey Cup Champions

The Argonauts defeated the Winnipeg Blue Bombers 35-0 in the most decisive Grey Cup final since 1923. In the eight years beginning in 1945, the Argos were to win the title five times.

7. HAMILTON TIGER-CATS, 1967 Grey Cup Champions

The Tiger-Cats decisively defeated the defending champion Saskatchewan Rough Riders by a score of 24-1. The Ticats won the Grey Cup four times between 1963 and 1972.

8. MONTREAL ALOUETTES, 1977 Grey Cup Champions

The Als defeated the Edmonton Eskimos 41-6 in the championship game. The Montreal team of 1977 was a tremendously effective unit, stable both offensively and defensively.

9. HAMILTON TIGER-CATS, 1963 Grey Cup Champions

The Tiger-Cats defeated the B.C. Lions in the final by a score of 21-10. After having lost in 1961 and 1962, this Hamilton team was determined enough to take the title from the western champion Lions.

10. BRITISH COLUMBIA LIONS, 1964 Grey Cup Champions

The Lions defeated the defending champion Tiger Cats, 34-24, to win their first Grey Cup in the team's history.

THE 10 GREATEST CANADIAN
FOOTBALL STARS

1. F. A. (CASEY) BALDWIN

A University of Toronto athlete who starred in many sports but excelled in football; in 1905 he captained the university team which defeated Ottawa Rough Riders in the Dominion final; after graduation he became involved in pioneer aviation.

2. BENJAMIN SIMPSON

A Hamilton school teacher who became a great punter and half-back with the Hamilton Tigers when that club was winning national football titles; honoured in Football Hall of Fame.

3. SMIRLE (the original "BIG TRAIN") LAWSON

A plunging half-back who starred with the University of Toronto team which became the first winner of the Grey Cup in 1909; honoured in Football Hall of Fame.

4. LIONEL P. (CONNY) CONACHER

Starred in eight sports and a professional in four of them; a member of two Stanley Cup winning teams but excelled in football in both United States and Canada; later became member in both provincial and federal parliaments; in 1950 was voted "Canada's all-round athlete of half-century."

5. JOSEPH BREEN

A versatile Toronto athlete who excelled in both baseball and athletics but especially in football, where he captained two University of Toronto teams which won both intercollegiate and national titles; member of Football Hall of Fame.

6. HARVEY PULFORD

An Ottawa athlete who won national fame and titles in football, rowing, boxing, paddling, and squash; also starred in hockey, where he was a member of three Stanley Cup winning teams.

7. EDWARD H. (TED) REEVE

Also affectionately termed "The Moaner"; an exceptional athlete who starred on two Canadian championship teams, each in a different sport (lacrosse and football); later became a successful football coach and prominent sportswriter, esteemed for his knowledge and sportsmanship; honoured in both football and lacrosse Halls of Fame.

8. JOSEPH (YOUNG JOE) WRIGHT

Son of famed father, early excelled in rowing where he won every available honour in Canada and United States, then captured the historic Diamond Sculls in England; with partner Jack Guest won the silver medal in pairs at Amsterdam Olympiad; also starred in football even during his rowing years and was a member of a Toronto Argonauts football team which won Grey Cup in 1933.

252

9. ALVIN RITCHIE

Played junior football in Regina, Saskatchewan, but earned recognition, not as a player, but rather for his coaching — managing and promoting the game in western Canada; for his untiring efforts he was elected to membership in Football Hall of Fame.

10. RUSS JACKSON

An Ottawa athlete who became Canada's outstanding football quarterback with Ottawa Rough Riders and was elected to membership in Football Hall of Fame; he later became a coach before returning to his teaching profession.

Henry Roxborough
Author
Great Days in Canadian Sport

Lionel Conacher was voted "Canada's all-round athlete of the half-century" in 1950.

4 AMAZING FACTS ABOUT SPORT AND CANADIAN FITNESS

1. Seventy-six percent of Canada's population over age thirteen spend less than one hour a week participating in sport.

2. Seventy-nine percent of Canada's population spend less than one hour per week in other physical activity, such as walking.

3. Eighty-four percent of the Canadian population over the age of thirteen watch four or more hours a week of television.

4. Thirty-six percent of the Canadian population spend in excess of fifteen hours a week watching television.

The Honourable Marc Lalonde
A New Perspective on the Health of Canadians

THE 10 MOST AMAZING INDIVIDUAL HOCKEY ACCOMPLISHMENTS

1. Paul Henderson's three game-winning goals, especially his historic winning shot in the dying seconds of the final game in Moscow in 1972. Team Canada edged the Soviet Union 4-3 in games, with one game tied.

2. Gordie Howe, at age 50, topping 1,000 career goals after 30 seasons in both the NHL and WHA and becoming hockey's only skating grandfather.

3. Darryl Sittler scoring six goals and four assists for a record 10 points in a single game, breaking the old record by two. Sittler's spree on Feb. 7, 1976, paced the Leafs to an 11-4 romp over Boston and rookie goalie Dave Reece.

4. Rocket Richard's record of 50 goals in 50 games, accomplished during the 1944-45 season.

5. One-eyed Frank McGee of the turn-of-the-century Ottawa Silver Seven. When a player from the challenging Dawson City team saw McGee score only twice in the first game of a two-game total goal series, he said, "McGee didn't look so hot to me." In the next game, McGee scored a record 14 goals in a 23-2 victory for Ottawa.

6. Bill Mosienko's famous scoring feat of three goals in 21 seconds. Mosienko, of the Chicago Black Hawks, scored at 6:09, 6:20, and 6:30 of the third period against the New York Rangers in New York. Chicago won the game 7-6. It happened on March 23, 1952.

7. Alex Connell, playing goal for the Ottawa Senators in 1927-28, stopped opposing players cold for 461 minutes, 29 seconds. Even though forward

Team Canada's victory over the Soviet Union in 1972 in Moscow remains Canada's most outstanding hockey accomplishment.

passing was not allowed in the attacking zones in that era, Connell's record of six consecutive shutouts is truly remarkable.

8. Until Bobby Orr came along, few defensemen ever scored more than 20 goals in a season. Orr once scored 46 goals in a single season and six times topped the 100-point mark — remarkable achievements for a hockey defenseman.

9. It's one thing for an established star to score 50 goals in a season. It's another thing for a rookie to do it. Mike Bossy, rookie with the New York Islanders, scored 53 goals in 1977-78. It may be decades before another rookie comes along to break Bossy's record.

10. It happened once. It'll never happen again. King Clancy, playing for the Ottawa Senators in a Stanley Cup game, played every position including goal. After shifts at all three forward positions and the two defence positions, Clancy was forced to take over in goal when the Ottawa goalie was given a two-minute penalty. In those days, the goalie served his own penalty time. Clancy played in goal and was not scored against.

Brian McFarlane
Author
Stanley Cup Fever

THE 10 GREATEST CANADIAN HOCKEY STARS

1. FRED (CYCLONE) TAYLOR
An Ontario-born hockey player who starred with many professional teams, member of two Stanley Cup winners — Ottawa and Vancouver; member of Hockey Hall of Fame; decorated with Order of British Empire.

2. LESTER PATRICK
Born in Drummondville, Quebec, an outstanding defenceman who later, with brother Frank, built artificial-ice rinks; played on and coached and managed their own teams and even founded leagues.

3. HOWARTH (HOWIE) MORENZ
Born in Mitchell, Ontario; later starred through 12 years with Montreal Canadiens; selected in 1950 as having been "Canada's outstanding hockey player during first half-century."

4. EDWARD W. SHORE
Played early hockey in western Canada; later joined Boston Bruins (N.H.L.) where he was elected to seven All-Star teams; later coached and owned minor league teams.

5. MAURICE (ROCKET) RICHARD
Sensational, high-scoring player; Montreal-born; played over 1,000 games with Montreal Canadiens; was named to 14 first or second all-star teams.

6. FRANK (KING) CLANCY
Colourful Ottawa-born hockey player, son of a great athlete, began professional career when only 18 years old; played with Ottawa Senators and

Bobby Orr is probably the greatest hockey defenceman Canada has ever seen.

Toronto Maple Leafs; later coached, managed, refereed through many years, and still holds high executive office.

7. GORDON HOWE

Saskatchewan-born hockey player; played 25 seasons with Detroit Red Wings, then joined W.H.A. clubs; still starring in his 50th year; has won every available hockey trophy and holds all scoring records.

8. JEAN BELIVEAU

Popular, talented player; born in Trois Rivières, Quebec; centered Montreal Canadiens for 18 seasons, then retired to become high executive in that club; respected for his ability and sportsmanship.

9. ROBERT M. HULL

Ontario-born hockey star; played 15 years in National Hockey League with Chicago Black Hawks and won every available honour including that of being top league scorer seven times. Later joined Winnipeg club in W.H.A.

10. ROBERT (BOBBY) ORR

Born in Parry Sound, Ontario; started playing professionally with Boston Bruins when only eighteen and became the highest-scoring defenceman in hockey history; won every available honour, including that of "Canada's top athlete of the year" (1970-71).

Henry Roxborough
Author
Great Days in Canadian Sport

THE 10 BEST CANADIAN HOCKEY TEAMS

1. MONTREAL CANADIENS, 1956-60

Five straight Stanley Cups with players Beliveau, Geoffrion, Moore, the Richards, Harvey, Plante.

2. MONTREAL CANADIENS, 1976-78

If the present-day Canadiens can make it five-for-five in Stanley Cup play, they'll be considered equal to the champions above.

3. DETROIT RED WINGS, 1949-55

Seven straight league championships and three Stanley Cups with Gordie Howe, Ted Lindsay, Sid Abel, and Terry Sawchuk leading the way.

4. BOSTON BRUINS, 1971-72

Cheevers and Johnston in goal, Orr, Esposito, Hodge, McKenzie, Cashman, Bucyk, and a reliable Derek Sanderson. All the way to the Stanley Cup.

5. TEAM CANADA, 1972

They were only together for a few weeks, but what a memorable climax to a once-in-a-lifetime series!

6. U.S.S.R., 1972

Fantastic team play and spectacular goaltending by Tretiak earned this team plaudits from hockey fans everywhere.

7. TORONTO MAPLE LEAFS, 1967

A team of youth and age, capably coached and managed by Punch Imlach, surged to the Stanley Cup in Centennial Year. A great "money" team.

8. PHILADELPHIA FLYERS, 1974-75

Toughness, determination, and talent; with Bobby Clarke's leadership standing out.

9. TORONTO MAPLE LEAFS, 1947-49

Hap Day and Conn Smythe moulded a team of champions that won five Stanley Cups in eight years. Day's final three Cup teams were his finest.

10. OTTAWA SILVER SEVEN, 1902-05

Let's not forget yesterday's heroes. After the turn of the century the Silver Seven beat everything in sight.

Brian McFarlane
Author
Stanley Cup Fever

THE 5 BEST HOCKEY GAMES INVOLVING CANADIANS

1. TEAM CANADA 6, RUSSIA 5. September 28, 1972. Lenin Central Stadium, Moscow

Paul Henderson, of the Toronto Maple Leafs, scored the winning goal with only 34 seconds to go in this game played before millions on world-wide TV from Russia. The win gave Canada a 4-3 victory (one game tied) in the seven-game series, the first such series pitting Canadian professionals against the best Russian players. No single game ever played before this time attracted as much interest. Fans were not disappointed, as they were treated to 60 minutes of nerve-tingling, high-scoring hockey.

2. MONTREAL CANADIENS 3, RUSSIAN CENTRAL RED ARMY 3. December 31, 1975. Montreal Forum.

From an artistic standpoint, an almost perfect hockey game. Sixty minutes of clean, fast-skating, pin-point passing hockey. Montreal outshot

Russia 38 to 13 and held 2-0 and 3-1 leads, but Russia finally tied the game for good at the 4:04 mark of the third period. Only seven minor penalties were called, 3 going to Montreal; 18,975 people were in the Forum and millions watched on television, after which most were too drained for regular New Year's Eve revelry.

3. CZECHOSLOVAKIA 1, TEAM CANADA 0. September 10, 1976. Montreal Forum

International hockey provided another spine-tingler as Czechoslovakia beat Canada in this meeting between the two teams during the first Canada Cup series. Although Canada outshot the Czechs 29 to 23, goalkeeper Dzurilla was unbeatable. Rogatien Vachon was almost as brilliant for Canada, allowing only Novy's goal at 15:41 of the third period. Canada went on to eliminate Czechoslovakia and win the tournament.

4. ST. CATHARINES TEE PEES 6, TORONTO ST. MICHAEL'S MAJORS 6. March 23, 1954. Garden City Arena, St. Catharines, Ontario

The 4,134 fans who went to the Ontario Hockey Association Junior "A" play-off game on that Tuesday night in 1954 expected a good game — there were more than a dozen future pro stars performing — but what they got was one of the most exciting games ever played, anywhere. With 20 seconds to go in the game, his team behind 5-4 and a face-off deep in his own zone, Tee Pee coach Rudy Pilous removed his goalie. Hugh Barlow scored with 12 seconds left to tie the game. In the standard 10-minute overtime period, Barlow scored again. But, with a minute to go in the overtime, St. Mike's coach Charlie Cerre removed *his* goalie. Jim Logan scored with 42 seconds left to again tie the game — this time for St. Mike's. Fittingly, that's how the game ended.

5. TORONTO MAPLE LEAFS 3, MONTREAL CANADIENS 2. April 21, 1951. Maple Leaf Gardens, Toronto

With 32 seconds left in this Stanley Cup final game and their goaltender removed for an extra attacker, Tod Sloan scored for the Leafs to send the game into overtime — the second time that night Sloan had tied the game and the fifth consecutive play-off game that year between these teams that went into overtime. The incomparable Maurice Richard had scored earlier for the Canadiens. Paul Meger, whose career was soon to be cut short by a tragic injury, had scored Montreal's second goal. At 2:53 of the first overtime period Leaf defenceman Bill Barilko, who, as it developed would never play again, scored. That single goal won the Stanley Cup for Toronto; it was Barilko's last ever (he was killed in a plane crash shortly after); and was the first important goal ever scored on a slap shot.

J. Lyman MacInnis
Hockey Historian

10 REASONS WHY CANADA CANNOT WIN A WORLD CHAMPIONSHIP IN HOCKEY UNDER PRESENT CONDITIONS *

1. TIMING

Canada does not have its top personnel available because they are involved in Stanley Cup play-off participation.

2. REFEREES

The quality of international refereeing is much below the quality to which our players are accustomed. The referees cannot skate quickly and are amateurs in every sense of the word.

3. RINK SIZE

The international size rink is difficult for our players in that it is about 20 percent larger than that on which they play during their regular North American hockey season.

4. THE WORLD CHAMPIONSHIP IS NOT IMPORTANT TO THE PLAYERS

The players still feel the Stanley Cup is the important prize in hockey.

5. THE SERIES IS UNIMPORTANT TO OWNERS

The owners share the views of the players with respect to the Stanley Cup.

6. THE SERIES IS UNIMPORTANT TO NORTH AMERICAN HOCKEY FANS

7. LACK OF PROPER TRAINING PERIOD

The players finish with their clubs on one day and have to assemble as a team within 48 hours and participate in crucial games. This is an impossible situation.

8. TRAVEL PROBLEMS

The players play in North America the entire season and then travel through a 6-to-8-hour time differential and have to adjust to that time change immediately.

---

*In spite of the reasons, Canada has come very close to winning a gold medal. In 1977 bad refereeing cost us a silver medal and if we had been able to defeat the Soviet Union once we would have won the gold medal. In 1978 Canada had the opportunity to win the gold medal again and lost to Russia after leading 2 to 1 with less than three minutes to play in the game. The more our players see of international competition, the better their chances are for a gold medal. One of these days everything will work out smoothly for Team Canada and we will come home with the World Championship.

9. THE SYSTEM OF CHOOSING REFEREES

The international Ice Hockey Federation tournament directorate chooses the referees on the basis of country rather than on the basis of ability. Each country in the Championships nominates a referee and each referee must referee at least one game even if that referee has no ability whatsoever.

10. SPONSORSHIP

Sponsors have to be available for Team Canada and must commit themselves to approximately $500,000 for each Championship. The problems of arranging sponsorship are becoming increasingly more difficult because of the large amount of money involved.

Alan Eagleson
Executive Director
National Hockey League Players' Association

THE 10 FASTEST WINNERS
OF THE QUEEN'S PLATE *

	Horse	Jockey	Owner	Year	Time
1.	Victoria Park	A. Gomez	Winfields Farm	1960	2:02
1.	Regal Embrace	S. Hawley	E.P. Taylor	1978	2:02
3.	Northern Dancer	W. Hartack	Winfields Farm	1964	2:02 1/5
4.	Lyford Cay	A. Gomez	E.P. Taylor	1956	2:02 3/5
4.	L'Enjoleur	S. Hawley	J.L. Levesque	1975	2:02 3/5
6.	Kennedy Road	S. Hawley	Mrs. A. Stollery	1971	2:03
6.	Jammed Lovely	J. Fitzsimmons	C. Smythe	1967	2:03
8.	Victoria Song	R. Platts	Green Hills Farm	1966	2:03 1/5
9.	Titled Hero	A. Gomez	P. K. Marshall	1966	2:03 3/5
10.	Whistling Sea	T. Inouye	Oliver Ranches	1965	2:03 4/5

*Since 1956, when the distance was changed from $1^1/_8$ miles to $1^1/_4$ miles.

Canadian Jockey Club

Northern Dancer won the Queen's Plate for industrialist E.P. Taylor in 1956 — but not in the fastest time.

Nijinsky has won more money than any other Canadian-bred racehorse.

THE 10 ALL-TIME BEST CANADIAN-BRED HORSES

1. Northern Dancer
2. Nijinsky
3. The Minstrel
4. George Royal
5. Victoria Park
6. Bunty Lawless
7. Northernette
8. Cool Reception
9. L'Enjoleur
10. Kennedy Road

Douglas Cooper
Retired Editor
Daily Racing Form

THE 10 CANADIAN-BRED
RACE HORSES THAT HAVE WON
THE MOST MONEY

		Amount Won
1.	Nijinsky	$667,163
2.	Northern Dancer	580,806
3.	La Prevoyante	572,417
4.	The Minstrel	570,748
5.	L'Enjoleur	546,079
6.	Kennedy Road	481,137
7.	Norcliffe	434,066
8.	Victorian Prince	356,611
9.	Reasonable Win	324,476
10.	George Royal	322,242

The Canadian Jockey Club

THE 10 HIGHEST
QUEEN'S PLATE PAYOFFS

		Year	*Win*	*Place*	*Show*
1.	Maternal Pride	1924	$193.35	95.45	43.65
2.	Paolita	1943	76.50	19.30	6.05
3.	Royal Chocolate	1973	48.10	14.50	9.00
4.	Blue Light	1961	39.50	10.60	4.80
5.	Moldy	1947	36.50	13.35	7.60
6.	Aymond	1930	30.20	11.25	6.15
7.	Shorelint	1929	28.30	10.50	8.10
8.	Epigram	1952	25.05	14.30	10.80
9.	Jammed Lovely	1967	24.90	8.50	5.10
10.	Collisteo	1954	24.20	5.40	2.20

Douglas Cooper
Retired Editor
Daily Racing Form

THE 10 GREATEST CANADIAN
RODEO PURSES

		Purse
1.	Calgary Exhibition and Stampede, Calgary, Alberta	$211,650
2.	Canadian Western Super Rodeo, Edmonton, Alberta	$ 27,000
3.	Manitoba Stampede, Morris, Manitoba	$ 26,000
4.	North American Chuck Wagon Races, High River, Alberta	$ 20,000
5.	Ponoko Stampede, Ponoko, Alberta	$ 19,700
6.	Medicine Hat Stampede, Medicine Hat, Alberta	$ 18,900
7.	Rodeo Royal, Calgary, Alberta	$ 18,900
8.	Cloverdale Rodeo, Cloverdale, B.C.	$ 18,750
9.	Williams Lake Stampede, Williams Lake, B.C.	$ 12,900
10.	Northwest Round-Up and Exhibition, Swan River, Manitoba	$ 10,750

Canadian Government Office of Tourism

10 GREAT CONTEMPORARY CANADIAN
RACING YACHTS

1. RED JACKET

Ah, so mean and hungry when Perry Connolly owned her in the late 1960s. And she cleaned up on Lake Ontario then, before winning everything in the Southern Ocean Racing Conference in 1968. The world treated Canadian ocean racers with new respect after that.

2. MANITOU

She's the homegrown product that trounced the Cleveland Yachting Club challenger for the Canada's Cup in 1969. Canadian Great Lakes sailors felt good about that. Her design (C & C Yachts Ltd.) was years ahead of its time.

3. DYNAMO

This 50-footer's silverware collecting habits in Lake Ontario waters could supplement supplies to the Royal Mint. She's also well-travelled, being on Canada's first (though ill-placed) Admiral's Cup team in Britain in 1975, with her skipper Gerry Moog as team captain.

4. BONAVENTURE V

Bernie Herman probably has put more miles on this fine 53-footer than any other Canadian racer. She's been a perennial at the SORC and before design rules out-sophisticated her, *Bonaventure* nearly had every success in home waters to her credit.

5. MIRAGE

Here's one of the toughest two-tonners built, an engineering joy. Sadly, she lost the Canada's Cup in 1972 when experiments of a twin with the same design didn't work out. She raced in the SORC to Jamaica in the Fastnet (Cowes-to-Ireland-to-Plymouth) and even in a big series in Brazil.

6. AMERICAN EAGLE

Not Canadian? Not originally, not now, but for a year she was when her owner Herb Wahl wanted to turn this 12-metre into the nucleus of a Canadian challenge for the America's Cup. Customs duty made things too tough so Ted Turner was allowed to make her famous in the U.S. What a joy to sail!

7. INTERLUDE II

The big aluminum yawl, Owen Sound built, that only dreams allow most sailors to deserve. She raced moderately well in Lake Ontario competition but she was a cruising joy on Toronto-to-Florida deliveries and gunkholing in the Bahamas.

8. NONSUCH

This chubby (30×11-foot) catboat fits on my list because it suits me, a chubby cat. It's also a daring new silhouette for the Canadian sailing scene. Designer Mark Ellis dipped into traditional and modern design theory to produce a nippy, easy sailer.

9. GRAYBEARD

Here's the boat that makes the news from exotic places. This is the maxi-boat joy of Lol Killam, Vancouver. It races to Hawaii, Tahiti, and Pacific ports where the Canadian flag is rarely flown. Some like 'em big. Some like 'em fast. Killam likes 'em big and fast.

10. ENDLESS SUMMER

The renamed *Gretel II* of Aussie America's Cup challenge fame, this boat, at the hands of George O'Brien, gave West Coast sailors a first look at how this 12-metre can move in their water. She won the Swiftsure Race and hearts went pitter-pat at the prospect of another Canadian challenge for the America's Cup.

Murray Burt
The Globe & Mail

10 GREAT CANADIAN
SAILBOATS OF THE PAST

1. INISHFREE

One of the most successful and most-travelled yachts of the century, this 54-footer designed by George Cuthbertson combined the best of wood construction and contemporary lines. In the early 1960s she was unbeatable in the Freeman race. She foundered off Cape Hatteras on a routine delivery trip to Florida.

2. NONSUCH

Chubby, but not to be confused with the aforementioned catboat, this *Nonsuch* was the vessel that Zachariah Gilliam piloted to James Bay in 1668, setting up the Hudson's Bay Company. A ketch, she cost her enterprising owners only £290.

3. SENECA

Grand old schooner *Seneca* was designed by Nat Hereshoff in 1906 for the Canada's Cup which she won for Rochester Yacht Club. Great as the first boat I sailed aboard in Canada, she was enchanting enough to keep me sailing long enough one week to get me fired from a job I hated and into a career I've stuck with ever since — newspapering.

4. PATRICIA

Some of the old hands genuflect in the RCYC clubhouse. This beautiful 53-foot P-class sloop, owned by Norman Gooderham, was first famous as winner of the Richardson Cup in 1912. It's her passing that was so classy, though. In a Viking-like funeral, she was towed out to Lake Ontario and ceremonially sunk.

5. CANADA

In 1896, the RCYC cutter *Canada* won the international trophy that bears her name. She was one of the "coffin" fleet of Canadian yachts which won everything in sight on the Great Lakes before the turn of the century. Coffin? Because they were boxy shaped, and painted black.

6. BLUENOSE

Without the *Bluenose,* Canada would be without a very important series of dimes and a delightful brand of beer. She would also lack justifiable pride in the most famous East Coast racing schooner ever built.

7. COUNTESS OF DUFFERIN

The schooner, entered by a Toronto syndicate, was Canada's first entrant in the America's Cup in 1876. She lost 2-0 to the American's *Madelaine*.

8. ATALANTA

A cutter from the Bay of Quinte challenged for the America's Cup in 1881 in an effort to retrieve Canada's honour. She lost two-zip to *Mischief*.

9. ST. ROCH

The Royal Canadian Mounted Police piloted this auxiliary schooner through the Northwest Passage to make Arctic history in 1942 — a sailing effort that is sadly unsung. The ship is now preserved in a museum setting in Vancouver. First ship to circumnavigate North America.

10. DRIFTWOOD

One of the first 12-foot Penguin-class sailboats built by George Hinterhoeller of Niagara-on-the-Lake. Meticulous cabinetwork finished as finely as a grand piano. Only an occasional race winner. Remembered by skinny dippers at an Algonquin Park girls' camp. It was *my* first boat in Canada.

Murray Burt
The Globe & Mail

10 GREAT CANADIAN SAILBOAT RACES

1. VICTORIA–MAUI

Raced on even years on Dominion Day morning over 2,300 miles of Pacific. Beginning in 1964.

2. HALIFAX–MARBLEHEAD

An odd-years event that sets the Boston crowd racing against the Nova Scotia crowd. Often foggy excitement.

3. PORT HURON–MACKINAC

A mid-July event each year which attracts all Great Lakes gung-ho ocean racers from both sides of the border.

4. THE LAKE ONTARIO INTERNATIONAL

Draws a big fleet for a big party when the 220 miles have been covered. Generally third week in August.

5. BLAKE VAN WINCKLE

An eye-opener for Toronto racers each spring. Short, 22 miles, but a joy. Nothing by international standards but fun.

6. SUSAN HOOD

Another Lake Ontario test. First overnight race of the season each June that drags out the biggest fleet.

7. SWIFTSURE

The tough West Coast bone-breaker each spring which attracts the sturdier types of the U.S. Northeast and British Columbia.

8. CORK

This is the clutch of smallboat competition which gets Canada's international racing teams in shape to face the world each August. Warmup for the Olympics (Canadian Olympic-Training Regatta, Kingston).

9. CANADA'S CUP

The ultimate test of match-racing skills by a U.S. and a Canadian Great Lakes 40-footer. Not more often than once in three years.

10. WATER RAT TRIATHLON

Some smallboat madmen who each winter ski-race downhill to sports cars, road-rally to their yacht club, chip the ice from their boats, and sail a no-rules triangular course. Cheese prizes.

Murray Burt
The Globe & Mail

THE 5 MOST OUTSTANDING FEMALE FIGURE SKATERS IN CANADA'S HISTORY

Barbara Ann Scott in one of the most outstanding female figure skaters in Canada's history.

1. BARBARA ANN SCOTT

1947 World Championships	Gold
1948 Olympic Games	Gold
1948 World Championships	Gold

2. PETRA BURKA

1964 Olympic Games	Bronze
1964 World Championships	Bronze
1965 World Championships	Gold
1966 World Championships	Bronze

3. KAREN MAGNUSSEN

1971 World Championships	Bronze
1972 Olympic Games	Silver
1972 World Championships	Silver
1973 World Championships	Gold

4. LINDA CARBONETTO

1968 Olympic Games	7th place
1969 World Championships	6th place

5. LYNN NIGHTINGALE

1976 Olympic Games	10th place
1976 World Championships	7th place
1977 World Championships	8th place

Ellen Burka
Figure Skating Coach

THE 5 MOST OUTSTANDING MALE FIGURE SKATERS IN CANADA'S HISTORY

1. LOUIS RUBENSTEIN

1890 World Championship	Gold (unofficial)

2. JACKSON HAINES

1863 American Skating Championships	1st
1864 American Skating Championships	1st

3. DONALD JACKSON

1959 World Championships	Silver
1960 Olympic Games	Bronze
1960 World Championships	Silver
1962 World Championships	Gold

4. DONALD MCPHERSON

1963 World Championships	Gold

5. TOLLER CRANSTON

1974 World Championships	Bronze
1976 Olympic Games	Bronze

Ellen Burka
Figure Skating Coach

THE 10 GREATEST SOLO MARATHON SWIMMERS IN CANADIAN HISTORY

1. GEORGE YOUNG

The Catalina Kid famous for exploits in late 1920s and early 30s; member of Canadian Hall of Fame.

2. WINNIE ROACH

   Greatest woman swimmer of 30s.

3. MARILYN BELL

   Great long-distance swimmer of the 50s. Swam Lake Ontario in 1954 when only 16 years old.

4. CLIFF LUMSDEN

   Great competitor of the 50s.

5. TOM PARK

   Great competitor of the 50s.

6. REGENT LACOURSIERE

   Great French-Canadian swimmer, recently inducted in Pro Hall of Fame.

7. CINDY NICHOLAS

   Fastest Lake Ontario crossing; double crossing in record time of English Channel.

8. GEORGE PARK

9. LORRAINE PASSFIELD

   Top-rated in current era.

10. DAN SHERRY

   Only truly great amateur (Olympian in 1964) and world-record holder in 1965 to make grade in pro races.

N.J. Thierry
Editor
Swim Magazine

THE 10 BEST SQUASH PLAYERS IN CANADA (MEN)

1. Sharif Khan   Victoria Village, Toronto

2. Clive Caldwell   Cambridge Club, Toronto

3. Mike Desaulniers   Montreal Amateur Athletic Association, Montreal

4. Aziz Khan   Toronto Cricket & Skating Club, Toronto

5. Gordon Anderson   Bay Street Racquet Club, Toronto

6. Victor Harding   Badminton and Racquet Club, Toronto

7. Colin Adair Montreal Amateur Athletic Association, Montreal

8. John McCrury Greenwin, Toronto

9. Barry Taylor Badminton and Racquet Club, Toronto

10. Phil Mohtadi University of Western Ontario, London

Canadian Professional Squash Association

THE 10 BEST TENNIS PLAYERS IN CANADA (WOMEN) *

1. Majorie Blackwood	Ottawa	6. Pam Gollish	Toronto
2. Wendy Barlow	Victoria	7. Susan Pridham	Oakville
3. Nina Bland	Victoria	8. Helen Pelletier	Quebec
4. Nicole Marois	Quebec	9. Pat Sinclair	Toronto
5. Kathy Morton	Cambridge	10. Lee Myers	Maple

*Ontario Lawn Tennis Association Rankings

Barry Taylor
Badminton and Raquet Club, Toronto

THE 10 BEST TENNIS PLAYERS IN CANADA (MEN) *

1. Harry Fritz	Toronto	6. Robert Bettauer	Vancouver
2. Dale Power	Toronto	7. Jim Boyce	Ottawa
3. John Picken	Vancouver	8. Richard Legendre	Quebec City
4. Don McCormick	Vancouver	9. Harry Brittain	Vancouver
5. Dave Brown	Mississauga	10. Nick Mohtadi	Calgary

*Ontario Lawn Tennis Association Rankings (neither Greg Halder nor Rejean Genois has played enough matches in Canada to warrant Canadian ranking)

Barry Taylor
Badminton and Racquet Club, Toronto

10 IMPORTANT TENNIS TIPS
FOR AMBITIOUS YOUNG PLAYERS

1. LOVE OF GAME

   Learn to like the game. You must like to play tennis before you can become good at it.

2. TEACHER

   Find a good and qualified professional to teach you the basic strokes and principles of the game and stop any bad habits you may be developing.

3. FITNESS

   Get in shape. If you are not fit you won't last through a tough match.

4. PRACTISE

   Learn to practise more than you play.

5. TACTICS

   Once you can play a match develop some tactical skills — it will make the difference between winning and losing.

6. CONDITIONS

   Before any match make yourself thoroughly familiar with your surroundings. Inspect the type of court, the scenery, and be conscious of weather conditions — important to make you feel at home.

7. GOOD PLAYERS

   Study the pros and how they play. You will learn a tremendous amount by watching good players, especially in match play.

8. RULES

   Learn the rules of tennis thoroughly, and play the game honestly.

9. EQUIPMENT

   Spend some time finding out how all tennis equipment — especially racquets — are made. It will give you a better understanding of how they work and why.

10. CONCENTRATE

   When you play, get everything else out of your head. Concentration will get you into the game and into that confident winning streak that all tennis players fight for.

Barry Taylor
Badminton and Racquet Club
Toronto

15
LIFE

10 GREAT CANADIAN
QUOTATIONS ON AGE

1. We're all fools till we get so old that what little sense we get does us no good.

   Merrill Denison, *Balm*

2. One can always tell when one is getting old and serious by the way that holidays seem to interfere with one's work.

   Robert C. Edwards, *Calgary Eye Opener*, 1913

3. Most people who are old enough to know better often wish they were young enough not to.

   Robert C. Edwards, *Calgary Eye Opener*, 1912

4. Sometimes very young children can look at the old, and a look passes between them, conspiratorial, sly and knowing. It's because neither are human to the middling ones....

   Margaret Laurence, *The Stone Angel*, 1964

5. We've lost some of our hair, some of our teeth. We're disintegrating slowly. When we stop breathing the process will quicken up. That's all.

   Leslie McFarlane, *A Matter of Principle*, 1936

6. From old men to children is but a step....

   Robert Service, *Ballads of a Bohemian*, 1921

7. Those that we envied at twenty we pity at thirty.

   Suzanne Marney, *The Unhappy House*, 1909

8. No man need blush at forty for the follies of one-and-twenty, unless indeed, he still perserveres in them.

   Thomas D'Arcy McGee, 1865

9. When a man is over fifty he has to expect to slow down a bit, but he doesn't want to have to remember it every waking hour of the day.

   Howard O'Hagan, *Trees Are Lonely Company*, 1958

10. You take advantage of your age, measuring it, in your convenient way, by years alone.

    W. H. Blake, *Brown Waters*

THE 10 BEST PLACES
TO LIVE IN CANADA *

1. Toronto
2. Niagara-on-the-Lake
3. Vancouver
4. Hockley Valley
5. Port Elgin (until it became too commercial)

6. Montreal
7. Jasper
8. Edmonton
9. Quebec City
10. Kelowna

*Picking the 10 best places to live in Canada is difficult because if
the question was to pick the ten best places to live all year around,
I would pick ten cities. I am assuming, however, that the list is
designed to give some leeway, and that is what I have taken.

Douglas Creighton
Publisher
The Toronto Sun

Niagara-on-the-Lake — the best place to live in Canada.

*Despite the scenic wonder of Niagara Falls, the city is probably the
worst place to live in Canada.*

THE 10 WORST PLACES TO LIVE IN CANADA

1. NIAGARA FALLS, Ontario

Despite the scenic wonders of the Falls, as the blurbs tell us, the downtown section has been devastated by cheap and shoddy shops selling cheap and shoddy souvenirs.

2. OTTAWA, Ontario

The oppressiveness of the bureaucracy overcomes the natural beauty of the landscape.

3. KITIMAT, British Columbia

A wondrous natural setting for a profitable one-industry town (aluminum), but the amenities of the good life are absent.

4. SPRINGHILL, Nova Scotia

Mining towns are not happy towns. And there's little else here.

5. WINDSOR, Ontario

Border towns are historically vulgar. With Detroit across the river, what can one expect?

6. DRUMHELLER, Alberta

At least it's on the road to Calgary.

7. CHURCHILL, Manitoba

Television by satellite and the intrusions of the white man make this northern city sombre and depressing.

8. MONTREAL, Quebec

This great cosmopolitan city is suffering an acute case of civic overspending on the wrong things, plus an equally acute case of cultural and linguistic schizophrenia. It might recover.

9. BRAMALEA, Ontario

Twentieth-century planned communities subvert the soul; unplanned cities are much more fun.

10. BIGGAR, Saskatchewan

A railroad town in the Prairies. Need one say more?

Jeremy Brown
Author
Dining Out in Toronto

10 ITEMS OF ETIQUETTE CANADIANS SHOULD ALWAYS REMEMBER

1. A man should remove his hat if he greets a woman with a kiss in a public place.

2. A woman, hostess, or wife should never help a man with his overcoat. Only a secretary can correctly perform this courtesy. This privilege is hers alone. A man should always help a woman with her coat.

3. Drivers should never announce their arrival by sounding the horn outside the house. One should alight from the car and ring the doorbell.

4. It is acceptable for a bachelor to entertain a woman alone in his apartment for luncheon, cocktails, or the evening. If she does not have her own car he is responsible for seeing her home, driving her, or providing a taxi. If he has no charge account he should give his woman guest sufficient cash for the trip and tip.

5. A woman travelling should never allow a stranger to pay for her meal.

6. When a man and wife are dining together in a public eating place, the wife should restrain her curiosity and never pick up and examine the check.

7. If calling on someone staying in a hotel, it is never correct to announce one's arrival by knocking on the door. As a hotel guest usually has one bedroom only, it is a rule of politeness never to arrive at the hotel without telephoning the person beforehand. It is equally important to announce your arrival in the lobby when calling on an apartment dweller.

8. When introducing his wife a husband should refer to her as "my wife" never as "Mrs.—." In speaking of his wife he should similarly always refer to her as "my wife" and never "the wife" or "Mrs.—."

9. When addressing one of equal status and asking for assistance or for a favour, the word "please" is obsolete. In making a request of a servant, "please" should never be used. The question should be worded, and then followed with "thank you."

10. In a restaurant, a man should always stand if a woman stops at his table to speak. (A lady should not unless it is necessary.) If she bows as she goes by, the man should make the gesture of standing or getting up half-way, bowing, and sitting down again.

Claire Wallace
Canadian Etiquette

THE 10 BEST PIECES OF ADVICE TO CANADIANS ON LIVING

1. Get married
2. Have children
3. Exercise regularly
4. Read everything
5. Laugh a lot
6. Travel frequently
7. Eat and drink in moderation
8. Take one lover
9. Do not sacrifice everything for money
10. Never retire

Jeremy Brown
Author
Dining Out in Toronto

10 FAVOURITE CANADIAN LOVES

1. BOOK
   The New Testament
2. MUSIC
   Bartok's Music for Strings, Percussion, and Celesta
3. ARTIST
   Pablo Picasso
4. SPECTATOR SPORT
   Professional Boxing
5. FILM
   Fellini's *La Strada*
6. PLAY
   Sean O'Casey's *Juno and the Paycock*
7. PIECE OF SCULPTURE
   St. Paul's, London
8. CITY
   London, England
9. FOOD
   Moules à la marinière
10. DRINK
    Corton-Charlemagne (Grivelet Chateau) 1973

Charles Templeton
Author, Broadcaster, Inventor

THE 10 WORST FADS IN CANADA IN THE LAST 10 YEARS

1. Polyester anything.
2. Nehru jackets.
3. Turtlenecks and peace symbol necklaces.
4. Duckbill shoes.
5. Drapes.
6. Leisure suits.
7. "Anything Goes"/"TVCelebrity Battle of the Sexes."
8. Hollywood mufflers.
9. Pink shirts with black knit ties.
10. 50-year-olds trying to look like 20-year-olds.

Terry O'Malley
President
Vickers & Benson (advertising agency)

THE TEN GREATEST CANADIAN AVERSIONS

1. Dark rum and orange juice
2. Soggy Caesar salad
3. Any team that beats the Argos
4. Any team that beats University of Michigan
5. People who dislike Brampton, Ontario
6. Dieting
7. Unresolved disagreements (domestic, political, etc.)
8. Taking out the garbage
9. Having to have a phone at the cottage
10. Self-righteous New Democrats

William G. Davis
Premier of Ontario

10 OUTRAGES FOR WHICH CANADIANS MAY GENUINELY BLAME AMERICANS

1. Chewing Gum
2. Coca-Cola
3. Hamburgers
4. Jeans
5. Mother's Day
6. Apple Pie
7. Big Anything
8. T-Shirts
9. Bourbon
10. Robert Nixon

David Scott-Atkinson
Public Relations Executive and
Canadian Trend Observer

10 GREAT CANADIAN QUOTATIONS ON MARRIAGE

1. Couples married for twenty years still have surprises for each other.
   Donald Cameron, *Love by the Book*, 1969

2. No woman can resist the opportunity to join in that most fascinating of all sports — man-hunting.
   Ralph Connor, *The Major*, 1917

3. There's more to marriage than four bare legs in a blanket.
   Robertson Davies, *A Jig for the Gypsy*, 1954

4. One may as well have some fun before marriage, one gets so little after.
   Frederick A. Dixon, *The Maire of St. Brieux*, 1875

5. All girls regard marriage as an enviable lot, or as a necessary evil.
   T. C. Haliburton, *Nature and Human Nature*, 1855

6. The burden of creating a happy marriage falls mainly on the wife.
   Marion Hilliard, *A Woman Doctor Looks at Love and Life*, 1957

7. People who have never married have not really lived.
   Stephen Leacock, *Woman's Level*

8. No man can deliberately exclude his wife from the centre of his life and hope to escape the hounds.
   Hugh MacLennan, *Each Man's Son*, 1951

9. It is all very well to marry for love ...if a fellow can afford it; but a little money is not to be despised; it goes a great way towards making the home comfortable.

Susanna Moodie, *Old Woodruff and His Three Wives*, 1847

10. In no other country on the face of the earth does the torch of wedded love beam brighter than in Canada, where the husband always finds "the wife dearer than the bride."

Samuel Strickland, *Twenty-Seven Years in Canada West*, 1853

10 IMPORTANT POINTS
OF ETIQUETTE TO REMEMBER
ABOUT CANADIAN WEDDINGS

1. Invitations to a wedding should be sent to close relatives and close friends — even though they live out of town and cannot attend.

2. A shower should never be given by any relative of the bride or groom.

3. It is not correct to congratulate a girl on her engagement, or a bride on her wedding day.

4. Women guests should always wear hats or a head covering during a wedding ceremony in a house, as they would in church. After the wedding for the reception, it is a matter of choice whether or not a woman guest keeps her hat on.

5. The bride's father should pay for the wedding and the reception afterwards.

6. The bachelor dinner, or stag, should be held three evenings before the wedding day.

7. Whether the wedding is held in church or at home, the bride should be on the spot 5 minutes before the ceremony — but she should be one minute late starting up the aisle with her father.

8. At the reception the bride should only be kissed by those guests who are intimate friends or relatives. If there is any doubt, the invitation should come from the bride or the groom. She should be kissed on the cheek, not the lips.

9. In a second marriage, formal white bridal attire is not worn. The bride may wear white but not the wedding veil. The first wedding ring is not worn after a second marriage.

10. Captains of British or Canadian ships are not authorized to perform wedding ceremonies.

Claire Wallace
Author
Canadian Etiquette

THE 10 PROVINCES
WITH THE MOST MARRIAGES
PER 1,000 PERSONS

		Marriage Rate
1.	ALBERTA	9.7
2.	NEW BRUNSWICK	9.2
3.	MANITOBA	9.1
4.	BRITISH COLUMBIA	9.1
5.	ONTARIO	9.0
6.	SASKATCHEWAN	8.8
7.	NOVA SCOTIA	8.7
8.	PRINCE EDWARD ISLAND	8.5
9.	QUEBEC	8.4
10.	NEWFOUNDLAND	7.9
Note:	YUKON	9.8
	NORTHWEST TERRITORIES	6.8

Statistics Canada

THE 10 MOST COMMON CAUSES
OF DIVORCE IN CANADA

1. Adultery

2. Going through a form of marriage with another person

3. Physical cruelty

4. Mental cruelty

5. Sodomy, bestiality, rape, homosexual acts

6. Imprisonment of respondent for a number of years

7. Gross addiction to alcohol or narcotics for not less than three years

8. Disappearance of respondent for not less than three years

9. Non-consummation of marriage for not less than one year; impotence or refusal to consummate

10. Living separate and apart for three to five years

Peter Kiviloo
Divorce Education Centre

THE 10 PROVINCES WITH THE MOST DIVORCES PER 1,000 PERSONS

		Divorce Rate
1.	QUEBEC	300.1
2.	ALBERTA	288.6
3.	BRITISH COLUMBIA	285.6
4.	NOVA SCOTIA	195.6
5.	ONTARIO	188.7
6.	MANITOBA	177.6
7.	SASKATCHEWAN	114.6
8.	NEW BRUNSWICK	114.1
9.	PRINCE EDWARD ISLAND	82.3
10.	NEWFOUNDLAND	55.5
Note:	YUKON	237.1
	NORTHWEST TERRITORIES	157.3

Statistics Canada

THE 10 MOST COMMON METHODS OF SUICIDE IN CANADA

1. Fire arms

2. Poisoning

3. Hanging

4. Suffocation

5. Carbon-monoxide poisoning

6. Drowning

7. Jumping from high places

8. The use of cutting or piercing instruments

9. Drugs

10. Domestic gases (usually gas stoves)

Statistics Canada

THE 10 HIGHEST LEVELS OF
UNEMPLOYMENT IN CANADA *

		Number *Unemployed*	*Percent* *Unemployed*
1.	NEWFOUNDLAND	37,000	18.5
2.	NEW BRUNSWICK	38,000	13.6
3.	QUEBEC	325,000	11.6
4.	NOVA SCOTIA	37,000	10.8
5.	PRINCE EDWARD ISLAND	5,000	9.7
6.	BRITISH COLUMBIA	92,000	7.6
7.	ONTARIO	307,000	7.3
8.	MANITOBA	30,000	6.2
9.	SASKATCHEWAN	22,000	5.1
10.	ALBERTA	39,000	4.1
	Total:	932,000	9.45

*1977 Statistics

Statistics Canada

16
EDUCATION

10 GREAT CANADIAN
QUOTATIONS ON EDUCATION

1. Education is the fruit of temperament, not success the fruit of education.

   Lord Beaverbrook, *The Three Keys to Success*

2. Of what use is a university education to a young man unless he comes under the influence of instructors who can astonish him?

   Robertson Davies, *A Voice from the Attic*, 1960

3. When you educate a woman late in life, it always sort of upsets her.

   Fred Jacob, *Man's World*, 1925

4. If French Canada is going to continue to insist that matters of education are exclusively the business of the provinces, then it will indeed be arguing that the rules are more important than the game.

   Gwethalyn Graham, *Dear Enemy*, 1963

5. There is no use in trying to train the mind of a child when his body is starved, or abused, or diseased.

   Nina Moore Jamieson, *The Hickory Stick*, 1921

6. A college education shows a man how devilish little other people know.

   T. C. Haliburton, *Sam Slick's Wise Saws*, 1853

7. It's all right to talk about education and that sort of thing, but if you want driving power and efficiency, get business men.

   Stephen Leacock, *Sunshine Sketches*, 1912

8. Education's a habit; you've got to start off with it, or it's no real use.

   Lister S. Sinclair, *Day of Victory* , 1945

9. Education unsettles a fellow — keeps him from enjoyin' his life as he finds it.

   Dora Smith Conover, *Winds of Life*, 1930

10. To attempt to educate the mind and heart, without educating the body, is more foolish than it would be to give a man all the learning of the ages, and then doom him to solitary confinement for the term of his natural life.

    Bliss Carman, *The Friendship of Art*, 1904

CANADA'S 10 FOREMOST INDEPENDENT SCHOOLS FOR GIRLS *

1. BISHOP STRACHAN SCHOOL, Toronto, Ontario

Established 1867. Long the "Grande Dame" of Canadian girls' schools; manages to strike a good balance between tradition and an open-minded approach to female education. BSS has also introduced a highly successful early childhood education program which includes boys from Nursery to Grade 4. Enrolment 700 students (Nursery to Grade 13).

Fees: Day, $2,500; Resident, $5,500.

2. TRAFALGAR SCHOOL, Montreal, Quebec

Established 1887. English-speaking Montreal's oldest independent school for girls, it is the product of a wealthy but childless couple's dream to create a "seminary for the education of the middle and higher ranks of female society." Although it no longer accepts boarders, it has preserved an image of basic conservatism and high academic expectations. Enrolment 250 students (Grades 7 to 11).

Fees: P.Q. government grant plus fee determined by the Ministry of Education.

3. HAVERGAL COLLEGE, Toronto, Ontario

Established 1894. A boarding and day school where traditions are lovingly preserved. There is a well-defined emphasis on academic excellence. Personal development and good sportsmanship are also essential aspects of the school's philosophy. Enrolment 700.

Fees: Day $2,800; Resident $5,500.

4. CROFTON HOUSE SCHOOL, Vancouver, B.C.

Established 1898. Begun on a shoestring with four pupils, Crofton House has emerged as one of B.C.'s most reputable schools for girls. It remains dedicated to the preservation of high education standards and Christian principles. Enrolment 400 girls, including 50 boarders (Grades 1 to 12).

Fees: Day, $2,500; Resident, $5,500.

5. ST. CLEMENT'S SCHOOL, Toronto, Ontario

Established 1901. A small and unpretentious day school with a sustained record of academic excellence. The school property is not extensive, therefore scholarship takes precedence over sports. A friendly but studious atmosphere prevails. Enrolment 350 girls (Grades 1 to 13).

Fees: $2,000.

6. BRANKSOME HALL, Toronto, Ontario

Established 1903. Its tartan-kilted girls appear keenly enthusiastic and loyal to their school. Branksome offers a sound basic education as well as excellent sports facilities to a broad range of students, without placing undue emphasis on academic achievement. Enrolment 700 (Grades 1 to 13).

Fees: Day, $2,300; Resident, $5,000.

*Member schools of the Canadian Association of Principals of Independent Schools for Girls — CAPISG Only

7. MISS EDGAR'S AND MISS CRAMP'S SCHOOL, Montreal, Quebec

Established 1909. Miss Edgar's, as it is more commonly known, still bears the stamp of its strong-minded founders who were determined that the development of moral fibre and a good education should go hand in hand. Enrolment 300 (Grades 1 to 11).

Fees: P.Q. government grant plus an amount determined by the Ministry of Education.

8. THE STUDY, Montreal, Quebec

Established 1915. A good school with a solid reputation for scholarship. Its rather unusual name stems from its origins in a Drummond Street rooming house. It became an almost instant success at the hands of its Oxford-educated founder. Enrolment 250 (Grades 1 to 11).

Fees: P.Q. government grant plus an amount determined by the Ministry of Education.

9. YORK HOUSE SCHOOL, Vancouver, B.C.

Established 1932. Begun as a private enterprise by seven women with the financial backing of their husbands and friends, York House has become a highly regarded day school which includes boys to the Grade 6 level. A distinctive bilingual program and an innovative approach to learning have contributed to its success. Enrolment 400 (Grades 1 to 12).

Fees: $2,500.

10. BALMORAL HALL, Winnipeg, Manitoba

Established 1950. The result of an amalgamation of two former girls' schools, Rupertsland (Anglican) and Riverbend (United Church), Balmoral Hall is now this city's only remaining school for girls. A limited number of residents are admitted to the senior level and a full academic program is offered. Enrolment 300 (Grades 1 to 12).

Fees: Day, $2,300; Resident $4,500.

Note: All fees and enrolments are approximations.

Carolyn Gossage
Author
A Question of Privilege

CANADA'S 10 FOREMOST INDEPENDENT SCHOOLS FOR BOYS *

1. KING'S COLLEGE SCHOOL, Windsor, Nova Scotia

*Member schools of the Canadian Headmaster's Association only.

Established 1788. The oldest existing Independent School in Canada, KCS now operates in affiliation with Edgehill School for Girls (Grades 7 to 12). It is a small country boarding school of 180 students where traditions are deep-rooted but lifetime sports are encouraged as well as competitive games. Fees: $5,000.

2. ST. JOHN'S-RAVENSCOURT, Winnipeg, Manitoba

Established 1820. Originally a Church of England Mission School for Indians, it soon attracted the children of Hudson's Bay Company personnel and Red River settlers. A merger with Ravenscourt Boys' School was effected in 1950 and qualified girls are now admitted at the Grade 10 level. Twelve Red River scholarships are offered annually. SJR has a distinctive western flavour. Enrolment 450 students (Grades 1 to 12).

Fees: Day, $3,000; Resident, $5,000.

3. UPPER CANADA COLLEGE, Toronto, Ontario

Established 1829. Without question Canada's best-known Establishment school. Its list of distinguished Old Boys is as long and impressive as its record of scholarship and community service. The excellence of its Preparatory School program is also a major strength. Enrolment 900 (Grades 3 to 13).

Fees: Day, $3,200 Resident $6,500.

4. BISHOP'S COLLEGE SCHOOL, Lennoxville, Quebec

Established 1836. For over a century Bishop's was a well-established and respected country boarding school for boys. Girls now comprise roughly one-third of the student body. However, the character of the school has remained relatively unchanged. Enrolment 300 (Grades 7 to 12).

Fees: $6,500.

5. TRINITY COLLEGE SCHOOL, Port Hope, Ontario

Established 1865. Staunchly Anglican, TCS follows Upper Canada as the second oldest of Ontario's famed "little big four" schools. It has maintained a solid reputation for scholarship and good sportsmanship which has stood it in good stead for many years. Enrolment 325 (Grades 7 to 13).

Fees $6,000.

6. LAKEFIELD COLLEGE SCHOOL, Lakefield, Ontario

Established 1879. A unique school, the "Grove" offers all the attributes of a small country boarding school at its best; high expectations without frills or pretension. The marked loyalty and affection of its Old Boys can be regarded as a measure of its success. Enrolment 235 boys (Grades 7 to 13).

Fees: $6,000.

7. RIDLEY COLLEGE, St. Catharines, Ontario

Established 1889. Another of the "little big four" schools, Ridley has preserved a keenly competitive atmosphere both in athletic and scholastic terms. Now it admits a very limited number of senior girls as day students. The school's rowing teams have established an international reputation of long standing. Enrolment 450 students (Grades 7 to 13).

Fees: $6,000.

In 1977 Prince Andrew was a student at Lakefield College School — one of Canada's best independent boys' schools.

8. ST. ANDREW'S COLLEGE, Aurora, Ontario

Established 1899. Last of the "little big four" group, considerable stress is placed on athletics and the development of leadership qualities. SAC buildings and grounds are exceptionally attractive and well maintained. Its Highland Cadet Corps is also a source of pride. Enrolment 400 (Grades 7 to 13).

Fees: $6,500.

9. LOWER CANADA COLLEGE, Montreal, Quebec

Established 1909. A day school with a long and strong tradition of academic and athletic achievement, LCC is English-speaking Montreal's oldest independent school for boys with roots dating back to the 1860s. Despite its unimposing premises, the school has developed exacting standards of excellence. Enrolment 600 boys (Grades 3 to 11).

Fees: $2,800.

10. ST. GEORGE'S SCHOOL, Vancouver, B.C.

Established 1931. The city's only remaining boarding and day school for boys provides its students with a varied and challenging school program. Its reputation as one of the West Coast's top-ranking schools appears to be well deserved. Enrolment 600 boys (Grades 2 to 12).

Fees: Resident, $4,500; Day, $2,500.

Note: All fees and enrolments are approximations.

Carolyn Gossage
Author
A Question of Privilege

THE 10 BEST UNIVERSITIES IN CANADA

1. UNIVERSITY OF TORONTO, Toronto, Ontario
   35,959 undergraduate students
   6,469 graduate students
   Basic academic fees range in a General Arts or Science course from $750
   to $850

2. McGILL UNIVERSITY, Montreal, Quebec
   15,203 undergraduate students
   4,019 graduate students
   Basic fees approximately $570 per year

3. QUEEN'S UNIVERSITY, Kingston, Ontario
   11,782 undergraduate students
   1,693 graduate students
   Fees average $790 per year

4. UNIVERSITY OF BRITISH COLUMBIA, Vancouver, British Columbia
   21,752 undergraduate students
   2,162 graduate students
   Fees range from $575 to $720

5. DALHOUSIE UNIVERSITY, Halifax, Nova Scotia
   6,969 undergraduate students
   1,269 graduate students
   Fees average $765 per year

6. UNIVERSITY OF WESTERN ONTARIO, London, Ontario
   19,760 undergraduate students
   2,291 graduate students
   Fees average $775 per year

7. UNIVERSITY OF NEW BRUNSWICK, Fredericton, New Brunswick
   7,150 undergraduate students
   629 graduate students
   Fees average $740 per year

8. UNIVERSITY OF MANITOBA, Winnipeg, Manitoba
   17,753 undergraduate students
   2,957 graduate students
   Fees average $450 per year

9. UNIVERSITY OF VICTORIA, Victoria, British Columbia
   6,876 undergraduate students
   586 graduate students
   Fees average $540 per year

10. ROYAL MILITARY COLLEGE, Kingston, Ontario
    626 undergraduate students
    26 graduate students
    Fees for Reserve Entry Cadets average $800

17
SCIENCE AND
HEALTH

THE 10 MOST FAMOUS
CANADIAN SCIENTISTS

1. SIR FREDERICK BANTING AND CHARLES BEST

Co-discoverers of insulin. Banting won the Nobel Prize for this work, but Best did not.

2. ALEXANDER GRAHAM BELL

Inventor of the telephone. There is an on-going dispute whether the phone was invented in Canada or in the United States, but Bell himself said he conceived the idea while visiting his father's home in Brantford, Ontario, in the summer of 1874.

3. REGINALD FESSENDEN

Born in East Bolton, Quebec. Known as the "father of radio," he succeeded in broadcasting voices through the air without wires, before Marconi. He achieved the first radio telephone conversation, the first two-way radio communication, and the first radio broadcast of music and voice.

4. SIR SANDFORD FLEMING

Invented standard time and the time zones. Until then each different location set its own time according to the sun, and travellers who went any distance at all would have to change their watches dozens of times.

5. ABRAHAM GESNER

Of Halifax, Nova Scotia. Invented kerosene and patented the process for manufacturing kerosene from petroleum. He is known as the forefather of the petrochemical industry.

6. GERHARD HERZBERG

Winner of the Nobel Prize for chemistry in 1971 for his work in exploring the structure of molecules through spectroscopy (a technique for studying the characteristic way in which atoms and molecules absorb and emit different wavelengths of light and other electromagnetic radiation).

7. WILDER PENFIELD

World-famous neuro-biologist at McGill University who developed new techniques for mapping the human brain.

8. SIR ERNEST RUTHERFORD

A British-born scientist who worked for many years at McGill Uni-

Alexander Graham Bell receives from Brantford, Ontario, the world's first one-way long-distance telephone call in Robert White's Boot and Shoe Store and Telegraph Office at Paris, Ontario, on August 10, 1876.

versity. While there, he developed the modern and still-accepted theory of radioactivity which laid the foundations for the whole field of nuclear physics. He won the Nobel Prize in Chemistry in 1908 for this work.

9. E. W. R. STACIE

President of the National Research Council from 1952 until his death in 1962. Stacie was highly successful in obtaining government funding for NRC grants to universities for basic research, thus laying the foundations for university research in Canada today.

10. TUZO WILSON

Currently head of the Ontario Science Centre. In 1978 Wilson won the $50,000 Columbia University Vetlesen Gold Medal — considered by geophysicists to be their Nobel Prize. His work led to widespread acceptance of the theories of continental drift and plate tectonics — theories which hold that the earth's crust is made up of thick moving plates that grind against each other, causing earthquakes, volcanoes, and mountain-building.

Lydia Dotto
Science writer

10 IMPORTANT CANADIAN SCIENTIFIC DISCOVERIES AND DEVELOPMENTS

1. CANDU NUCLEAR REACTOR

The only kind in the world to use natural uranium and heavy water.

2. COBALT-60 TREATMENT FOR CANCER

Made possible by the inexpensive production of cobalt in Canada's first pilot plant nuclear reactor. The treatment was tried for the first time in two Canadian hospitals in London, Ontario, and Saskatoon, Saskatchewan, in 1951.

3. ELECTRON MICROSCOPE

Developed at the University of Toronto by James Hillier of Brampton, Ontario, Albert Prebus and C.E. Hall of Edmonton, Alberta. Their microscope is capable of much greater magnification than normal optical microscopes. The first one was built in Toronto in 1938.

4. INSULIN

The isolation of insulin produced by the pancreas has allowed millions of diabetics to lead normal lives.

5. SLICK-LICKER

Invented by Richard Sewell of the Defense Research Board, this is a device for cleaning up oil spills on water. It was used to clean up Chedabucto Bay.

6. SNOWMOBILE

Invented by J. Armand Bombardier of Valcourt, Quebec.

7. STANDARD TIME

Invented by Sandford Fleming in 1878. He suggested that there should be a prime meridian and that the the world should be divided into 24 time zones 15 degrees of longitude apart. Standard time took a great deal of confusion out of long-distance travel.

8. TELEPHONE

Invented by Alexander Graham Bell, who said he got the idea in Brantford, Ontario.

9. VARIABLE PITCH PROPELLER

Invented by W. R. Turnbull in 1922. The variable pitch propeller essentially opened up the commercial air transport field by making it economically profitable to carry large loads. A propeller set for maximum performance in take-off is not good for cruising because it wastes too much energy; on the other hand, if the propeller was set for cruising, it couldn't get the plane off the ground with a full load. Turnbull's invention allowed the prop to be set for take-off and then altered in flight.

10. WHEAT

The development of red fife and marquis wheat by David Fife and Charles Saunders made Canada a breadbasket of the world, as these wheats were adapted to the short growing season in Canada.

Lydia Dotto
Science writer

CANADA'S 10 MOST FAMOUS PSYCHIC MYSTERIES

1. THE SHAKING TENTS

Since the time of Samuel de Champlain observers, including artist Paul Kane, various anthropologists, and police and government officials have testified to the ability of Ojibway, Blackfoot, and other Canadian Indians to set large wigwams vibrating powerfully and shaking without physical contact.

2. FIRE-EATING

In 1637, Père le Jeune, a Jesuit priest in New France, witnessed 24 Montagnais lifting red hot stones the size of goose eggs with their bare hands and placing them in their mouths where they held them for some time between their teeth without blistering or injury.

3. PRECOGNITION

The Venerable Mère Marie de l'Incarnation was astonished by an Indian girl who in 1663 said she had heard a voice warning of an earthquake to occur three days later at five in the afternoon, which it did —the great Quebec Earthquake of 1663.

4. THE APPARITION OF JOHN WYNYARD

On October 15, 1785, a figure in the exact likeness of John Wynyard walked through the quarters of his brother George Wynyard in Sydney, Nova Scotia, and vanished to the surprise of George and his brother-officer John Sherbrooke (later Governor-General). John was dying in India at that very moment.

5. THE GHOST PICTURE

This picture of the first Legislature of British Columbia and on view in the Parliament Buildings at Victoria was taken on January 13, 1865, when one member, Charles Good, was at home seriously ill, yet his face, though transparent, appears quite distinctly in the place he would have occupied!

6. THE GREAT AMHERST MYSTERY

In 1878 Esther Cox at Amherst, Nova Scotia, was the center of mysterious events in the family home. Lighted matches would "materialize" in mid-air. Writing appeared on the walls and loud rapping noises were heard. Witnesses saw objects move as if carried by invisible hands.

7. THE TALKING POLTERGEIST

In 1889 on a farm at Clarendon, Quebec, numerous witnesses heard a mysterious deep harsh voice, speaking out of thin air, both inside the house and outdoors, carrying on long conversations.

8. THE GHOST OF CANOE LAKE

The spectre of the famous painter Tom Thomson of the Group of Seven has been seen paddling a conoe or landing it on the beach at Canoe Lake in Algonquin Park where he was found dead on July 15, 1917.

9. THE GLEN HAMILTON SEANCES

From 1928 until his death in 1934, Dr. T. Glendenning Hamilton, the distinguished and respected Winnipeg physician, photographed remarkable ectoplasmic and materialization phenomena in weekly experiments with three mediums.

10. THE MACKENZIE HOUSE GHOST

Occupied from 1859 to 1861 by William Lyon Mackenzie, the "Great Rebel" who died there, 82 Bond Street, Toronto, first became known as haunted a century later. Reported happenings include the sounds of phantom footfalls and the apparition of a small, bald-headed man.

Donald C. Webster
President
Helix Investments Limited

8 GREAT CANADIAN INVENTIONS

1. THE PADDED BASEBALL GLOVE

Invented by Arthur Irwin in 1884.

2. PABLUM

Invented by three doctors — Dr. Alan Brown, Dr. T. G. H. Drake, and Dr. F. F. Tisdall in 1930.

3. BASKETBALL

The *game* of basketball was invented by James Naismith in 1922.

4. ZIPPER

Invented by Gideon Sundback in 1891.

5. KEROSENE

Invented by Dr. Abraham Gesner in 1846.

6. TELEPHONE

Invented by Sir Alexander Graham Bell in 1874.

The game of basketball was invented by a Canadian, James Naismith, in 1922.

7. POLIO VACCINE

    Invented by Dr. Joseph Salk in 1954.

8. SNOWMOBILE

    Invented by J. Armand Bombardier in 1922.

THE 15 MOST SERIOUS SELF-IMPOSED CANADIAN HEALTH RISKS

DRUGS

1. ALCOHOL ADDICTION

    Leading to cirrhosis of the liver, encephalopathy, and malnutrition.

2. SOCIAL EXCESS OF ALCOHOL

    Leading to motor vehicle accidents and obesity.

3. CIGARETTE SMOKING

    Ensuring chronic bronchitis, emphysema, and cancer of the lung, and aggravating coronary-artery disease.

4. ABUSE OF PHARMACEUTICALS

    Leading to drug dependence and drug reactions.

5. ADDICTION TO PSYCHOTROPIC DRUGS

    Leading to suicide, homicide, malnutrition, and accidents.

6. SOCIAL USE OF PSYCHOTROPIC DRUGS

    Leading to social withdrawal and acute anxiety attacks.

DIET AND EXERCISE

7. OVEREATING

    Leading to obesity and its consequences.

8. HIGH-FAT INTAKE

    Possibly contributing to atherosclerosis and coronary-artery disease.

9. HIGH CARBOHYDRATE INTAKE

    Contributing to dental caries.

10. FAD DIETS

    Leading to malnutrition.

11. LACK OF EXERCISE

    Aggravating coronary-artery disease, leading to obesity, and causing lack of physical fitness.

12. MALNUTRITION

Leading to numerous health problems.

13. LACK OF RECREATION AND LACK OF RELIEF FROM WORK AND OTHER PRESSURES

Associated with stress diseases such as hypertension, coronary-artery disease, and peptic ulcers.

OTHER

14. CARELESS DRIVING AND FAILURE TO WEAR SEATBELTS

Leading to accidents and resultant deaths and injuries.

15. PROMISCUITY AND CARELESSNESS

Leading to syphilis and gonorrhea.

The Honourable Marc Lalonde
*A New Perspective on the
Health of Canadians*

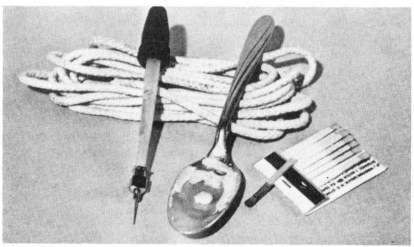

Drug addiction leads to suicide, homicide, and malnutrition, and is one of the 15 most serious self-imposed Canadian health risks.

10 FACTS CANADIANS SHOULD KNOW ABOUT MARIJUANA AND ITS EFFECTS

1. According to a recent survey, men who smoked an average of five marijuana cigarettes a week had greater lung damage than men who smoked an average of sixteen or more cigarettes a day.

Marijuana is potentially one of the most harmful drugs available in Canada, and its smoke has been shown to contain 50 percent more tar than smoke from cigarettes.

2. Prime Minister Trudeau has promised that if his Liberal Government is re-elected, it will move ahead with legislation to remove simple possession of marijuana from the Criminal Code. Conservative leader Joe Clark has also said that there should not be a criminal record attached to the possession of marijuana.

3. According to a survey taken in Canada's largest urban centres, 60 percent felt that it would be a bad thing to legalize marijuana and 33 percent thought it would be a good thing. The Atlantic and Quebec regions were most decidedly against legalization while the Prairie Provinces were most strongly in favour.

4. Approximately one out of five students are reported to have used cannabis in the preceeding six months. Approximately one out of twelve adults are reported to have tried cannabis.

5. The first short-term effect is the "high" — a feeling of euphoria, and a tendency to talk and laugh much more than usual. Similar in many ways to mild alcohol intoxication.

6. Next, reddening of the eyes and an increase in the pulse rate.

7. Later on the user becomes quiet, reflective, and sleepy.

The following are long-term effects observed in some cannabis users *(cannabis sativa* is the hemp plant from which marijuana and hashish are obtained):

8. Regular use, especially by teenagers and young adults, may lead to loss of energy and drive, slow confused thinking, impaired memory, and lack of interest in any planned activity. This is known as the "amotivational syndrome."

9. In some cases physical discomforts occur, such as diarrhoea, cramps, weight loss or gain, blockage of blood vessels, and loss of sex drive.

10. Tolerance develops — more of the drug is needed to produce the same effect.

Addiction Research Foundation

4 AMAZING FACTS ABOUT CANADIAN HEALTH ABUSE

1. Forty percent of all alcoholic beverages in Canada are purchased by seven percent of the drinking population.

2. There are at least 67 children under the age of fifteen with a diagnosis of alcoholism in Canadian mental hospitals.

3. One-quarter of all first male admissions to psychiatric hospitals are due to alcoholism and alcohol abuse makes a heavy contribution to motor vehicle accidents, poisonings, accidental fire deaths, cirrhosis of the liver, and falls.

4. Absenteeism due to alcohol abuse costs Canadian industry a million dollars a day.

The Honourable Marc Lalonde
*A New Perspective on the
Health of Canadians*

10 IMPORTANT FACTS CANADIANS SHOULD KNOW ABOUT CIGARETTES AND SMOKING

1. Smokers' babies are likely to be smaller and stay smaller — that is, if they are not stillborn.

2. Smoking during pregnancy has been linked to disorders fatal to babies during the prenatal period. The prenatal death rate between mother and child has been found to be 81 percent higher in women who smoke.

3. Cigarette smoking can be blamed for 37 percent more early heart attack deaths, and 19 percent more early lung cancer deaths. Total mortality is twice as high in cigarette smokers as in non-smokers.

4. Almost 43.3 percent of Canadian men over 15 are regular cigarette smokers, and 31.3 Canadian women over 15 are regular cigarette smokers. In recent years, however, 12 percent of Canadian smokers have managed to kick the habit.

5. Women who both smoke and use oral contraceptives run an increased risk of a heart attack or stroke.

6. Nicotine increases the viscosity, or stickiness, of the smoker's blood, slowing down the blood supply to the heart and other organs. This may lead to damage to the heart or other organs, caused by a blood clot.

7. Cigarette smoking is one of the few definitely proven environmental causes of cancer.

8. Each day 4,000 U.S. children and teenagers are enticed by advertising to start smoking.

9. If women quit smoking, this can be predicted to eventually result in an approximate 70 percent reduction in lung cancer, and an overall reduction of 7 percent in incidence of the five most frequent female cancers: breast, colon, corpus uterus, cervix, uterus, and lung.

10. Ninety percent of smokers say they would like to give up cigarettes while on 12 percent manage to do it.

THE 10 MOST COMMON (REPORTED) DISEASES IN CANADA

		Number of *Cases Reported*
1.	Venereal diseases	56,344
2.	Streptococcal sore throat and scarlet fever	18,512
3.	Measles	9,158
4.	Rubella	4,167
5.	Hepatitis, infectious (including serum hepatitis)	4,165
6.	Whooping cough	3,002
7.	Salmonella infections, other	2,929
8.	Tuberculosis	2,601
9.	Dysentery, bacillary	1,654
10.	Amoebiasis	870

Statistics Canada

THE 10 MOST COMMON DISEASES IN CANADIAN CHILDREN

1. INJURIES

The commonest cause of illness after age 5.

2. INFECTIONS

a) Respiratory infections: colds, tonsillitis, pneumonia, croup, otitis media.

b)Urinary Tract Infections: infections of the bladder and kidneys (much more prevalent in female children).

c) Chicken pox, whooping cough.

3. FEEDING PROBLEMS

The inability of children to handle certain foods because of allergies, lack of enzymes which digest the food, or improper feeding habits.

4. GASTROENTERITIS

Diarrhoea and vomiting because of infection in the bowel, either viral or bacterial.

5. ALLERGIC DISEASES

Eczema, asthma, hayfever. There are numerous causes such as prematurity, immaturity of the lungs, mechanical obstructions, and congenital deformities.

6. RESPIRATORY DISTRESS IN THE NEWBORN

7. OBESITY

Practically always from overeating. Endocrinological causes are practically unknown. This is extremely important in view of the fact that obesity is probably a contributing factor to the development of heart disease in adults.

8. EMOTIONAL DISORDERS

An ever-increasing cause of illness; the disappearance of the close family unit and increasing social pressures are contributing factors.

9. LEARNING DISABILITIES

Certain children who used to be considered backward are actually of normal intelligence but are handicapped either by hyperactivity or the inability to relate their visual or auditory input to motor output.

10. DRUGS AND ALCOHOL

An increasingly disturbing phenomenon.

Bernard Laski, M.D., F.R.C.P.

CANADA'S 10 BEST-KNOWN DOCTORS

1. SIR FREDERICK BANTING

Nobel Prize winner; insulin discoverer

2. CHARLES BEST

Co-Nobel Prize winner; insulin dicoverer

3. SIR WILLIAM OSLER

Professor of Medicine at Oxford, writer

4. PROFESSOR J. GRANT

Great anatomist; author of classical textbook (a Scot originally)

5. PROFESSOR WILLIAM BOYD

Great pathologist; author of classical textbook (a Scot originally)

6. DR. RAE FARQUHARSON

Professor of Medicine at University of Toronto

7. WILLIAM COLLIP

Discoverer of parathormone, affiliated with University of Western Ontario

8. DR. WILLIAM BIGELOW

Pioneer cardiac surgeon

9. DR. JOHN EVANS

Ex-president of the University of Toronto

10. DR. BETTE STEPHENSON

President of the Ontario Medical Association, Minister of Labour in the Ontario Legislature

Dr. Daniel Cappon
Professor in Environmental Studies
York University

THE 14 MOST IMPORTANT BREAKTHROUGHS IN PEDIATRICS IN CANADA

1. ANTIBIOTICS

The discovery of antibiotic agents, such as penicillin and many other drugs, has literally saved millions of lives, for example:

Pneumonia, which had a mortality in young infants as high as 50 percent, now practically never causes death except when present as a complication of another serious disease.

Meningitis, which was a hundred percent fatal, has a tremendously improved outlook, with most children being saved.

Tuberculosis, with its resulting chronic, lifelong lung disease and the necessity of living in a sanatorium, can now be treated in the home with a complete cure in a relatively short time.

The incidence of rheumatic fever has been cut down dramatically by the judicious use of penicillin.

2. IMMUNIZATION

Smallpox vaccine has finally eradicated this disease. German measles can be prevented; this is a extremely important as German measles is a potent cause of congenital deformities, such as deafness, blindness, and heart disease, if the mother contracts the disease before the fifth month of pregnancy. The discovery of polio vaccine has practically eradicated this dreaded cause of death and maiming due to paralysis.

There are many other examples.

3. CARDIAC CATHETERIZATION

Done by injecting dye into the heart through a blood vessel. Following this, X-rays are taken which demonstrate the actual defect in the heart. The X-rays show the flow of the dye through an abnormal passage, allowing a definitive diagnosis of the actual deformity to be made.

4. CARDIAC SURGERY

By use of improved surgical techniques and anesthesia, the defects which have been demonstrated can be corrected. Much of this has been made possible due to the ability to isolate a heart and make it bloodless by using a pump outside the body which oxygenates the blood during the operation. Further aid is given by cooling the body to abnormally low temperatures to slow down the body's metabolism and thus decrease the need for oxygen.

5. CORTISONE

The discovery of this hormone secreted by the adrenal gland has revolutionized the treatment of many previously untreatable diseases. Its powerful anti-inflammatory and many other effects are still not clearly understood.

6. THE C.A.T. SCANNER (COMPUTERIZED AXIAL TOMOGRAPHY)

A relatively new diagnostic tool, it enables doctors to diagnose soft tissue abnormalities such as tumors and abscesses, which they were previously unable to delineate by available methods.

7. ANTI-MALIGNANT AND ANTI-LEUKEMIC THERAPY

Cortisone and various immuno-suppressive drugs prolong and in some cases cure children with leukemia and cancer.

8. INTRAVENOUS THERAPY AND FLUID AND ELECTROLYTE BALANCE

The discovery of abnormal chemistries in many acute diseases in children, such as gastroenteritis (diarrhoea) and diabetic coma, and the resultant ability to correct these with intravenous replacement of fluid and chemicals, have saved the lives of countless numbers of infants. This has been made easier by micromethods (the ability to do chemical analysis on minute quantities of blood).

9. MONITORING NEWBORNS

The improved ability to monitor the newborn prenatally and postnatally has allowed doctors to prevent death and to prevent brain damage in high-risk infants. This had been made possible by improved methods of determining acid-base balance, the levels of gases, such as oxygen and carbon dioxide in the blood, and continual monitoring of the heart by electrocardiogram.

10. THE DISCOVERY OF THE Rh FACTOR IN RED BLOOD CELLS

Opened up a whole new field in the diagnosis of anemia and jaundice in the newborn infant, and has led to decreased incidence because of methods of prevention, which have been developed.

11. CHROMOSOME ABNORMALITIES

Techniques to demonstrate chromosomes, which are present in every cell of the body, have enabled doctors to associate certain diseases with abnormalities of chromosomes, for example mongolism or Down's Syndrome.

12. PRE-NATAL DIAGNOSIS BY AMINOCENTESIS

This has enabled diagnosis of certain serious diseases to be made in the early months of pregnancy by examining the amniotic fluid (the fluid in the sac surrounding the baby in the mother's uterus). If the outlook for the infant is either early death or severe physical or mental deformity, then termination of the pregnancy can be considered.

13. THE TREATMENT OF HYDROCEPHALY

This condition, in which the fluid in the brain increasingly damages the brain by expanding and putting pressure on the brain tissue, was formerly a hundred percent fatal. By improved diagnostic methods and new surgical techniques, such as the use of various types of shunts which allow a normal flow of fluid in the brain, the enlargement of the head can be prevented and the child can grow up with normal intelligence.

14. ANTI-HEMOPHILIAC TREATMENT

The development of improved blood products, such as cryoprecipitate, a preparation which concentrates the anti-hemophiliac material in 500 cc of blood into 5 cc of active material. The development of a product such as this has revolutionized the treatment of hemophilia, preventing crippling bone deformities, and also allowing life-saving surgical techniques to be performed.

Bernard Laski, M.D., F.R.C.P.

THE 10 MOST COMMON POISONS TAKEN BY CANADIAN CHILDREN *

1. Children's Acetyl Salicylic Acid

2. Bleach

3. Adult Acetyl Salicylic Acid

4. Diaper Pail Deodorizer

5. Laxatives

6. Antipyretics (non A.S.A.)

7. Cough Syrup

8. Tranquilizers

9. Birth Control Pills

10. Cigarette Butts

* Telephone inquiries to Hospital for Sick Children, Poison Control Centre

** The mushroom is the leading cause of poisoning in the summer months of June, July, and August.

Bernard Laski, M.D., F.R.C.P

THE 10 PROVINCES WITH THE HIGHEST BIRTH RATES

		Birth Rate per 1,000
1.	NEWFOUNDLAND	18.9
2.	ALBERTA	17.4
3.	NEW BRUNSWICK	17.3
4.	MANITOBA	17.1
5.	SASKATCHEWAN	16.7
6.	PRINCE EDWARD ISLAND	16.6
7.	NOVA SCOTIA	15.9
8.	ONTARIO	15.3
9.	BRITISH COLUMBIA	14.8
10.	QUEBEC	14.0

Statistics Canada

10 REASONS IN SUPPORT OF FREEDOM OF CHOICE ON ABORTION

1. The assertion that abortion is murder stems from a particular religious dogma. There is no consensus among scientists, theologians, and lay people as to when human life can be said to begin.

2. In a democratic secular society, it is unthinkable that the religious beliefs of some be imposed by law on all.

3. A large majority of Canadians support the right to legal abortion. Even if this were not the case, a majority should not have the power to force any woman into motherhood against her will.

4. In a humane and caring society, every child should be a wanted child.

5. In general, those who support strict abortion laws have also opposed the right of men and women to contraception.

6. At present there is no contraceptive that is a hundred percent safe and a hundred percent effective. As well, human beings are not infallible. Safe, legal abortion is essential as a backup for contraceptive failure and human error.

7. Early abortion by a qualified practitioner is a safe medical procedure, ten times safer than childbirth.

8. Harsh and repressive laws have never stopped abortions. They merely force women to seek illegal and often dangerous abortions.

9. The population policies of a nation should not be accorded a higher priority than the right of a woman to govern her life and her fertility.

10. The Canadian abortion law has been shown to be unworkable and unevenly and unfairly applied. Abortion should be *removed* from the Criminal Code so that *all* Canadians may be free to act according to their consciences in this most important matter.

The Canadian Association for Repeal of the Abortion Law (CARAL)

10 REASONS WHY ABORTION SHOULD BE ABOLISHED IN CANADA

1. Abortion is the killing of an actually living human being. Remove abortion from the Criminal Code and there is no protection for the lives of unborn, immature human beings.

2. Legalizing abortion logically leads to attacks on other vulnerable people and groups, to the killing of the defective and the aged, and to infanticide.

3. Legal abortion has deleterious effects on the health of women and their subsequent offspring.

4. Legal abortion tends to corrupt some members of the medical profession (the profit motive) and also threatens the civil liberties of doctors, nurses, and other hospital personnel who do not want to take part in abortion procedures.

5. Legal abortion diminishes sexual responsibility — where there are liberal abortion laws, abortion is used as a method of birth control.

6. Legal abortion is contrary to the interests of women — it results in women being pressured into having abortions by parents, husbands, boy friends, and doctors.

7. Legal abortion is often a superficial attempt to solve what are really deep social (housing) or personal (the need to be loved) problems — the problems are left untouched, or are even worsened.

8. Legal abortion is based on a false notion of freedom — freedom to do just anything, which amounts to licence.

9. Legal abortion increases the overall abortion rate.

10. Legal abortion does not prevent the birth of unwanted children. There is no evidence that an unwanted pregnancy results in the birth of an unwanted child.

Right to Life Association

THE 10 PROVINCES WITH THE HIGHEST ABORTION RATES

		Rate per 1,000 females 15-44 yrs. old
1.	BRITISH COLUMBIA	19.3
2.	ONTARIO	14.2
3.	ALBERTA	11.9
4.	NOVA SCOTIA	6.9
5.	MANITOBA	6.3
6.	SASKATCHEWAN	5.9
7.	QUEBEC	4.8
8.	NEWFOUNDLAND	3.5
9.	NEW BRUNSWICK	2.6
10.	PRINCE EDWARD ISLAND	2.2

Statistics Canada

THE 10 MOST IMPORTANT WARNINGS AND THINGS CANADIANS SHOULD KNOW ABOUT ARTHRITIS

1. CORRECT DIAGNOSIS

The foundation of proper treatment. Only a doctor can make the diagnosis on which the treatment program for the patient must be based.

2. EARLY DIAGNOSIS

The key to successful treatment. The earlier any form of arthritis is diagnosed and treated, the better the final result will be.

3. THERE ARE NO ABSOLUTE CURES

No drug, diet, or other remedy will cure any of the more serious forms of arthritis. Treatment now available can prevent and check disability, but does not eliminate the disease completely and permanently.

4. KNOWN TREATMENT MEASURES ARE EFFECTIVE

Modern treatment concentrates on the prevention of disability. Relief of most joint inflammation can often be achieved within a matter of weeks. Nevertheless, treatment may have to be carried on for many years. The patient should not be disappointed if after 5, 10, or even 15 years, he still has some difficulty. Instead, he should recognize that because of his persistence, he is still active and not in a wheelchair or an invalid's bed.

5. SIMPLE MEDICATIONS ARE VALUABLE

Salicylates (Aspirin-like drugs) are the safest, most predictably beneficial drugs in the treatment of rheumatoid arthritis. The kind and amount of salicylates for each patient must be prescribed by a doctor. In proper dosage they do more than relieve pain, they act directly on the joints to lessen inflammation.

6. OTHER DRUGS MAY BE USEFUL

Other drugs may be prescribed for special purposes for some patients. Among these are gold salts, colchicine, and chloroquine. Cortisone and cortisone-like drugs are used occasionally, usually for brief periods, for the control of acute episodes. All drugs may have harmful side effects. Their use will be planned specially by the doctor, who balances the benefits to be hoped for against the hazards to be encountered.

7. SURGERY MAY BE INDICATED

Steady advances are being made in the development of surgical techniques for the reconstruction of damaged joints, particularly the knees, hips, hands, and feet. In most patients with arthritis, surgery may produce dramatic improvement.

8. DIET MAY HELP

There is no evidence that any special form of food or diet causes or cures arthritis. Nevertheless, a well-balanced and nutritious diet is beneficial. This is particularly true in rheumatoid arthritis.

In osteoarthritis, excessive weight may make the joint disorder worse, and the doctor may prescribe a reducing diet.

9. CLIMATE MAY HELP

There is no evidence that any particular kind of climate either causes or cures arthritis. But some people feel a little more or less pain depending on such conditions as temperature, humidity, and barometric pressure. In general, moving to another country or climate will not significantly affect the underlying disease.

10. GENERALIZATIONS ARE DANGEROUS

Some people will tell a patient with arthritis "keep going at all costs." Others will say "go to bed and stay there." Such generalizations are dangerous. If a patient with severe rheumatoid arthritis keeps going at all costs — walks with bent, swollen, and painful knees — he invites permanent disability. If, on the other hand, such a patient goes to bed and neglects therapeutic exercises designed to keep the joints moving freely and the muscles strong, he also invites trouble.

The Arthritis Society of Canada

THE 10 PROVINCES WITH THE LONGEST LIFE EXPECTANCY (AT BIRTH) (WOMEN)

		Life Expectancy
1.	SASKATCHEWAN	76.45
2.	ALBERTA	76.24
3.	MANITOBA	76.11
4.	BRITISH COLUMBIA	75.84
5.	ONTARIO	75.53
6.	PRINCE EDWARD ISLAND	75.51
7.	NEW BRUNSWICK	75.26
8.	NOVA SCOTIA	74.80
9.	NEWFOUNDLAND	74.43
10.	QUEBEC	73.91

Statistics Canada

THE 10 PROVINCES WITH THE LONGEST LIFE EXPECTANCY (AT BIRTH) (MEN)

		Life Expectancy
1.	SASKATCHEWAN	70.45
2.	ALBERTA	70.10
3.	MANITOBA	69.80
4.	BRITISH COLUMBIA	69.21
5.	NEWFOUNDLAND	68.94
6.	ONTARIO	68.71
7.	NEW BRUNSWICK	68.53
8.	NOVA SCOTIA	68.34
9.	PRINCE EDWARD ISLAND	68.32
10.	QUEBEC	67.88

Statistics Canada

THE 10 LEADING
CAUSES OF HOSPITALIZATION
FOR WOMEN IN CANADA

		Number of *Women Hospitalized*
1.	Delivery	358,855
2.	Uterus, other female genital	129,314
3.	Liver, gall-bladder, pancreas	79,386
4.	Other, upper respiratory tract	76,280
5.	Supplementary	76,272
6.	Symptoms, systems, or organs	64,168
7.	Abortion	63,952
8.	Complications of pregnancy	63,942
9.	Neuroses	55,994
10.	Ischemic heart	54,141

Statistics Canada

THE 10 LEADING
CAUSES OF HOSPITALIZATION
FOR MEN IN CANADA

		Number of *Men Hospitalized*
1.	Ischemic heart	87,244
2.	Other, upper respiratory tract	80,718
3.	Hernia, abdominal cavity	58,350
4.	Symptoms, systems, or organs	56,191
5.	Male genital organs	53,283
6.	Acute respiratory	50,380
7.	Neuroses	50,132
8.	Osteomyelitis, other bone, joint	46,516
9.	Bronchitis, emphysema, asthma	45,114
10.	Pneumonia	41,494

Statistics Canada

THE 10 LEADING CAUSES
OF DEATH IN CANADA

		Male	Female
1.	Heart disease	34,576	23,434
2.	Cancer	19,529	15,303
3.	Cerebrovascular	7,361	8,603
4.	Respiratory	7,504	4,297
5.	Accidents	8,009	3,242
	Motor vehicle	3,770	1,402
	Other	4,239	1,840
6.	Diseases of arteries	3,059	2,814
7.	Diabetes melitus	1,342	1,603
8.	Suicide	2,108	827
9.	Cirrhosis of liver	1,941	850
10.	Congenital anomalies	857	738

Statistics Canada

THE 10 PROVINCES THAT
SPEND THE MOST ON DENTAL SERVICES

		$ per capita
1.	BRITISH COLUMBIA	25.19
2.	ONTARIO	21.01
3.	ALBERTA	18.56
4.	MANITOBA	15.65
5.	SASKATCHEWAN	11.78
6.	PRINCE EDWARD ISLAND	11.12
7.	QUEBEC	10.07
8.	NOVA SCOTIA	10.03
9.	NEW BRUNSWICK	9.45
10.	NEWFOUNDLAND	5.63

Statistics Canada

THE 10 PROVINCES
THAT SPEND THE MOST
ON PRESCRIPTION DRUGS

		$ per capita
1.	NEW BRUNSWICK	26.98
2.	PRINCE EDWARD ISLAND	24.63
3.	NOVA SCOTIA	23.84
4.	ONTARIO	23.73
5.	QUEBEC	23.52
6.	BRITISH COLUMBIA	22.38
7.	ALBERTA	20.45
8.	MANITOBA	19.19
9.	SASKATCHEWAN	17.55
10.	NEWFOUNDLAND	14.95

Statistics Canada

THE 10 PROVINCES THAT SELL
THE MOST ALCOHOL

		Volume of Sales *('000 gallons)*	*Value of Sales* *($ '000)*
1.	ONTARIO	15,011	547,220
2.	QUEBEC	6,967	264,019
3.	BRITISH COLUMBIA	5,595	207,963
4.	ALBERTA	3,677	149,842
5.	MANITOBA	2,024	76,425
6.	SASKATCHEWAN	1,831	70,047
7.	NOVA SCOTIA	1,391	56,790
8.	NEW BRUNSWICK	874	36,157
9.	NEWFOUNDLAND	707	29,288
10.	PRINCE EDWARD ISLAND	227	9,161

Statistics Canada

THE 10 BEST-SELLING DRUGS IN CANADA*

Brand name	Manufacturer	Type
1. Inderal	Ayerst Laboratories	Anti-hypertensive
2. Acetophen Compound with Codeine	Charles E. Frosst & Co.	Analgesic
3. Ortho-Novum	Ortho Pharmaceuticals (Canada) Ltd.	Oral-Contraceptive
4. Naprosyn	Syntex Ltd.	Anti-inflammatory/Analgesic
5. Amoxil	Ayerst Laboratories	Antibiotic
6. Valium	Hoffman-La Roche Limited	Tranquilizer (semi-synthetic penicillin)
7. Ventolin	Allan & Hanburys	Broncho dilator
8. Aldomet	Merck, Sharpe & Dohme Canada, Limited	Anti-hypertensive
9. Anturan	Geigy Pharmaceuticals	Urico Surick (Cardiovascular agent)
10. Dextrose Intravenous Solution	Abbott Laboratories Ltd.	Hospital Solution (I.V.)

*According to dollar sales volume to drug stores and hospitals for 1977.

Pharmaceutical Manufacturers' Association of Canada

13 OF THE MOST HARMFUL DRUGS AVAILABLE IN CANADA

1. ALCOHOL
(Sedative Depressant)

Short-term Effects: initial relaxation, loss of inhibitions, impaired co-ordination, slowing down of reflexes and mental processes (reactions); attitude changes, increased risk-taking to point of bad judgment/danger; acute overdose may lead to death due to respiratory depression.

Long-term Effects: regular, heavy use increases the possibility of gastritis, pancreatitis, cirrhosis of the liver, certain cancers of the gastro-intestinal tract, heart disease; upon withdrawal following regular heavy use convulsions and delirium tremens may occur.

2. AMPHETAMINES
(Stimulants)

Short-term Effects: reduced appetite, increased energy and postponement of fatigue, increased alertness, faster breathing, increased heart rate and blood pressure which lead to increased risk of burst blood vessels or heart failure, dilation of pupils.

With Larger Doses: talkativeness, restlessness, excitation, sense of power and superiority, illusions and hallucinations frequently occur; some frequent users become irritable, aggressive, paranoid, or panicky; high blood pressure, dry mouth, fever, sweating, and sleeplessness.

Long-term Effects: malnutrition, increased susceptibility to infections, tolerance develops with high doses, psychological dependence; after stopping, there usually follows a long sleep and then depression.

3. ASA
(Acetylsalicylic Acid)

Short-term Effects: reduces pain, fever, and inflammation; one out of 500 people experiences undesirable side effects.

Possible Adverse Side Effects: asthma, chronic urticaria (hives), irritation and bleeding of the gastrointestinal tract.

4. CAFFEINE
(Stimulant)

Short-term Effects: increased alertness and sleeplessness, spontaneous tremor of hands.

Long-term Effects (of heavy use — more than 8 average cups a day): caffeine dependence (withdrawal symptoms include irritability, restlessness, and headache); insomnia, anxiety, stomach and duodenal ulceration; also heart disease, bladder cancer, and birth defects are under suspicion.

5. CANNABIS
(Marijuana, Hashish, "Hash Oil")

Short-term Effects: euphoria — a "high" feeling, increase in pulse rate, reddening of the eyes; a later stage in which the user becomes quiet, reflective, and sleepy; the whole experience is usually over in a few hours; combined with alcohol and certain other drugs, cannabis increases their effects on thinking and behaviour; impairs short-term memory, logical thinking, and ability to drive a car or perform other complex tasks; with larger doses, perceptions of sound, colour, and other sensations may be sharpened or distorted and thinking becomes slow and confused.

In very large doses, the effects of cannabis are similar to those of LSD and other hallucinogens — confusion, restlessness, excitement, and hallucinations — which may cause anxiety and panic, or may even precipitate a psychotic episode.

Long-term Effects: moderate tolerance, possible psychological dependence, loss of drive and of interest in sustained activity; marijuana smoke has been shown to contain 50 per cent more tar than smoke from a high-tar cigarette; with regular use, risk of lung cancer, chronic bronchitis, and other lung diseases increases.

6. COCAINE
(Stimulant)

Cocaine, though chemically not related to amphetamine, has actions so closely similar it is considered a stimulant, although it is legally classed as a narcotic.

Short-term Effects: same as amphetamines.

With Larger Doses: stronger, more frequent "highs"; bizarre, erratic, sometimes violent behaviour; paranoid psychosis (disappears if discontinued); sometimes a sensation of something crawling under the skin; similar to amphetamines.

Long-term Effects: strong psychological dependence, destruction of tissues in nose if sniffed, other effects like amphetamines.

7. LSD
(Lysergic Acid Diethylamide)

Short-term Effects: initial effects like those of amphetamine — rapid pulse, dilated pupils, arousal, excitation; later, distortions of perception — altered colours, shapes, sizes, distances; this may produce exhilaration, "mind expansion," or anxiety and panic, depending on user; feeling of panic or of unusual power or importance may lead to behaviour which is especially dangerous to the user; occasionally mental illness follows use of LSD — prolonged anxiety and depression; occasionally convulsions occur; profound tolerance develops very rapidly and disappears very rapidly.

Long-term Effects: unknown.

8. OPIATES
(Opium, Morphine, Codeine, Heroin)

Short-term Effects: relief from pain; produces a state of contentment, detachment, and freedom from distressing emotion; large doses create euphoria; sometimes nausea and vomiting; therapeutic dose lasts from 3-4 hours; acute overdose can result in death due to respiratory depresssion.

Long-term Effects: rapid development of tolerance and physical and psychological dependence; abrupt withdrawal results in moderate to severe withdrawal syndrome (cramps, diarrhoea, "gooseflesh," running nose, etc.)

9. PCP
(Phencyclidine)

Short-term Effects: euphoria, increase in rate of breathing, shallow respiration, increase in blood pressure and pulse rate, flushing and profuse sweating, muscular incoordination, generalized numbness of the extremities.

With Larger Doses: a fall in blood pressure, pulse rate, and respiration; nausea, vomiting, blurred vision, rolling movements and watering of eyes, loss of balance, and dizziness; large amounts can cause convulsions,

314

coma, and sometimes death; effects of PCP can mimic certain primary symptoms of schizophrenia, hallucinations; delusions, mental confusion, and amnesia are common; feeling of distance from one's environment.

Long-term Effects: possibility of flashbacks, possibility of prolonged anxiety or severe depression.

10. SEDATIVE HYPNOTICS
(Barbiturates, Non-Barbiturates)

Short-term Effects: a small dose relieves anxiety and tension, producing calmness and muscular relaxation; a somewhat larger dose produces effects similar to alcohol intoxication, e.g. a high feeling, slurred speech, staggering, produces sleep in a quiet setting; otherwise sleep may not occur; these effects make it dangerous to drive a car or perform other complex tasks while affected by barbiturates; much larger doses produce unconsciousness; acute overdose can be fatal due to respiratory depression.

Long-term Effects: tolerance and dependence develop rapidly if large doses are used; sedative hypnotics do not produce completely normal sleep, user may feel tired and irritable even though a sleeping state occurs; upon withdrawal, temporary sleep disturbances occur which may lead the user to incorrectly decide that more of the drug is required; abrupt withdrawal leads to progressive restlessness, anxiety, and possibly delirium, convulsions, and death.

11. SOLVENTS
(Gasoline, nail polish remover, lighter fluid, cleaning fluids, and airplane cement)

Short-term Effects: exhilaration and disorientation; confusion, slurred speech and dizziness, distortions of perception; visual and auditory hallucinations; poor muscular control.

With Larger Doses: drowsiness and unconsciousness; risk increases with fume concentration; large doses of solvents may produce death from heart failure.

Long-term Effects: dependence may occur which includes craving and habituation; upon withdrawal, the user may experience restlessness, anxiety, and irritability; with some solvents it is possible that extensive exposure may lead to liver and kidney damage.

12. TOBACCO
(Smoke is made up of some 500 compounds the most important of which are nicotine and tars)

Short-term Effects: increased pulse rate, rise in blood pressure, drop in skin temperature, relaxed feeling in regular smokers, increased acid in stomach, reduced urine formation; stimulates, then reduces brain and nervous system activity; loss of appetite, physical endurance.

Long-term Effects: narrowing or hardening of blood vessels in heart, brain, etc., shortness of breath, cough, more respiratory infections (e.g. colds, pneumonia), chronic bronchitis, emphysema; risk of cancer of lungs, mouth, larynx, esophagus, bladder, kidney, pancreas; stomach ulcers; risk of thrombosis in users of birth control pills.

13. TRANQUILIZERS
(Depressants)

Short-term Effects: calms hyperactivity, tension, and agitation; diminished emotional responses to external stimuli, e.g. pain; muscle relaxation, reduced alertness, gives short-term relief of anxiety, combats severe withdrawal effects of other depressant drugs; with larger doses, possible impairment of muscle coordination, dizziness, low blood pressure, and/or fainting; increases effect of alcohol and sedatives.

Long-term Effects: physical dependence; withdrawal reaction like that of sedative hypnotics.

The Alcohol and Drug Addiction
Research Foundation

THE 10 MOST POPULAR
BRANDS OF CIGARETTES IN CANADA

1. Export 'A', Regular

2. Rothmans King Size, Filter

3. Players Filter, Regular

4. du Maurier, King Size

5. du Maurier, Regular

6. du Maurier, King Size

7. Craven 'A', King Size

8. Number 7

9. Mark 10 Filter, Regular

10. Peter Jackson

Exclusive to *The Canadian Book of Lists*

THE 10 MOST POLLUTED CITIES IN CANADA

		Micrograms per cu. metre
1.	MONTREAL	128
2.	CALGARY	122
3.	WINDSOR	122
4.	HAMILTON	105
5.	QUEBEC CITY	101
6.	LONDON	92
7.	OTTAWA	91
8.	SARNIA	89
9.	MEDICINE HAT	88
10.	TORONTO	81

Statistics Canada

317

18
WAR

THE 10 BEST CANADIAN COMMANDING OFFICERS IN CANADA'S MILITARY HISTORY *

1. LT.-GEN. GUY GRANVILLE SIMMONDS C.B., C.B.E., D.S.O., C.D.

Regarded by British general officers and by military historians as the most capable and innovative of all Canadian generals in World War II. This tall, austere man conducted the Battle of the Schedlt late in 1944, one of the bitterest of the war, with cool brilliance. He concluded his career as Chief of the General Staff in Ottawa (from 1951 to 1955), feuding frequently with politicians.

2. COL. JOHN BUTLER

The American Revolution sent Col. Butler to Canada as a United Empire Loyalist. Here he formed Butler's Rangers and waged a hugely successful war against the American forces in Maryland, Kentucky, and along the Mohawk Trail. One of his feats was the capture of Daniel Boone at Blue Licks, Kentucky, in 1782. He had been a Lieutenant-Colonel in the Mohawk Militia before the Revolution. He later settled in the Niagara Peninsula. Ironically, he was a cousin of George Washington.

3. LT.-COL. GEORGE T. DENNISON

This veteran of the Fenian Raids of 1866 was a brilliant military theoretician and in 1868 wrote *Modern Cavalry* , acknowledged as one of the best books ever written about cavalry tactics. He was a founder of the Governor General's Body Guard, later the Governor General's Horse Guards. One of the few Canadian military writers ever to gain international recognition.

4. GEN. J.A. DEXTRASE, C.B.E., C.M.M., D.S.O., C.D.

He commanded the Fusiliers Mont-Royal in 1944 in Europe, winning the D.S.O. for his brilliant tactics. He was later summoned from private life to command the 2nd Battalion, Royal 22nd Regiment, in Korea. The first French Canadian to be named Chief of the General Staff, he kept the Canadian forces functioning through a long period of post-war government neglect.

5. GABRIEL DUMONT

Dumont was Louis Riel's cavalry commander. Military historians believe that if Riel had given Dumont his head, the story of the Northwest

---

* Although British General Wolfe is not listed among the 10 best commanding officers, he certainly became the most famous general connected with Canadian history after his victory over General Montcalm on the Plains of Abraham in 1759.

Rebellion might have ended as a bloody disaster for the Canadian forces. At Duck Lake in March of 1885, although badly outnumbered, he defeated a force under Major Crozier. Then, in April 1885, with a handful of Métis, he trapped a force under Maj. Gen. Frederick Middleton (Commander of the Canadian Militia), leaving 10 killed and 40 wounded.

6. ADAM DOLLARD, SIEUR DES ORMEAUX

In May 1660, Dollard, with a party of 16 volunteers and 42 loyal Indians, held off a large force of invading Iroquois at the Long Sault on the Ottawa River. His five-day battle, frequently called a Canadian Thermopylae, probably saved the colony of New France from being overwhelmed. He helped create the legend of the citizen-soldier in New France, although his victory has been largely ignored in Canadian history.

7. LT.-GEN. MAURICE A. POPE, C.B., M.C.

A grandson of Sir Henri Taschereau, Chief Justice of Quebec, Pope won the military cross in World War I, then stayed in the army and became a member of the Canadian General Staff in England from 1940-41. Successive-

Air Marshall William (Billy) Bishop was a leading air ace in World War I and won the Victoria Cross.

319

ly, he was Chairman of the Canadian Joint Staff Mission to Washington, 1942-44, Military Staff Officer to Mackenzie King, 1944-45, head of the Canadian Military Mission in Germany, 1945-50, Ambassador to Belgium, 1950-53, and Ambassador to Spain, 1953-56. His great strength was making the Canadian presence felt in Washington when Americans were singularly disinterested.

8. COL. WILLIAM OTTER

Otter saw action during the Fenian Raids and later at Cut Knife Hill, Saskatchewan, in 1885 during the Northwest Rebellion. He commanded the 2nd Service Battalion of the Royal Canadian Regiment during the Boer War, serving with skill both British Imperial Officers and Canadian politicians. He fashioned a motley collection of soldiers into a reasonably effective fighting force, with little support from subordinates. His thorough professionalism and distaste of partisan politics led him to be the first Canadian named as Chief of the General Staff, in 1908. The position was formerly held by British officers seconded to the Canadian Militia.

9. AIR MARSHALL WILLIAM AVERY (BILLY) BISHOP, V.C., D.S.O., M.C.

A graduate of the Royal Military College, Bishop was one of the leading aces of World War I, shooting down 72 German planes. He was named Air Marshall in 1938, and Chief of the Air Staff, Royal Canadian Air Force, in 1939. He held this post until 1945. A prolific writer (*Winged Warfare,* 1918; *Winged Peace ,* 1944) he epitomized the dashing concept of Canadian airmen. No other flyer ever achieved his fame.

10. LT.-GEN. SIR ARTHER CURRIE

A former schoolteacher, Currie was a Lieutenant-Colonel when World War I broke out. He shot up to command a battalion in Europe, was promoted to Major-General in 1916, and became Commander of the Canadian Corps. He was the only militia officer ever to command a Canadian force in a major conflict. Because of his administrative skill, there was no British officer he could not have replaced in the field, and when David Lloyd George was Prime Minister, there was talk of his being made Commander-in-Chief of the British Expeditionary Force in France.

Peter G. Silverman
Historian, News Correspondent
Global TV

THE 10 MOST FAMOUS CANADIAN WAR HEROES

1. PIERRE LEMOYNE D'IBERVILLE

An eighteenth-century French Canadian soldier and sailor who swept

Hudson Bay of the British, led raiding parties against the American colonies, and ended as Governor of Louisiana.

2. JEAN-BAPTISTE FALCON

A Métis from White Horse Plain who commanded his people in the epic battle of Grand Coteau when 77 Métis fought off twenty times their number of Sioux.

3. WILLIAM AVERY BISHOP

The third most successful fighter pilot on any side in World War I, who shot down 72 enemy aircraft. He was the first Canadian airman to win the Victoria Cross.

4. LAURA SECORD

With or without her cow, she walked from Queenston to Beaver Dam to warn Lieutenant James Fitzgibbon that an American force was moving in his direction.

5. GEORGE RANDOLPH PEARKES

A Victoria Cross winner for his leadership in the terrible battle of Passchendaele in 1917, renowned for his fearlessness and cool leadership under fire.

6. DAVID VIVIAN CURRIE

He won his Victoria Cross for heroic leadership at St-Lambert-sur-Dives on August 19, 1944, when he and his fellow Albertans helped close the Falaise Gap to retreating Germans.

7. ISAAC BROCK

In 1812 his courage transformed a defeatist Upper Canada. His whirlwind victory over a much larger American force at Detroit gave us a breathing space. His death at Queenston Heights gave us our first military hero.

8. JEAN-VICTOR ALLARD

Canada's youngest brigadier in World War II, and her ablest brigade commander in Korea, General Allard was the most distinguished soldier of modern French Canada.

9. ARTHUR CURRIE

A portly businessman of questionable commercial judgment, Currie proved to be the most successful, imaginative, and effective Canadian general in World War I. His Canadian Corps was the finest fighting force Canada has every created.

10. ANDREW MYNARSKI

If heroism means self-sacrifice, this air gunner who stayed in his burning Lancaster bomber struggling to rescue another crew member can represent many thousands of brave Canadians. When he finally jumped, he was too badly burned to live.

Desmond Morton
Dean of Humanities and Academic
Vice-Principal
Erindale College, University of Toronto

Vimy Ridge, 1917 — the greatest day in Canadian military history.

THE 10 BEST-KNOWN CANADIAN BATTLES

1. CHATEAUGUAY, 1813

French Canadian voltigeurs and militia under Colonel Charles de Salaberry did most of the fighting, when an American invasion force advancing on Montreal was routed.

2. LUNDY'S LANE, 1814

The bloodiest battle of the War of 1812 was really a stalemate. American and British regulars did most of the fighting on each side, but Canadian-incorporated militia had by then achieved the quality of regular soldiers and shared in the heavy casualties.

3. BATOCHE, 1885

After a four-day siege, Canadian militia grew impatient and finally attacked the Métis positions against the wishes of their British commander. The result was a sudden victory and a tragic end to Métis dreams.

4. SECOND YPRES, 1915

The first important Canadian battle of World War I was also one of the most glorious. The Canadians in the 1st Contingent survived the first gas attack in modern warfare, held off an attack by some of the finest German soldiers, and established an heroic reputation for Canada.

5. VIMY RIDGE, 1917

The capture of the impregnable German position made April 9 the greatest day in Canadian military history. All four divisions of the Canadian Corps participated in a battle which was a perfect model of planning, preparation, discipline, and co-ordination. For an army of amateurs which had once sneered at military discipline, it was a marvellous transformation.

6. MOREUIL WOOD, 1918

A brilliant and courageous battle by the Canadian Cavalry Brigade in the struggle to slow down the German offensive in March 1918, Moreuil Wood is still commemorated by the three participating regiments on March 30 each year.

7. DIEPPE, 1942

Needless tragedy or necessary experiment, the Dieppe raid is probably the best-remembered Canadian battle in World War II. The heavy losses may have been a useless sacrifice, but they also showed that the courage and self-sacrifice of Canadians had not diminished since the previous war.

8. ORTONA, 1943

Of many hard battles in the Italian campaign, the struggle for Ortona in the last month of 1943 was a brutal house-to-house battle against the toughest German paratroopers. It recalled the trench fighting of the previous war.

9. OPERATION "PARTICIPATE," 1944

It should never have worked but it did. Fed up with futile, mismanaged operations of his raw Canadians against the Germans, General Guy Simonds collected the 4th Armoured Division and simply rolled it at the German lines. It could have been a massacre; it turned out to be a triumph as tanks and infantry simply poured over an astonished enemy.

10. SCHELDT ESTUARY, 1944-45

The Allies could not advance into Germany without supplies from the port of Antwerp. The port could not be used while the flooded islands and polder land of the Estuary were held by German troops. General Crerar's 1st Canadian Army took on the thankless and costly task of clearing out resistance. It was a Cinderella operation, with armoured and air support unavailable. It was done.

Desmond Morton
Dean of Humanities and Academic
Vice-Principal
Erindale College, University of Toronto

10 GREAT
CANADIAN MILITARY HUMILIATIONS

1. RIDGEWAY, 1866

Two battalions of Canàdian militia had almost routed some Fenian raiders when Colonel Alfred Booker suddenly gave the orders to form a square. The inexperienced Canadians panicked and fled from the enemy.

2. DUCK LAKE, 1885

Major Garnet Crozier led out a hundred North West Mounted Police and militia to teach Louis Riel and the Métis a lesson. Trapped between trees and snowbanks, Crozier lost a quarter of his men in a few minutes. The rest were lucky to escape.

3. CUT KNIFE HILL, 1885

Lieutenant-Colonel William Otter marched out of Battleford to punish Poundmaker and his Crees. The Indians were not where he expected them to be. His men climbed Cut Knife Hill to eat breakfast and found themselves surrounded. The punishers were sorely punished. Only Poundmaker's restraint allowed them to escape.

4. THE ST. ELOI CRATERS, 1916

General Richard Turner's 2nd Canadian Division attacked and captured what it thought were the St. Eloi Craters. Unfortunately, the real craters were somewhere else. General Turner had not checked. When the Germans counter-attacked, artillery support came down on the real craters, not in front of the Canadians. The result? Almost a thousand casualties.

5. REGINA TRENCH, 1916

The 1st and 3rd Canadian Divisions lost two thousand men trying to capture a German trench because the wire entanglement had not been cut.

6. STRATFORD, 1933

One of the peacetime duties of the Canadian army used to be supporting the police during strikes. The Royal Canadian Regiment decided to take its new machine gun carriers to Stratford. These were promptly labelled "tanks" and provided the strikers with a gigantic propaganda victory. That was the end of "strike duty" for Canadian soldiers in peacetime.

7. HONG KONG, 1941

Two battalions of raw, ill-equipped Canadians were sacrificed to the theory that a few thousand men could somehow deter the Japanese from going to war.

8. DIEPPE, 1942

The best-known Canadian battle of World War II was the most tragic disaster. Less than half the 5,000 men who landed managed to return to England.

9. THE BOMBER OFFENSIVE, 1941-45

The Allied bomber offensive against Germany, designed to destroy German industrial power at minimal casualties, did neither. The Germans lost half a million — most of them women and children — for a drop of 1.2 percent in war production. The RAF Bomber Command lost 47,000 dead, over 8,200 of them Canadians, in a triumph of technological idiocy.

10. BRETTEVILLE, 1944

Inexperience led to many Canadian military disasters in the Normandy invasion. The worst was Bretteville, where a Canadian tank regiment, through bad map reading, blundered into German defences and lost every tank.

Desmond Morton
Dean of Humanities and Academic
Vice-Principal
Erindale College, University of Toronto

10 GREAT BATTLES OF THE WORLD IN WHICH CANADA TOOK PART

1. QUEBEC, 1759

The battle on the Plains of Abraham and the subsequent fall of Quebec was a minor pawn exchange in the Seven Years' War, but it had decisive consequences, including the American Revolution. Canadian militia were blamed for Montcalm's defeat.

2. BALACLAVA

In their assault on Turkish and British positions in the Crimean War, the Russians came close to destroying the Allied invasion force. In the subsequent charge of the Light Brigade, a Canadian, Lieutenant James Dunn, won a Victoria Cross.

3. PAARDEBERG, 1900

In the decisive battle of the Boer War, the British captured most of a Boer army and broke the myth of Afrikaner invincibility. The 2nd Battalion, Royal Canadian Regiment, under Colonel William Otter, played a distinguished role in the battle.

4. SECOND YPRES, 1915

If the Germans, using poison gas for the first time, had broken through the British and French line, the result could have been a decisive defeat. The raw 1st Canadian Division met the brunt of the German attack, held ground, and won Canada a military reputation.

5. PASSCHENDAELE, 1917

This terrible and needless offensive through the Flanders swamps almost broke the morale of the British Army. The terrible tragedy was allowed to end only when the village of Passchendaele was captured. The Canadian Corps did the job.

6. AMIENS, 1918

Ludendorf called it the "Black Day of the German Army." For the first time, a carefully planned combination of tanks, infantry, and aircraft shattered the German line. The Canadian Corps was half the British spearhead.

7. BATTLE OF BRITAIN, 1940

If the German Luftwaffe had wiped out Britain's air defences, the Nazi triumph in Europe would have been complete. The Royal Air Force narrowly won. Hundreds of its pilots were Canadian. A single, ill-equipped squadron of the Royal Canadian Air Force did its utmost.

8. BATTLE OF THE ATLANTIC, 1939-45

Without the Atlantic bridge of heavily laden convoys, there could have been no victory over Germany. The Royal Canadian Navy, ill-equipped and inexperienced, slowly learned to cope with German submarines and eventually commanded its own sector of the North Atlantic.

9. THE NORMANDY INVASION, 1944

As one of six Allied divisions to hit the Normandy beaches on June 6, 1944, the 3rd Canadian Division was part of the most important and riskiest Allied operation of World War II.

10. KAPYONG, 1951

The Chinese attempt to break through the United Nations line in Korea in April 1951 ran into the British Commonwealth's 27th Brigade. Canadians and Australians took the attack and after bitter fighting threw it back. The 2nd Battalion, Princess Patricia's Canadian Light Infantry, was awarded a U.S. Presidential Citation.

Desmond Morton
Dean of Humanities and Academic
Vice-Principal
Erindale College, University of Toronto

General Wolfe, on the Plains of Abraham in 1759, became the most famous general in Canadian history.

19
HERITAGE

10 GREAT CANADIAN
QUOTATIONS ON CANADA

1. Canada is under such handicaps: it is full of natural disadvantages, like the French and the savages.

   Nathaniel A. Benson, *The Paths of Glory,* 1927

2. There isn't any one Canada, any average Canadian, any average place, any type.

   Miriam Chapin, *They Outgrew Bohemia,* 1960

3. Sometimes for us in Canada it seems as though the United States and the United Kingdom were cup and saucer, and Canada the spoon, for we are in and out of both with the greatest freedom, and we are given most recognition when we are most a nuisance.

   Robertson Davies, *A Voice from the Attic,* 1960

4. There would be nothing distinctive in Canadian culture at all if there were not some feeling for the immense searching distance, with the lines of communication extended to the absolute limit, which is a primary geographical fact about Canada....

   Northrop Frye, *Letters in Canada,* 1952

5. Canadians ask themselves whether they have become free of Britain's colonial influence only to fall under the spell of the United States' economic imperialism.

   Walter Gordon, *A Choice for Canada*

6. Where else in the world could you find another case like ours — three thousand miles of forts and not a single frontier?

   Stephen Leacock, *All Right, Mr. Roosevelt*

7. The trouble with this whole country is that it's divided up into little puddles with big fish in each one of them.

   Hugh MacLennan, *Two Solitiudes,* 1945

8. Canada is no longer a child, sleeping in the arms of nature, dependent for her very existence on the fostering care of her illustrious mother.

   Susanna Moodie, *Roughing It in the Bush,* 1871

9. No person need starve in Canada, where there is plenty of work and good wages for every man who is willing to labour, and who keeps himself sober.

Samuel Strickland, *Twenty-Seven Years in Canada West,* 1853

10. Canada persevering energy and industry with sobriety will overcome all obstacles, and in time will place the very poorest family in a position of substantial comfort that no personal exertion alone could have procured for them elsewhere.

Catharine Parr Traill, *The Canadian Settler's Guide,* 1855

THE 10 LARGEST ETHNIC GROUPS IN CANADA

	Number of Persons

1. British Isles
 includes English
      Irish
      Scottish
      Other
	9,624,115

2. French	6,180,120
3. German	1,317,200
4. Italian	730,820
5. Ukrainian	580,660
6. Netherlands	425,945

7. Scandinavian
 includes Danish
      Icelandic
      Norwegian
      Swedish
	384,795

8. Polish	316,430
9. Indian and Eskimo	312,760
10. Jewish	296,945

Statistics Canada

2 IMPORTANT ITEMS OF NATIONAL ETIQUETTE CANADIANS SHOULD RESPECT

1. Canada's National Anthem is "O Canada"; the Royal Anthem is "God Save the Queen." When either is played one should stand with head up and hands hanging straight at the sides. No one should turn, speak, sit down, or leave, until the last note has been played. When Canada's flag is displayed at the same time, the audience should face the flag if singing the anthem.

2. The flag of any country should never be allowed to touch the ground when it is being handled. Nothing should be placed on the flag except the Bible, and it should never be hung where it can be struck by a gavel or any other object. The flag should not be flown after dark.

Claire Wallace
Canadian Etiquette

THE 5 GREATEST CANADIAN QUOTATIONS ON NATIONALISM AND NATIONALITY

1. Political nationalism has little to do with the cultural traditions of peoples.

    George Woodcock, *Views of Canadian Criticism*, 1966

2. Nationality is of no consequence. In the things of the spirit there is no such barrier.

    John Marlyn, *Under the Ribs of Death*, 1957

3. Any process of blending implies confusion to begin with; we are here at the making of a nation.

    Sara Jeannette Duncan, *The Imperialist*, 1904

4. Each mountain
    its own country
    in the way a country
    A state of mind.

    Sid Marty, *Each Mountain*, 1971

5. A country too sharply divided against itself may be culturally no more healthy than it is politically.

    George Woodcock, *A Commonwealth of Literature*, 1963

THE 10 LARGEST RELIGIOUS DENOMINATIONS IN CANADA

		Number of persons
1.	Roman Catholic	9,974,895
2.	United Church	3,768,800
3.	Anglican	2,543,180
4.	Presbyterian	872,335
5.	Lutheran	715,740
6.	Baptist	667,245
7.	Greek Orthodox	316,605
8.	Jewish	296,945
9.	Pentecostal	220,390
10.	Jehovah's Witnesses	174,810

Statistics Canada

THE 10 YEARS WITH THE MOST IMMIGRANT ARRIVALS IN CANADA

	Year	Number of Arrivals		Year	Number of Arrivals
1.	1913	400,870	6.	1907	272,409
2.	1912	375,756	7.	1967	222,876
3.	1911	331,288	8.	1974	218,465
4.	1910	286,839	9.	1906	211,653
5.	1957	282,164	10.	1966	194,743

Statistics Canada

10 INTERESTING FACTS
ABOUT ESKIMOS AND INDIANS

1. Carrier Indians of British Columbia decree that when a woman becomes a widow she must carry the bones of her dead husband on her back.

2. According to an Eskimo proverb, "A man's best friend is his dog, better even than his wife."

3. The Indians of the West Coast measured their wealth in terms of numbers of blankets owned. To redistribute their wealth, a ceremony known as the "potlach" was performed. A potlach was held for events of social significance, such as births, deaths, or marriages. The individual whose potlach it was would distribute all his blankets among a selected number of guests, who would then be compelled to invite him to their potlach. The secret of success was to invite the wealthiest guest, so that when it came time for their potlachs the initial investment would be returned a hundredfold.

4. The Netsilik people of Northern Canada refer to their fishing location as "The Sacred Spot." While at the river a pregnant women cannot leave her tent, for it she did the "Sacred Spot" would be polluted and the fish inedible.

5. The Eskimo divide the year into 13 periods of 28 days each, according to the lunar cycle. These periods correspond to natural cycles of wildlife and weather.

6. According to native traditions, an Indian could never really own anything living. Live possessions had to be deserved and could be taken away if the owner faltered in merit.

7. In the 1700s it was not uncommon for an Indian trapper to get two combs in exchange for a beaver pelt.

8. Early French settlers were encouraged by Roman Catholic priests to intermarry with the Indians for two reasons. First, to spread themselves across more of the land and second, to convert "the heathen."

9. In 1752 British General Amherst suggested: "You will be well advised to infect the Indians with sheets upon which smallpox patients have been lying, or by any other means which may serve to exterminate this accursed race."

10. Status Indians, that is Indians who are defined as Indian under the Indian Act and are registered as band members, who leave the reservation lose their legal right to be Indians, as do their wives, children, and all descendants.

10 INTERESTING FACTS
ABOUT CANADA

1. Since 1961 the taxpayers' burden has increased 239 percent.

2. Four million dollars' worth of Canadian dollar bills are burned every day at the Bank of Canada.

3. Canadians spend $40 a year per person on lotteries.

4. In 1867 the first members of Parliament made $6.00 a day.

5. Alexander Graham Bell, besides inventing the telephone, also invented the photophone, forerunner of the modern film sound track; a solar still to take the salt from sea water; the first working hydrofoil craft in the world; a metal detector to find bullets within the body; and the first airplane to fly, albeit rather briefly, in our country.

6. John Buchan, author of *The Thirty-Nine Steps,* was Governor General of Canada from 1935 to 1940.

7. Twelve states come into contact with the Canadian border. They are, from east to west: Maine, New Hampshire, Vermont, New York, Pennsylvania, Ohio, Michigan, Minnesota, North Dakota, Montana, Idaho, and Washington.

8. In 1867 an unmarried man could get 100 acres of land free, a married man 200, and a top quality piece of property cost only a dollar per acre.

9. Over 32 million people cross the U.S.-Canadian border every year.

10. Until 1922 people in British Columbia drove on the left hand side of the road.

THE LONGEST 10 IN CANADA

1. THE LONGEST AND MOST DEVASTATING HEAT WAVE

For seven days in July, 1936, in southern Ontario, Canada experienced its worst heat wave. Temperatures for the week were 104.9°F, 105°F, 104.9°F, 96°F, 92°F, 100°F, and 92°F. Approximately 230 Ontario deaths were attributed to the heat wave.

2. THE LONGEST TIME SPENT IN OFFICE BY A PRIME MINISTER

William Lyon Mackenzie King was Prime Minister of Canada for twenty-one years, five and one-half months.

3. THE LONGEST RUNNING NEWSPAPER IN CANADA

The Quebec Gazette, which was founded in 1764, survives as part of the *Quebec Chronicle-Telegraph.*

4. THE LONGEST STREET

Yonge Street begins at the lakeshore in Toronto and runs north as Highway Eleven for more than sixty miles.

5. THE LONGEST DAY

On August 19, 1942, during World War II in the legendary Dieppe Raid, 3,350 casualties out of 5,000 soldiers were recorded.

6. THE LONGEST BRIDGE

The Pierre Laporte bridge in Quebec has a centre span of 2,190 feet. It connects Quebec City with l'Ile d'Orleans.

7. THE LONGEST DROUGHT

In 1949 Arctic Bay, Northwest Territories, received only one-half inch of rain.

8. THE LONGEST HOCKEY GAME

In 1936 the Montreal Maroons played the Detroit Red Wings in the Stanley Cup semi-finals. Detroit won the game 1-0 in the sixth overtime period after a total of 176 minutes and 30 seconds. Detroit won the best-of-five semi-final three games to zero.

9. THE LONGEST BAR

Canada's and probably the world's longest bar at 76 feet long runs the entire 76-foot length of the main floor in the Kazabazua Hotel in Kazabazua, a small town in the Gatineau, Quebec.

10. THE LONGEST RIVER

The Mackenzie River is 2,635 miles long. It runs between Great Slave Lake and the most northeasterly corner of the N.W.T. where it meets the Arctic Ocean.

David Ondaatje
Exclusive to *The Canadian Book of Lists*

THE 10 MOST APPEALING BUILDINGS OR STRUCTURES IN CANADA

1. UNIVERSITY COLLEGE, University of Toronto, Toronto

An eclectic building with wonderful stonework, a memorable entrance way, and amusing carvings in both wood and stone.

The Shaw Festival Theatre in Niagara-on-the-Lake — one of the 10 most appealing buildings in Canada.

2. NATHAN PHILLIPS SQUARE, Toronto

A genuine civic space in the centre of downtown Toronto, providing a place for public activities as well as skating in the winter and sunning in the summer. In addition, it provides a view of the handsome old City Hall, the new City Hall which has become a symbol of Toronto, and Osgoode Hall, with its elegant nostalgic fence along Queen Street.

3. THE CITADEL, Halifax

An historic fortification which still dominates Halifax today, providing both a focus for the city and fine views of Halifax and its harbour.

4. THE WINNIPEG ART GALLERY, Winnipeg

An interesting sculptural building effectively exploiting an odd-shaped lot to form unusual and interesting galleries.

5. THE SUBWAY SYSTEM, Montreal

Vibrant, colourful, spacious, and pleasant.

6. THE ANTHROPOLOGICAL MUSEUM, Vancouver

An elegant showcase for a spectacular collection of totems and other Northwest Coast artifacts.

7. THE WATERFRONT, Halifax

A fine collection of old industrial structures, both the excellent stone brewery and warehouse buildings, and the simple wooden waterfront structures — some of which have recently been pleasantly renovated into shops.

8. SHAW FESTIVAL THEATRE, Niagara-on-the-Lake

A very human structure, appropriate in scale, warm in treatment, and modestly focusing on the theatrical events.

9. THE PROVINCIAL LEGISLATURE, Charlottetown, P.E.I.

A gem of a building — awash with history and sentiment — very simple and human in scale and character.

10. THE LOCKS, Trent Canal System

The handsome ruggedness of unselfconsciousness; nineteenth-century engineering structures, with the careful functional detailing which was a precursor of the twentieth-century modern movement.

Henry Sears
Architect
Klein and Sears, Toronto

10 QUESTIONS YOU COULDN'T ANSWER IF WE DIDN'T HAVE A CANADA

1. Where else would you get a West that gives you Calgary redeye and Winnipeg goldeye?

2. What other country has a real Old Man River?

3. Who else has pubs with table shuffleboard; with waitresses who make change from a fistful of dollars folded lengthwise?

4. What is there about the Maritimes that spawns a Beaverbrook, a Nathan Cohen, and a Gordon Pinsent?

5. Who else would admit to having the silliest airport in the world, name it after a plum (Mirabelle), and then make its official symbol a flying white elephant?

6. Who else would discourage subway interlopers with signs which say "Trespassers May Be Electrocuted"?

7. Where else could you get a government that sends out jets and honour guards for leaders of countries with suburb-size populations, yet treats mayors of cities with over two million inhabitants like wetbacks?

8. What is it in the air that makes the music of Gordon Lightfoot, Joni Mitchell, Neil Young, Murray McLaughlin, and The Band so unmistakably Canadian?

9. What other country would define itself by what it is not?

10. What other country that sells long tons of steel, board-feet of wood, and bushels of wheat, would rush into metric measurement so fast that no one over 21 knows how fast he's going, how much he's had to drink, how much he's overweight, and how cold he is?

Bill Marshall
Film Producer
Outrageous

10 CANADIANS TO INVITE TO DINNER TO UNDERSTAND THE MEANING OF CANADA AND ITS ROOTS

1. GABRIEL DUMONT

A key strategist for the Métis. If Riel had listened, Canadian history would have been very different, because he understood the heritage of his people.

2. SIR JOHN A. MACDONALD

Spent most of the nineteenth century putting the whole country together.

3. J. S. WOODSWORTH

Provided a social conscience for twentieth-century Canada.

4. GILLES VIGNEAULT

He has put passion into our understanding of *pays*.

5. WILLIAM VAN HORNE

You need at least one rascal at dinner. He was one of Canada's great entrepreneurs, and he knew how to get things done.

Sir William Van Horne, perhaps Canada's greatest entrepreneur, knew how to get things done.

6. STEPHEN LEACOCK

Many people don't know that he was a political economist with a very conservative view of Canada. He had a great sense of place — a world of small towns and neighbourhoods.

7. JOHN G. DIEFENBAKER

He elevated a sense of roots into a national conscience.

8. RALPH ALLEN

He's helped a generation of journalists to write clearly and fairly.

9. SUSANNA MOODIE

Her sharp tongue and critical eye tell us about the bitter and the sweet of life as a pioneer.

10. ANDRÉ LAURENDEAU*

Even for Tories in Toronto, the French language took on new significance for the future of Canada, thanks to this Quebec patriot.

David Crombie
Politician

10 CANADIAN LEGAL PROBLEMS WHICH SHOULD BE SOLVED

1. Amend the British North America Act to accommodate regional needs, and enshrine civil liberties.

2. Settle native land claims.

3. Outlaw strikes in vital public industries.

4. Reform abortion laws.

5. Set and enforce land-zoning laws to protect prime farmlands and to establish an economic basis for adequate domestic food production.

6. Clarify police powers, modify the Official Secrets Act, and implement freedom of information policies.

7. Settle offshore territorial fishing rights.

8. Revise laws to further encourage investment by Canadians in Canada.

9. Reform postal communications by restoring confidence in the Post Of-

fice, prohibit postal strikes, and give back to the Post Office its monopoly on mail delivery.

10. "Make the punishment fit the crime" by prescribing public flogging for rapists and capital punishment for first-degree murderers, hijackers, and terrorists.

J.P. Boyer and J.S. Elder
Lawyers
Fraser, Beattie, Toronto

10 UNUSUAL CANADIAN FESTIVALS

1. INTERNATIONAL DEW WORM CONTEST
   Held in Sardis, British Columbia, during August.

2. SHAKEYS FROG RACE
   Held in Prince George, British Columbia, during August.

3. THE CANADIAN INVITATIONAL BED RACING CHAMPIONSHIPS
   Held in Vancouver, British Columbia, during May.

4. THE OUTHOUSE RACE
   Held in Fort St. John, British Columbia, during June.

5. THE GREAT INNERTUBE RACE
   Held in Victoria, British Columbia, in August.

6. THE GREAT SNOW, EARTH, AND WATER RACE
   Held in Whistler, British Columbia, in May.

7. THE ANNUAL WORLD WHEELBARROW CHAMPIONSHIPS
   Held in Ladner, British Columbia.

8. THE WORLD CHAMPIONSHIP CANNONBALL AND BELLYSLOP RACE
   Held in Vancouver, British Columbia.

9. THE NANAIMO BATHTUB RACE
   Held in Nanaimo, British Columbia.

10. THE GREAT OYSTER EATING CONTEST
    Held in Campbell River, British Columbia.

Canadian Government Office of Tourism

THE 12 BEST TEMPERATURES IN CANADA

1	100°C	212°F	Water boils
2.	0°C	32°F	Water freezes
3.	82.2°C	180°F	The best temperature for brewing coffee
4.	100°C	212°F	The best temperture for brewing tea
5.	37°C	98.6°F	Normal body temperature
6.	44.4°C	112°F	The best temperature for a hot bath
7.	12.8°C	55°F	The best temperature for a cold bath
8.	20°C	68°F	The most comfortable room temperature
9.	6.7°C	44°F	The ideal temperature for a dry martini (straight up)
10.	3.3°C	38°F	The ideal temperature for a cold beer
11.	20°C	68°F	The best temperature for claret
12.	17.8°C	64°F	The best temperature for sex (indoor)

Exclusive to *The Canadian Book of Lists*

20
HISTORY

THE 10 MOST HISTORIC
SITES IN CANADA

1. NEWFOUNDLAND

Located on the northern tip of Newfoundland, *L'Anse aux Meadows* was the site of what was probably the first European colony in North America. Norsemen from Greenland came ashore late in the 10th century A.D. and established a colony which was not discovered until the 1960s.

2. PRINCE EDWARD ISLAND

On September 1, 1864, representatives from the British North American colonies of Nova Scotia, New Brunswick, and Canada met in the Legislative Council chamber of the *Colonial Building* in *Charlottetown*, Prince Edward Island, to discuss a proposed union of the colonies, a proposal that came to fruition on July 1, 1867, with the formation of the Dominion of Canada.

3. NEW BRUNSWICK

In early May 1783, on the heels of the American War of Independence, some 3,000 refugee Loyalists, packed in seven sailing ships, sat off the mouth of the Saint John River waiting for orders that would permit them to land on the rough, forested shoreline. Commencing May 18 and lasting several weeks, these Loyalists put ashore to establish a settlement, which two short years later would become the City of *Saint John*, the first in Canada to be incorporated by charter.

4. NOVA SCOTIA

Built in 1605 by Acadian governor Pierre de Monts and destined to become the first successful white settlement north of Florida, *Port Royal* was plundered and set afire in 1613 by Captain Samuel Argall who was carrying out the orders of the governor of Virginia "to destroy all French settlements on land claimed by England."

5. QUEBEC

On July 3, 1608, Samuel de Champlain and his 30 men stepped ashore at a place where the St. Lawrence River narrowed, a site which in the Algonkian language translates—"kébec." From this simple, unassuming event we can trace the earliest continuous settlement of a country we now call Canada.

6. ONTARIO

At the foot of the present-day thoroughfare called Dufferin Street stands a weathered obelisk announcing to those who happen upon it that this was the site of *Fort Toronto*, a French fur-trading outpost built in 1750. It was the first white settlement established in the area we now call Metropolitan Toronto.

Prince Edward Island — the site of the meeting that eventually led to Confederation.

7. MANITOBA

In 1812, Thomas Douglas, the Earl of Selkirk, and a large number of Scottish highland farmers established a settlement in the heart of the present-day city of *Winnipeg*, a land then known as "Assiniboia." Four years later, twenty-one of these Red River colonists were butchered in one of Canada's bloodiest massacres.

8. SASKATCHEWAN

Métis leader Louis Riel tried unsuccessfully to establish a government that would be recognized by the new Dominion of Canada and that would protect the rights and guarantee the prosperity of his people. Riel's dream was shattered when his forces were defeated at *Batoche* on May 12, 1885, thereby ending the ill-fated Northwest Rebellion.

9. BRITISH COLUMBIA

A plaque on a cairn situated at *Craigellachie* in Eagle Pass states: "A nebulous dream was a reality; an iron ribbon crossed Canada from sea to sea." When the last spike was driven on November 7, 1885, to unite the rails of the Canadian Pacific Railway, Canada truly extended from sea to sea.

10. ALBERTA

On February 13, 1947, while exploring for oil south of Edmonton, a drilling crew made the greatest oil deposit discovery in Canadian history. The Leduc oil field ushered in Alberta's golden age of oil.

Mike Filey
Author, Broadcaster

THE 10 MOST FREQUENTED CANADIAN HISTORIC SITES

		Number of Visitors
1.	Signal Hill, Newfoundland	921,072
2.	Halifax Citadel, Nova Scotia	724,107
3.	Fortress of Louisbourg, Nova Scotia	300,440
4.	Alexander Graham Bell Museum, Nova Scotia	205,688
5.	Lower Fort Garry, Manitoba	121,575
6.	Fort Beauséjour, New Brunswick	106,960
7.	Citadel Hill, Newfoundland	106,118
8.	Cartier-Brébeuf, Quebec	105,526
9.	Fort George, Ontario	99,647
10.	Grand Pré, Nova Scotia	less than 99,000

Department of Indian Affairs
and Northern Development

CANADA'S 10 MOST HISTORIC MONUMENTS

1. BRITISH COLUMBIA TOTEM POLES

The West Coast native peoples, the original inhabitants of British Columbia, were the only ones to carve the totem poles which told their stories, myths, and legends. The most outstanding examples are those of the Kwakiutl Tribe in Victoria's Thunderbird Park, the Squamish at Vancouver's Stanley Park, and the Haida and Kwakiutl at the University of British Columbia in Vancouver.

2. CARTIER-BRÉBEUF MONUMENT AND REPLICA OF LA GRANDE HERMINE (at the junction of the St. Charles and Lairet rivers, Quebec City, Quebec)

Jacques Cartier, official explorer to King Francis I of France, sailed here in his flagship, *La Grande Hermine* in 1534-35, seeking the northwest passage to Asia. Instead, he discovered Canada, and sailed up the St. Lawrence River to the site of Montreal. On May 3, 1536, he planted a cross and *fleur de lis* at the spot now commemorated by a monument. The monument also honours Father Jean de Brébeuf and the Jesuit missionaries who came here in 1625.

3. MONUMENT TO SAMUEL DE CHAMPLAIN (on the Dufferin Terrace near the Château Frontenac, Quebec City, Quebec)

Samuel de Champlain, the great explorer who first came to North America in 1603, is commemorated as the founder of Quebec and New France, where he served many years as Governor. He also explored inland along what would become the main trade route to the West, and was the first European to visit the Huron tribes in the Georgian Bay area of Ontario.

4. STATUE TO THE ACADIANS, GRAND PRÉ (near Wolfville, Nova Scotia)

These early Nova Scotians settled around the Minas Basin, about 60 miles from present-day Halifax, in the 1670s. The unique community persisted for years, despite constant struggles over Acadia between the English and the French and feuds among their French leaders. In 1755 when war broke out with France, the English expelled the Acadians from their land for refusing to take the oath of allegiance to the British crown. Many of them returned, however, and their descendants today populate parts of Nova Scotia.

5. MONTCALM-WOLFE MONUMENT (Quebec City, Quebec)

A two-sided monument, erected in 1827-28 and rebuilt in 1871, honours Major General James Wolfe and Louis Joseph Marquis de Montcalm, both fatally wounded on September 13, 1759, at the Battle of the Plains of Abraham, as a result of which Canada was gained for the British Empire. The Latin inscription on the monument translates: "Valour gave them a common death, history a common fame, and posterity a common monument."

6. BROCK'S MONUMENT (Queenston Heights, Queenston, Ontario)

This impressive monument, the second on the site, was erected in 1854 to the memory of Major General Sir Isaac Brock, Administrator of the Province of Upper Canada during the War of 1812, who, having brilliantly won the Battle of Fort Detroit, led the English defenders against American invaders in the Battle of Queenston Heights on October 13, 1812. Major General Brock was fatally wounded in the battle, later won by the English. He is buried beneath the monument. It was designed by the well-known nineteenth-century Toronto architect, William Thomas.

7. GRAVESTONE OF WILLIAM LYON MACKENZIE (Necropolis, Winchester Street, Toronto, Ontario)

A political activist, rabid reformer, and writer of scathing editorials, William Lyon Mackenzie (1795-1861) left his mark on Canadian history as an indefatigable champion of responsible government. While not all would agree with his means — he led the Upper Canada Rebellion of 1837 — his goals were clear and he fought for them with spirit. He was elected a member of the Provincial Legislature in 1829 and served as first mayor of Toronto in 1834. His last house stands at 82 Bond Street, Toronto.

8. PROVINCE HOUSE (Charlottetown, Prince Edward Island)

The birthplace of Confederation, this building, erected in 1843-47 to the design of Isaac Smith, was the setting in 1864 for a meeting of members of the coalition government of the provinces of Upper and Lower Canada, together with representatives of the Maritime Provinces who had previously planned to discuss only Maritime union. This conference led to the Quebec Conference and to the passing of the British North America Act by which Canada was created. The Confederation Chamber has been preserved with what are believed to be the original table and chairs used at the historic conference.

9. THE LAST SPIKE (Craigellachie, in Eagle Pass, 300 miles east of Vancouver, British Columbia)

A cairn was erected to mark the site where the last spike was driven to complete the Canadian Pacific Railway across Canada on November 7, 1885. The spike, iron, not gold as was rumoured, was driven by Lord Strathcona. Also in attendance were two of those in charge of the building of the great railway — William Van Horne and Sandford Fleming. A year later regular transcontinental train service commenced.

10.THE ST. ROCH (Vancouver Marine Museum, Vancouver, British Columbia)

Built in 1928 in Vancouver of Douglas fir, this schooner served for 26 years as a Royal Canadian Mounted Police supply and patrol vessel, doing much to establish Canada's sovereignty in the North. She was the first ship to sail the Northwest Passage in both directions, with her crew enduring a voyage of 28 months through heavy arctic ice on the way from Vancouver to Halifax. The St. Roch is on display in a building built specially for the purpose.

George Rust-D'Eye
Toronto Historical Board

10 SIGNIFICANT DATES IN CANADIAN HISTORY

1. 1000 A Norse sailor, Herjulf, sights Canada for the first time.

2. 1689 Bill of Rights passed by British Parliament. Decreed that each person had individual liberties and legal rights.

3. 1759 The Battle of the Plains of Abraham. The British, under Wolfe, defeat the French.

4. 1848 The first responsible government in the British Empire overseas formed in Nova Scotia.

5. 1867 The Confederation of Canada. Nova Scotia, New Brunswick, Ontario, and Quebec form the Union of the Province of Canada.

6. 1885 The last spike of the Canadian Pacific Railway is nailed, connecting Canada by rail from coast to coast.

7. 1914 Canada becomes involved in World War I.

8. 1920 First exhibition of the Group of Seven, a group of artists who changed the history of Canadian art. The seven were:

   Franklin Carmichael, Lawren S. Harris, Alexander Young Jackson, Frank Johnston, Arthur Lismer, James E. H. Macdonald, and Frederick Horsman Varley.

9. 1939 Canada becomes involved in World War II.

10. 1976 Election of the Parti Québécois government in Quebec, committed to remove Quebec from Confederation.

THE 10 MOST HATED
CANADIANS IN CANADIAN HISTORY

1. FRANCOIS BIGOT

The last intendant of New France, he profiteered while Canada burned, horded grain while people starved; his name has come to represent the most vile and irresponsible corruption, to suggest a man who would sell out his country for personal gain.

2. CHARLES LAWRENCE

Lieutenant-Governor of Nova Scotia, who, in 1755, decided on the expulsion of the Acadians; his policy led to the destruction of the 150-year-old Acadian coummunity and the dispersion of some eight to ten thousand Acadians to the far corners of North America, the Caribbean, and Europe.

3. MARIE-JOSEPHE CORRIVEAU

Convicted of the brutal axe-murder of her second husband (though she almost got away with letting her father take the blame in her place), "La Corriveau" was hanged at Quebec in 1763 and her body publicly displayed for a month, chained up in an iron cage. For over a century popular accounts portrayed her as a witch, told of her ghost assailing passers-by near the place of her execution and dragging them off to witches' sabbaths, and increased the number of her alleged murders to seven or more, each more ghastly than the others.

4. JOHN LAMBTON, LORD DURHAM

Author of the famous report urging the complete assimilation of the French Canadians: "a people with no history, and no literature"; his recommendations led to the English-only union of Ontario and Quebec in 1840, frequently referred to by French Canadians as a "second conquest," and Durham himself has been remembered by French Canadians as the arch-enemy of their national survival.

5. SIR JOHN A. MACDONALD

Despite the attempts of modern-day patriots to turn him into the "father of his country," the bibulous "Old Fox" has been thought of by too many as the crafty politician who cynically decided to let Louis Riel hang "though every dog in Quebec bark in his favour"; who, after the Fathers of Confederation had agreed on a constitution, tried to have drastic changes written into the British North America Act behind the backs and against the wills of his colleagues; who refused to enforce those sections of the BNA Act that protected minority school rights; and about whom the dying George-Etienne Cartier was said to have warned a comrade: "Watch out for Sir John Macdonald. He hates the French Canadians."

6. LOUIS RIEL

A hero today, Riel was feared and hated in his lifetime as the fomenter of two rebellions, the murderer of Thomas Scott ("laid still groaning into his

Louis Riel was 41 years old when he was hanged by Sir John A. Macdonald's government in 1885.

grave"), the man who stirred up savage tribes of Indians to murder innocent settlers and missionaries. Some feared he wanted to overthrow Canadian institutions and institute a French and Catholic rule over the whole country; others saw him as a greedy and cynical man who was willing to sell out his own Métis people for a bribe of $35,000. When he was hanged at Regina in 1885, a reporter was heard to exclaim with relief: "Well, the God-damned son of a bitch is gone at last!"

7. SIR JOSEPH FLAVELLE

Multimillionaire meat-packer "Old Black Joe, the Methodist bacon bandit," was accused of outrageous profiteering during World War I, at a time of general hardship and sacrifice. Though his biographer declares the charges to be without foundation, Flavelle's name still conjures up the image of a man who grew enormously wealthy supplying rotten meat to the Canadian boys in the trenches.

8. ARTHUR MEIGHEN

Unloved to begin with because of his harsh and intolerant personality and manner, Meighen earned the hatred of a great part of the population as the chief champion of conscription in World War I; in 1919 he incurred the wrath of labour by using troops and vicious emergency power to crush the Winnipeg general strike and thus set back the cause of collective bargaining; as leader of the federal Conservatives, he antagonized western farmers by opposing their demands for tariff reduction, annoyed nationalists by seeming to be too servile in his attitude toward Britain, and infuriated Quebeckers by again calling for overseas military conscription in 1942.

9. W. L. MACKENZIE KING

Although Canadians voted for him again and again, they seemed to do so, as one observer put it, while "holding their noses." He was anathema to intellectuals because of his reputation for deviousness and obfuscation, for disguising shallow thought in elaborate language, and for refusing to take clear stands on important issues. His failure to remedy effectively the evils of the Depression made those who suffered from them look on him as callous and cynical; his centralization of power at Ottawa angered the provinces; and his reorientation of Canadian life and policy away from Britain and toward the United States angered Anglophiles and nationalists alike.

10. PIERRE ELLIOTT TRUDEAU

Even if we were to disregard the deception caused by his failure to nip separatism in the bud, the fury provoked by his bilingualism policies, the bitterness of the unemployed and of those whose incomes don't keep up with the cost of living, the animosity created by his personal manner or style, the detestation of Quebec separatists, the hatred of civil libertarians, and all the factors of one sort and another which lead people to put bumper stickers on their cars saying "Certain destruction with Trudeau" — even if we were to disregard all this, the principle of "Throw the rascals out" must lead us to maintain that the man actually in office should always be among the most hated in his country.

A.I. Silver
History Department
University of Toronto

THE 6 MOST HATED FOREIGNERS IN CANADIAN HISTORY

1. SATAN

The Prince of Darkness must stand as the greatest villain in our past. He has been blamed for everything from rainstorms to invasions, marital infidelity, to the influx of Irish. Most important, the poor devil was an object both Catholics and Protestants could loathe, hence an instrument of national unity.

2. GEORGE WASHINGTON

For a couple of generations this revolutionary who split the British Empire and launched American republicanism remained a marvellous ogre, at least in Tory circles. Time and U.S. propaganda, though, eventually rehabilitated his image.

3. JOSEF STALIN

Another man all could hate — native-born as well as immigrant—for his Communist empire threatened our survival and our God, or so it seemed in the happy days of the Cold War.

4. WILLIAM OF ORANGE

King Billy may have been a hero to Orangemen, but he was cursed by generations of French and Irish Catholics — no wonder, given the prejudices that flourished in his name.

5. ANY POPE

Nineteenth-century Protestants saw this officeholder as the head of a worldwide conspiracy against liberty, true Christianity, and the Canadian way (the British type, anyway). The onset of religious indifference has consigned this hatred to the dustbin of history.

6. LORD DURHAM

Whatever his present reputation, he was bitterly hated in the 1840s (and beyond) by Tories because his Report condemned their oligarchical rule and by French Canadians because that same Report denied the legitimacy of their nationality.

Paul Rutherford
Chairman, History Department
University of Toronto

10 VIOLENT CANADIAN DEATHS

1. GEORGE BROWN, Statesman

In 1873 Brown was murdered by an angry employee of *The Globe*, whom Brown had recently fired.

2. HENRY HUDSON, Explorer

In 1611 Hudson's crew mutinied and set him and his son adrift in an open boat. No trace of them was ever found.

3. PIERRE LAPORTE, Member of Parliament, Cabinet Minister

In 1970 during the FLQ crisis in Montreal, Laporte was found murdered in the trunk of a car at Montreal International Airport.

4. D'ARCY McGEE, Statesman

In 1868 McGee was shot by a young Fenian, just after making a speech in Parliament. It was Canada's first and only political assassination.

5. LOUIS RIEL, Rebel

In 1885 Riel was hanged after leading two Métis rebellions — in 1869 and 1885.

6. TOM THOMSON, Artist

Died mysteriously in 1917 in a canoeing accident. Many believe that Thomson was murdered, as his body, although not indubitably identified, was later discovered tangled in fishing line.

7. ISAAC BROCK, British Soldier and Lieutenant-Governor of Upper Canada

Brock was killed in battle during the War of 1812. Despite the loss of their general, the British scored a key victory over the Americans at Queenston Heights.

8. MARQUIS DE MONTCALM, French Commander

In 1759, just after the British victory over the French on the Plains of Abraham, Montcalm died of injuries received.

9. TECUMSEH, Indian Chief and Brigadier-General

In 1813 Tecumseh, a Shawnee Indian Chief, was killed in the British defeat at Moraviantown. He had attempted to organize a confederacy of tribes which would stretch from Florida to Canada.

10. JAMES WOLFE, British Commander

Died in 1759, during the Battle on the Plains of Abraham.

Pierre Laporte was found murdered in the trunk of a car at Montreal's International Airport in 1970. The longest bridge in Canada (centre span 2190 ft.), which links Quebec with L'Isle d'Orleans, is named after him.

THE 10 MOST IMPORTANT CANADIAN NATION BUILDERS

1. JOHN A. MACDONALD

The closest approximation to the Father of Canada — a master of the political arts, including corruption, who managed to inspire some and suborn others sufficiently to generate a common, if self-interested, support for a transcontinental dominion.

2. GEORGE ETIENNE CARTIER

An oft-forgotten ally of John A., the French Canadian whose conservative views and political skills wedded a suspicious Quebec to the Canadian Confederation.

3. WILLIAM LYON MACKENZIE KING

He carried on John A.'s work. Mackenzie King made national unity a Canadian fetish, avoiding all manner of measures (from conscription to social welfare) until events or a consensus made them inevitable. He may not have supplied inspired leadership, but he did offer sound government.

4. WILLIAM VAN HORNE

The American-born general manager of the Canadian Pacific Railway, Van Horne built the country's "bond of steel" that was, incidentally, a great profit-making enterprise.

5. NELLIE McCLUNG

The irrepressible prairie lady who gave Canada its own suffragist tradition and helped to bring a huge body of Canadians into our political democracy.

6. LEONARD BROCKINGTON

First master of the Canadian Broadcasting Corporation, who established this major nationwide cultural enterprise on a firm foundation. Can he be blamed if things haven't worked out as well as some pundits predicted?

7. JOHN GRIERSON

Scottish-born filmmaker, famed for his pioneering development of the documentary, who moulded a National Film Board during World War II that is renowned for its depictions of the Canadian reality.

8. HAROLD INNIS

Supposedly Canada's intellectual giant whose historical theories justified the country's independent existence in North America. His impenetrable prose, however, has limited his direct influence to a few academic zealots.

9. PIERRE ELLIOTT TRUDEAU

He tried to re-design the Canadian nation-state. His success looks questionable, but the effort was surely worthwhile.

10. RENÉ LÉVESQUE

He may stand as Quebec's "national father" — in which case he will, of course, contribute to the emergence of a new Anglo-Canadian nation.

Paul Rutherford
Chairman, History Department
University of Toronto

THE 10 MOST PROMINENT FATHERS OF CONFEDERATION

1. GEORGE BROWN (1818-1880)

His enthusiasm and energy were unequalled. But because of conflict with Sir John A. Macdonald, Brown withdrew before Confederation became a fact.

2. SIR ALEXANDER CAMPBELL (1822-1892)

In 1864 Campbell became Commissioner of Crown Lands and in the same year he served in the Quebec Conference. In 1867 he was appointed the first Postmaster General of Canada.

3. SIR GEORGE ETIENNE CARTIER (1814-1873)

Cartier had a dominant hold over the French-speaking people of Canada from 1858-1873. It was largely because of him that French Canada accepted the Federation's proposals.

4. JAMES COCKBURN (1819-1883)

Cockburn became the first Speaker of the House of Commons and he held that post until 1874. Much of the tradition upheld in the House of Commons today can be credited to Cockburn's tact and courtesy.

5. SIR ALEXANDER TILLOCH GALT (1817-1893)

Galt and Cartier together virtually dominated all of Lower Canada — Cartier the French and Galt the English.

6. SIR JOHN A. MACDONALD (1815-1891)

Macdonald played a leading part in the "Great Coalition" which led to the Confederation of the British North American provinces. He was the dominant figure in the Quebec Conference of 1864 and in the London Conference of 1866. He is regarded as the "Father of Confederation."

7. THOMAS D'ARCY McGEE (1825-1868)

McGee was the main orator. His speeches, delivered nationwide, roused much patriotic fervour. Later assassinated.

Sir Charles Tupper, "The Grand Old Man of Canada" was one of the most prominent Fathers of Confederation.

8. WILLIAM McDOUGALL (1822-1905)

McDougall preached federal unity in *The Globe*—a newspaper for which he was the chief writer—as well as in brilliant public speeches. He, like McGee, did much to rouse patriotic fervour.

9. SIR SAMUEL LEONARD TILLEY (1818-1896)

Tilley and Charles Tupper were the two men responsible for getting the Atlantic provinces to join. Tilley was a delegate at the London Conference of 1866 and in 1867 became the Minister of Customs in Canada's first Cabinet.

10. SIR CHARLES TUPPER (1821-1915)

Prime Minister of Nova Scotia from 1864 to 1867. In 1868 he played a crucial part in the defeat of the anti-confederationists in Nova Scotia. He was Minister of Public Works and Minister of Railways and Canals in the first Cabinet.

8 NICKNAMES OF CANADA'S GREAT LEADERS OF THE PAST

1. **THE AXE-GRINDER**

   John Sandfield Macdonald (1812-1872); Premier of Ontario (1867-1871)

2. **THE BEAVER**

   Lord Beaverbrook (1879-1964); William Maxwell Aitken

3. **BLUE RUIN DICK**

   Sir Richard Cartwright (1835-1912); Member of Parliament (1863-1912)

4. **THE FATHER OF BRITISH COLUMBIA**

   Sir James Douglas (1803-1912); Governor of Vancouver Island (1851-1863) and British Columbia (1858-1864)

5. **THE GOOD SAMARITAN OF LABRADOR**

   Sir Wilfred Grenfell (1865-1940)

6. **THE GRAND OLD MAN OF CANADA**

   Sir Charles Tupper (1821-1915); Prime Minister of Canada (May 1 - July 8, 1896)

7. **OLD MAN ELOQUENT**

   Joseph Howe (1804-1873)

8. **OLD TOMORROW**

   Sir John A. Macdonald (1815-1891); Prime Minister of Canada (1867-1873, 1878-1891)

Sir Wilfred Grenfell (1865-1940) — The Good Samaritan of Labrador.

Lord Beaverbrook, from New Brunswick, attained enormous power and wealth — mostly in England.

THE FIRST 10
PRIME MINISTERS OF CANADA

1. Sir John Alexander Macdonald — July 1, 1867 - Nov. 5, 1873
   Oct. 18, 1878 - June 6, 1891

2. Alexander Mackenzie — Nov. 7, 1878 - Oct. 16, 1878

3. Sir John Joseph Caldwell Abbott — June 16, 1873 - Nov. 24, 1892

4. Sir John Sparrow David Thompson — Dec. 5, 1892 - Dec. 12, 1894

5. Sir Mackenzie Bowell — Dec. 21, 1894 - Apr. 27, 1896

6. Sir Charles Tupper — May 1, 1896 - July 8, 1896

7. Sir Wilfrid Laurier — July 11, 1896 - Oct. 6, 1911

8. Sir Robert Laird Borden — Oct. 10, 1911 - Oct. 12, 1917

9. Arthur Meighen — July 10, 1920 - Dec. 29, 1921
   June 29, 1926 - Sept. 25, 1926

10. William Lyon Mackenzie King — Dec. 29, 1921 - June 28, 1926
    Sept. 25, 1926 - Aug. 6, 1920
    Oct. 23, 1935 - Nov. 15, 1948

Since June 1926 there have been five Prime Ministers of Canada:
Richard Bedford Bennett, Aug. 7, 1930 - Oct. 23, 1935
Louis Stephen St. Laurent, Nov. 15, 1948 - June 21, 1957
John George Diefenbaker, June 21, 1957 - Apr. 22, 1963
Lester Bowles Pearson, Apr. 22, 1963 - Apr. 20, 1968
Pierre Elliott Trudeau, Apr. 20, 1968-

Christopher Ondaatje
Author
The Prime Ministers of Canada

THE FIRST 10 PROVINCES
TO JOIN CONFEDERATION

		Date of Admission	Seat of Provincial Government
1.	Ontario	July 1, 1867	Toronto
2.	Quebec	July 1, 1867	Quebec City
3.	Nova Scotia	July 1, 1867	Halifax
4.	New Brunswick	July 1, 1867	Fredericton
5.	Manitoba	July 15, 1867	Winnipeg
6.	British Columbia	July 20, 1871	Victoria
7.	Prince Edward Island	July 1, 1873	Charlottetown
8.	Saskatchewan	Sept. 1, 1905	Regina
9.	Alberta	Sept. 1, 1905	Edmonton
10.	Newfoundland	March 31, 1949	St. John's

Statistics Canada

THE FIRST 10 GOVERNORS-GENERAL
OF CANADA

		Assumed Office
1.	The Viscount Monck of Ballytrammon	July 1, 1867
2.	The Baron Lisgar of Lisgar and Bailieborough	Feb. 2, 1869
3.	The Earl of Dufferin	June 25, 1872
4.	The Marquis of Lorne	Nov. 25, 1878
5.	The Marquis of Lansdowne	Oct. 23, 1883
6.	The Baron Stanley of Preston	June 11, 1888
7.	The Earl of Aberdeen	Sept. 18, 1893
8.	The Earl of Minto	Nov. 12, 1898
9.	The Earl Grey	Dec. 10, 1904
10.	The Duke of Connaught	Oct. 13, 1911

Since 1916 there have been eleven further Governors-General of Canada:
The Duke of Devonshire, Nov. 11, 1916
The Baron Byng of Vimy, Aug. 11, 1921
The Viscount Willingdon of Ratton, Oct. 2, 1926
The Earl of Bessborough, Apr. 4, 1931
The Baron Tweedsmuir of Elsfield, Nov. 2, 1935
The Earl of Athlone, June 21, 1940
The Viscount Alexander of Tunis, Apr. 12, 1946
The Rt. Hon. Vincent Massey, Feb. 28, 1952
General the Rt. Hon. Georges P. Vanier, Sept. 15, 1959
The Rt. Hon. Roland Michener, Apr. 17, 1967
The Rt. Hon. Jules Leger, Jan. 14, 1974

THE 6 MOST IMPORTANT EVENTS IN CANADIAN HISTORY BEFORE CONFEDERATION

1. THE ESTABLISHMENT OF PORT ROYAL

Samuel de Champlain was responsible for the establishment of the first permanent colony in New France, the event that confirmed France's presence in the New World and marked the beginning of the struggle for supremacy in the New World by England and France.

2. THE QUEBEC ACT, 1774

This act guaranteed the French Canadian linguistic, religious, and legal rights in Quebec. It was an amazingly liberal act for its time. It also confirmed French Canada as an entity in a primarily English-speaking continent.

3. THE EFFECT OF THE AMERICAN REVOLUTION

The invasion of Quebec by American troops early in the war was a fiasco mainly caused by the refusal of the newly conquered inhabitants of Quebec to join the rebels in their fight for independence. This ensured a British presence in North America.

4. THE IMMIGRATION OF THE UNITED EMPIRE LOYALISTS

Those who supported England during the American Revolution found themselves displaced refugees after the British defeat. A large number of them settled in virgin territory of what is now Ontario. This group of skilled, primarily middle-class individuals established the second of Canada's "Two Solitudes."

5. THE DEFINING OF CANADA'S BORDERS

The most important result of the War of 1812 occurred in 1818 when the borders of Canada and the United States were peacefully partitioned. They have remained unguarded and untouched since that time.

6. THE REVOLTS OF 1837

Although these revolts were no more than minor skirmishes, the results were to be of major importance. In effect, the ruling class of rigid, British-oriented aristocrats was replaced by individuals who represented the new type of Canadian citizen whose home and heart were in Canada and who resented bitterly the class structures that tried to prevent him from upward social mobility. This replacement meant that it was only a matter of time before Confederation.

Paul A. Kates
Historian

THE 10 MOST IMPORTANT EVENTS IN CANADA'S HISTORY SINCE CONFEDERATION

1. 1867   Act of Confederation passed by British Parliament. Upper and Lower Canada (Ontario & Quebec), New Brunswick, and Nova Scotia form a union.

2. 1885   Execution of Métis leader Louis Riel.

3. 1890   Manitoba enacts Official Language Act abolishing use of French in law and in the Legislature.

4. 1917   Halifax explosion. Every building in the city is damaged and 1,630 people are killed.

    Coalition Government of Liberals and Conservatives wins election on conscription issue. Quebec opposes and stands alone.

5. 1919   Winnipeg General Strike.

6. 1939   Canada enters World War II as a partner nation of Britain and Commonwealth and issues a separate declaration of war.

7. 1945   Igor Gouzenko, cipher clerk at Soviet Embassy, defects.

8. 1947   Oil is discovered at Leduc, Alberta.

    Canadian citizenship is defined for the first time without regard to British nationality.

9. 1967   Centennial of Canada's Confederation and the staging of Expo, outstanding world's fair.

10. 1970   FLQ crisis and the murder of Quebec Cabinet Minister Pierre Laporte.

Lloyd Robertson
CTV Newscaster

CANADA'S 10 WORST DISASTERS

1. THE HALIFAX EXPLOSION—DECEMBER 6, 1917—2,000 DIED

Early in the morning of December 6, 1917, two steamships, the *Mont Blanc* and the *Imo*, collided in Halifax Harbour. The ensuing explosion injured 8,000 people and left 10,000 homeless. The estimated property damage was 50 million dollars. That night, Halifax suffered its worst blizzard in 20 years and many people froze to death. As a result of the blizzard and the explosion, 2,000 died.

2. THE ST. LAWRENCE SHIPWRECK—MAY 29, 1914—1,012 DIED

At 1:55 A.M. May 29, 1914, two ocean liners, the *Empress of Ireland*, bound for Liverpool, and a Norwegian ship, the *Storstad*, collided in the Gulf of St. Lawrence. The *Empress* sank in 14 minutes and 1,012 of her passengers drowned. One million dollars' worth of silver bars was also lost.

3. THE TORONTO PLANE CRASH —JULY 5, 1970—109 DIED

An Air Canada DC-8 jet bound for Los Angeles from Toronto plunged into a corn field three miles north of Toronto International Airport and 109 persons died.

4. ROCKSLIDE IN ALBERTA—APRIL 29, 1903—100 DIED

At 4:10 A.M. on April 29, 1903, a huge wedge of limestone 1,300 feet high, 4,000 feet wide, and 500 feet thick crashed down from Turtle Mountain on to the town of Frank in Alberta. Seventy million tons of rock swept over two miles of valley in 100 seconds. Seventeen coal miners were entombed for thirteen hours inside Turtle Mountain and a hundred died—10 percent of the total population of Frank.

5. THE NEWFOUNDLAND FIRE—DECEMBER 12, 1942—99 DIED

During a barn dance at the Knights of Columbus Hotel in St. John's, Newfoundland, a fire broke out and killed 99 people. It is believed that the fire was started by an enemy agent. (There were reputed to be a great number of foreign agents in St. John's at that time.)

6. HURRICANE HAZEL—OCTOBER 15, 1954—83 DIED

Hurricane Hazel began in the Caribbean on October 6, 1954. In nine days it swept through half of North America and then struck Toronto. Gales were measured of up to 70 miles per hour and a record 4 inches of rain fell in 12 hours. Eighty-three people from Toronto died and an estimated 25 million dollars' damage was done. Hazel herself died on October 17, 1954, over the Hudson Strait.

7. SPRINGHILL MINE DISASTER—NOVEMBER 6, 1958—75 DIED

In Springhill, Nova Scotia, on November 6, 1958, North America's

George V, in 1901, became the first member of the British royal family to visit Canada.

deepest coal mine collapsed, trapping 174 miners two miles below the surface of the earth for two weeks. Seventy-five died. The hardships experienced by the 99 surviving men make for one of the greatest endurance feats in Canada's history. The Cumberland Mines in Springhill have taken an average of over 6 lives per year since the turn of the century.

8. THE REGINA TORNADO—JUNE 30, 1912—65 DIED

At 4:50 P.M. on June 30, 1912, a tornado swept through Regina, Saskatchewan, six blocks wide, zig-zagging erratically, turning over freight cars, and destroying entire blocks of houses. It was all over five minutes later.

9. VANCOUVER BRIDGE COLLAPSE—JUNE 17, 1958—19 DIED

On June 17, 1958, a bridge that was to link North Vancouver with Main Vancouver collapsed. It was to be two miles long, with a six lane highway running across it. A 35-ton train carrying several tons of steel and a 155-ton crane both on the bridge at the same time caused the collapse, which killed 19 and caused approximately 23 million dollars damage.

10. THE WINNIPEG FLOOD—MAY 5, 1950

Amid 50 mile per hour winds the Red River broke through protective dikes and flooded much of Winnipeg. The river had already turned 600 square miles of Manitoba farmland into swamp and inland sea. Although only one person died, one-third of Winnipeg's population was forced to flee their homes and an estimated 100 million dollars' worth of damage was done.

THE FIRST 10 VISITS TO CANADA
BY MEMBERS OF THE
ROYAL FAMILY *

1. 1901   George V as the Duke of York, with his wife

2. 1919   Edward VIII as the Prince of Wales

3. 1924   Edward VIII as the Prince of Wales

4. 1927   Edward VIII as the Prince of Wales

5. 1939   King George VI and Queen Elizabeth. The first time a ruling British Monarch visited Canada

6. 1951   Elizabeth II, as Princess Elizabeth, with her husband, the Duke of Edinburgh

7. 1957   Queen Elizabeth II

8. 1957   Queen Elizabeth II

9. 1957   Queen Elizabeth II

10. 1957   Queen Elizabeth II

*Since Confederation

Queen Elizabeth II, as Princess Elizabeth, visited Canada for the first time in 1951 with her husband the Duke of Edinburgh.

21
POLITICS

10 GREAT CANADIAN QUOTATIONS ON POLITICS AND POLITICIANS

1. The success of Canada has been that we turned war into politics. The wars of the French and English, of the Americans and Canadians, of the Indians and whites, have all been converted into issues, elections, debates, and solutions.

   James Bacque, *Notes for a Native Land*, 1970

2. Canadian political parties have no policies at all; they cultivate the art of electioneering.

   Louis Dudek, *Editorial*, 1958

3. What need has a man of brains when he goes into politics? Brainy men make the trouble.

   Nellie L. McClung, *Sowing Seeds in Danny*, 1911

4. The ambitions and actions of politicians, if one does not stand too near to them, are powerfully romantic.

   Robertson Davies, Preface to *A Jig for the Gypsy*, 1954

5. Party leaders are admired for their keen knowledge of the winds of opinion, and their capacity for "compromise."

   Louis Dudek, *Editorial*, 1958

6. Why is it... that when people have no capacity for private usefulness they should be so anxious to serve the public?

   Sara Jeannette Duncan, *The Imperialist*, 1904

7. I know what a statesman is. He is a dead politician. We need more statesmen.

   Robert C. Edwards, *Calgary Eye Opener*

8. We be all humbugs, but the greatest of all is the politician.

   Francis W. Grey, *The Curé of St. Philippe*, 1899

9. A democrat can't condescend. He's down already. But when a conservative stoops, he conquers.

   Stephen Leacock, *My Remarkable Uncle*

10. There are two classes of politicians: those who sit still, and make all the money; and those who go about the country, and make all the speeches.

    J. J. Procter, *The Philosopher in the Clearing*, 1897

10 GREAT CANADIAN QUOTATIONS ON FRENCH CANADA AND FRENCH CANADIANS

1. French Canada is almost without curiosity about the literature and culture of English Canada.

   E. K. Brown, *The Problem of Canadian Literature*, 1943

2. The tragedy of French Canada is that you can't make up your mind whether you want to be free-choosing individuals or French-Canadians choosing only what you think your entire race will approve.

   Hugh MacLennan, *Two Solitudes*, 1945

3. What a mine of inspiration there is in the history of French Canada! Fit theme indeed for poet, novelist, historian, and painter!

   Thomas O'Hagan, *Canadian Essays*, 1901

4. French genius and French taste on the banks of the St. Lawrence differ little from French genius and French taste on the banks of the Loire or the Seine.

   Thomas O'Hagan, *Canadian Essays*, 1901

5. A French Canadian will accomplish as much with an axe as a man of any other race with a full outfit of tools.

   Henry M. Ami, *Canada and Newfoundland*, 1915

6. The majority of French Canadians remained... semi-literate, under the tutelage of a repressive clergy.

   Louis Dudek, *The Two Traditions*, 1962

7. We are French Canadians, but our country is not confined to the territory overshadowed by the citadel of Quebec; our country is Canada.

   Edwin R. Procunier, *Granite and Oak*, 1962

8. We cannot ask more of them; their sin is one of omission rather than commission.

   Roy Daniells, *High Colonialism in Canada*, 1969

9. Our good Canadians, as you will find, attach more value to the simple word of a priest — than to the command of any lay authority.

   William McLennan and J. N. McIlwraith, *The Span o' Life*, 1899

10. They have ... founded a literary microcosm of their own — created a literature with a colour, form and flavor all its own, which must be considered in itself a greater marvel than their material preservation.

    Thomas O'Hagan, *Canadian Essays*, 1901

SIR JOHN A. MACDONALD'S
10 GREATEST QUOTES

1. Whatever you do, adhere to the Union — we are a great country, and shall become one of the greatest in the Universe if we preserve it; we shall sink into insignificance and adversity if we suffer it to be broken. (1861)

2. Given a parliament with a big surplus, and a big majority and a weak opposition, and you could debauch a committee of archangels. (1869)

3. Anybody may support me when I am right. What I want is a man that will support me when I am wrong. (1874)

4. Until that road is built to British Columbia and the Pacific...until bound by the iron link, as we have bound Nova Scotia and New Brunswick by the Intercontinental Railway, we are not a Dominion in fact. (1875)

5. As to myself, my course is clear. A British subject I was born — a British subject I will die. (1875)

6. A compliment is a statement of an agreeable truth; flattery is the statement of an agreeable untruth. (1876)

7. The task of the politician is to climb the tree and shake down the acorns to the pigs below. (1876)

8. Any election is like a horse-race, in that you can tell more about it the next day. (1882)

9. Let us be English or let us be French; but above all let us be Canadians. (1890)

10. I will let you know tomorrow. (1891)

SIR WILFRID LAURIER'S
10 GREATEST QUOTES

1. The eternal principles of justice are far more important than thousands of millions of acres of land. (1882)

2. For us, sons of France, political sentiment is a passion; while, for the Englishman, politics are a question of business. (1884)

3. More revolutions have been caused by Conservative obstinacy than by Liberal exaggeration. (1887)

4. You cannot legislate against geography. (1887)

"The eternal principles of justice are far more important than thousands of millions of acres of land."

Sir Wilfred Laurier

5. It is not enough to have good principles; we must have organization also. Principles without organization may lose, but organization without principles may often win. (1893)

6. The nineteenth century was the century of the United States. I think we can claim that it is Canada that shall fill the twentieth century. (1904)

7. We have found that our Canadian independence is quite comfortable with our dependency as a colony. (1904)

8. We are in the year 1904. We are a nation of six million people already; we expect soon to be twenty-five, yes, forty millions. There are men living... who will see this country with at least sixty million people. (1904)

9. The proper basis of the British Empire was that it was to be composed of a galaxy of nations under the British Crown. (1907)

10. What great and enduring achievement has the world every accomplished that was not based on idealism? (1916)

Prime Minister John Diefenbaker claimed that he never campaigned, but merely visited with the people!

JOHN G. DIEFENBAKER'S
10 GREATEST QUOTES

1. We shall be Canadians first, foremost, and always, and our policies will be decided in Canada and not dictated by any other country. (1962)

2. I'd never have been Prime Minister if the Gallup Polls had had their way. (1962)

3. As long as there is a drop of blood in my body they won't stop me from talking about freedom. (1962)

4. The duty of the Opposition is to turn out the government. (1964)

5. I have always been a House of Commons man. (1964)

6. I never campaign. I just visit with the people. (1965)

7. They criticized me sometimes for being too much concerned with the average Canadian. I can't help that. I'm just one of them. (1967)

8. I believe in Canada — a Canada undivided. A Canadian I was born, a Canadian I will die. (1967)

9. Nothing I ever do is political. (1968)

10. Don't get me started on history because then you shall know the meaning of eternity. (1969)

PIERRE ELLIOTT TRUDEAU'S 10 GREATEST QUOTES

1. I wouldn't lift a finger to get rid of the monarchy. I think the monarchy, by and large, has done more good than harm to Canada. (1967)

2. There's no place for the state in the bedrooms of the nation. (1967)

3. We must remain whole, and we must remain complete. National unity is the framework to which everything else is knit. (1968)

4. Canada will be a strong country when Canadians of all provinces feel at home in all parts of the country, and when they feel that all Canada belongs to them. (1968)

5. Canada is the product of understanding, not conflict. (1969)

6. Americans should never underestimate the constant pressure on Canada which the mere presence of the United States has produced. We're a different people from you, and a different people because of you. (1969)

7. If we don't solve our own problems, other people will — and the world of tomorrow belongs to the people who will solve them. (1969)

8. Mangez de la merde! (1970)

9. It is more important to maintain law and order than to worry about those whose knees tremble at the sight of the army. (1970)

10. Separation is against the gut interest and the gut feeling of the average Canadian. (1971)

10 IMPORTANT STATEMENTS
ON CANADIAN UNITY *

1. I believe in the unity of Canada. I believe that Canada is one country and that Canadians are one people.

2. All Canadians are builders and founders of Canada and it is wrong to suggest that there are only two founding races or two founding peoples.

3. It is a mistake to believe that the increased use of the French language will somehow increase national unity. Most Canadians want unity and will do whatever is necessary to achieve it.

4. It is important for all of us to understand the difference between individual bilingualism, which is essential to Canadian unity, and national bilingualism, which is the primary cause of national disunity.

5. We must all try to remember that we are nation-building, not province-building, and that if Canadians are to achieve their destiny as one people, Canada must ultimately be united by language and not divided by language.

6. Western Canadians want a country of goodwill; a Canada in which there is understanding of the difficulties experienced by others, a Canada in which we attempt to overcome by joint effort the problems and handicaps of all Canadians.

7. It is essential that Quebeckers and all Canadians achieve equality, but there must be more clarity of thought on how this equality is to be achieved. Legislating a greater use of the French language throughout Canada will not achieve equality for French-speaking Canadians.

8. A reality of North America which none of us can do anything about, is the fact that an essential ingredient in the achievement of equality is the ability to speak the common language. Most Quebeckers recognize that the road to equality in North America is to join the mainstream.

9. There is a great Canada deep in the hearts of all Canadians. Once we have corrected the fundamental errors in our thinking, we can continue to build together what I believe can be the model nation of the world. The twentieth century can still belong to Canada!

10. For all of us the cause is Canada and, for most of us, Canada is one country and Canadians are one people.

*From a speech to the Task Force on Canadian Unity, Winnipeg
January 13, 1978

The Honourable James Richardson
Member of Parliament, Winnipeg South

THE 10 BEST OR MOST ENIGMATIC QUOTES ON SEPARATISM BY RENE LÉVÉSQUE

1. We are not a small people. Perhaps we come close to being a great people.

    La Presse, November 15, 1976

2. For a small people such as we, a minority status on an Anglo-Saxon continent already creates the permanent temptation of self-denial. This self-denial has all the appeal of an easy ride down the hill. At the foot of this hill we could comfortably drown in the "great whole."

    Un Québec souverain dans une nouvelle Union canadienne, M.S.A., September 15, 1967

3. If we ever came to a sad end, our own impotence would be to blame for the dejection which would follow.

    de l'Homme, 1968

4. French-Canadian nationalism must make an extremely complicated and laborious effort so as to adjust to today's world, using independence as a tool. It must emerge from futuristic illusions of a second French conquest of America.

    La Presse, January 9, 1969

5. Independence is possible; economically, politically, and humanly. Anyone who is not convinced of this must either be blind or intent on protecting his own interests and his own career.

    La Presse, May 11, 1964

6. We believe that we can get along better without Canada than Canada can without us.

    Le Devoir, February 25, 1964

7. A sovereign Quebec means, first of all, the complete recovery and the absolute property of the taxes that we pay.

    La Presse, January 9, 1969

8. We endorse Mr. Toynbee's prediction, when he wrote that at the end of time, China and the French Canadians would still be around.

    La Presse, January 9, 1969

9. Pristine socialism, as it was conceived by 19th century philosophers, is as outdated as capitalism. We must now face 20th century problems that even Karl Marx's theories cannot solve.

    Naturally, changes won't fall in our laps like pennies from heaven. For years we of the Parti Québécois have been repeating that we have only ourselves to count on.

    Point de Mire Magazine, November 27, 1971

10. General de Gaulle's "Vive le Québec libre" did more for Quebec's publicity than ten million dollars spent by an ad agency could ever have done.

Agence France-Presse, November 22, 1976

10 REASONS WHY THE PROVINCE OF QUEBEC MAY WELL SEPARATE FROM CANADA

1. For more than two hundred years the Québécois have considered themselves a conquered people. The election of a government dedicated to independence is a major step in a process that will ultimately succeed.

2. Canadian unity outside Quebec lacks definition and dedication, while independence for Quebec is a clearly defined objective. Unless and until national unity becomes more than a propaganda slogan, separation will have more achievable appeal — not only for Québécois, but for other provinces as well.

3. The Québécois have justifiably felt uncomfortable and unwelcome outside their own patch. They recognize that they have been considered to be "different" because of language and religion, and can only achieve a sense of satisfaction in their own place.

4. Bilingualism, as a national policy, now has little appeal to the Québécois. It has come years too late, and now faces the unilingual policy of the present Quebec government. Many Québécois consider the Federal bilingual policies as condescending and opportunist.

5. While the present Quebec leader is certain to remain dedicated to democratic principles and reliance on persuasion, less democratic and more radical elements are likely to succeed him should he fail to achieve independence.

6. The cause of independence has remained a burning issue for a part of the population for much longer than Canada has been a country. By comparison, national unity as a concept is little more to them than a costly ritual to disguise various regional economic interests.

7. A great many people outside Quebec really have little interest in whether or not Quebec remains. The unthinking attitude of "let them go their own way if they want to" is sensitively realized by the Québécois.

8. The events of 1970 showed that there were at least a few people inside Quebec who were prepared to die for their objective. Such dedication, if maintained and organized, must ultimately prevail over indifference.

9. Public pressure from the rest of Canada against perceived favour toward Quebec in the distribution of government spending may force the Federal Government to change the pattern, in turn making the case for remaining within Canada less attractive to Quebec.

10. Assumption: that more Québécois are prepared to accept the risks of independence and hostility than those willing to continue to negotiate for a new status.

John P. S. Mackenzie
Investment Counsellor, Author

10 REASONS WHY THE PROVINCE OF QUEBEC IS UNLIKELY TO SEPARATE FROM CANADA

1. The Québécois are essentially conservative, although there has been a radical element since the first defeat in 1759. While this element has grown significantly in the last 20 years, it is not now, nor is it likely to be, strong enough to carry the majority.

2. The Catholic Church no longer wields the political power it once did, but much of the population remains devoutly religious. The religious influence is essentially conservative and, while not dedicated to unity, is opposed to radical change.

3. The present Government of Quebec is made up of people dedicated to democratic principles. It is unlikely that a democratically based government can achieve by influence what, to succeed, can probably only be achieved by power.

4. The economics are all wrong. The Parti Québécois has produced doubtful projections to illustrate that economic viability can be maintained. It appears to be perceived by a large element that economic independence is unlikely.

5. The *curé* and the *notaire* have been replaced as the principal power in the villages by the managers of the *caisses* or credit unions. The financial influence is likely to be the more persuasive in the practical considerations of economic survival. .

6. The present Government of Quebec appears to have assumed that economic union with the rest of Canada would be welcomed. The government and people of Quebec have been quickly and emphatically disabused of this assumption by other provincial governments.

7. The power base of the Parti Québécois appears to remain in only some 20 percent of the population despite the dedication of the government to the cause of independence since coming to office.

8. The 1976 election success was based primarily on the dreadful perfor-mance of the previous government rather than on a belief in the cause of separation. It is thought than many who voted for the Parti Québécois will vote *"non"* to the referendum.

9. Recognizing that Quebec has genuine aspirations to its own identity and its "differentness," Canada will find constitutional compromises which will satisfy the majority in Quebec. This, in turn, will reduce the internal pressure for independence.

10. Assumption: that more Québécois will wish to maintain a position with-in Canada than to experience the loneliness of an independent state in the midst of indifferent, if not hostile, neighbours.

John P. S. Mackenzie
Investment Counsellor, Author

THE 10 WORST POLITICAL SCANDALS IN CANADIAN HISTORY

1. THE PACIFIC SCANDAL, 1872

Through Sir Hugh Allan, American contractors contributed heavily to the Tory election fund in 1872 in return for a controlling interest in Can-ada's proposed Pacific railway. When Sir John A. Macdonald balked at their demands, they tried blackmail and, finally, with a lot of help from the Liber-als, brought the facts to light. Even the hardened political consciences of the time were shocked, and the "Pacific Scandal" drove Macdonald from office for all his claims that "these hands are clean."

2. THE BEAUHARNOIS SCANDAL, 1930

Whoever won the hydro power rights to the Beauharnois section of the St. Lawrence River would have made the deal of the century. A House of Commons committee found that the successful syndicate had been remark-ably generous to the sanctimonious but tight-fisted William Lyon Mackenzie King and two top Liberals. As graft goes, the amounts paid to King were trifling but they were enough to send him and the Liberals, in King's words, into "the valley of humiliation."

3. THE MANITOBA LEGISLATURE SCANDAL, 1915

For most of a year, Manitoba voters followed the details of how the price of their new Legislature had doubled with the proceeds going to a shab-by network of contractors, officials, and Conservative fund raisers. The Tor-ies were swept from office and the Premier, Sir Rodmond Roblin, and three ministers faced trial. Others escaped by fleeing to the United States. The chief contractor, Thomas Kelly, went to jail but the politicians had their charges dropped because of ill health.

4. THE LANGEVIN-MCGREEVY SCANDALS, 1891

J. Israel Tarte, the Conservative organizer in Quebec, kept all his secrets in a little black bag. When he opened it, the revelations of kickbacks, pay-offs, and fraud sent Thomas McGreevy, the Tories' Quebec fund raiser, to jail. It took all the efforts of a weakened Conservative government to save the eminent Sir Hector Langevin, Minister of Public Works, from the same fate. For the Tories, leaderless after the death of Sir John A. Macdonald, the scandal could well have been fatal.

5. THE BAIE DE CHALEUR SCANDAL, 1891

If the Tories were saved, it was because the same black bag contained enough scandal to destroy the Nationalist regime of Quebec's premier, Honoré Mercier. Payoffs for a contract to build a railway to Baie de Chaleur helped pay Mercier's expenses on a lavish trip to Paris and Rome. Mercier's personal ruin helped the career of another Quebec Liberal, Wilfrid Laurier.

6. THE BROWNLEE SCANDAL, 1934

The Chief Justice of Alberta did not believe the claim of pretty Vivian MacMillan that her boss, Premier John Brownlee, had had a three-year affair with her. The people of drought-stricken, puritannical Alberta preferred to believe Miss MacMillan. What they really wanted was vengeance against a bankrupt, ineffective government. Within a year, they had William Aberhart and Social Credit.

7. THE SQUIRES SCANDAL, 1932

It did not take much of a scandal to destroy a government during the Depression. Major Peter Cashin's claim that Newfoundland's Premier, Sir Richard Squires, had falsified Cabinet minutes to conceal illegal payments to himself and Cabinet cronies was enough to send the hungry, desperate people of St. John's on a rampage of destruction through the House of Assembly. Squires barely escaped with his life. A British cruiser hurried to St. John's, and Newfoundland's bankrupt government surrendered the island's Dominion status to a British-appointed commission.

8. THE RIVARD SCANDAL, 1964

An assistant to the Liberal Minister of Citizenship and Immigration offered a $20,000 bribe to a Montreal lawyer to get bail for Lucien Rivard, a narcotics smuggler. There was also a promise of money for Liberal party funds. The Prime Minister, Lester Pearson, claimed that his Minister of Justice, Guy Favreau, had told him nothing of the affair. It did not help that Rivard later escaped with amazing ease from his Montreal prison. It was even less helpful that most of those contaminated were French Canadian Liberals. Those who raised the scandal were accused of anti-French bias.

9. THE NORTHERN ONTARIO NATURAL GAS SCANDAL, 1958

Three Ontario Tory cabinet ministers, a mayor of Sudbury (later a federally-appointed judge), and several other favoured people were allowed to buy NONG stock before public sales began. They just happened to be the people who had most influence over where the natural gas line would run. But times were good and Ontario voters were loyal to their belief that scandals only happen elsewhere in Canada.

10. THE SOLDIER VOTE SCANDAL, 1917

As part of their efforts to win victory for the pro-conscription Union government in the war-time election of 1917, organizers persuaded military voters to switch their ballots to ridings where the Unionist candidates needed help. This disgraceful proceeding enraged the Liberals and led them to cry corruption. Almost all historians have echoed the claim. None of them ever bothered to check the fact that all of these switched ballots were disallowed by election officials. This persistent laziness by historians is, in itself, a scandal.

Desmond Morton
Dean of Humanities and Academic
Vice-Principal
Erindale College, University of Toronto

THE 10 WORST CANADIAN POLITICAL DISASTERS IN THE LAST 10 YEARS

1. THE SECRET TRIAL OF NATO

Electronics whiz, Dr. Peter Treu charged under the Official Secrets Act — the first all-secret trial in English common law history.

2. THE URANIUM CARTEL

Instigated by Canada in 1971 and involving the Rothschild's firm in Britain, South Africa, France, and Australia to undercut American uranium prices. An Order-in-Council guaranteed protection to the cartel member-firms from prosecution and went a step further and made it against the law for anyone to mention uranium sales, their purchases, or even the agreement, on pain of fines and imprisonment.

3. THE SALE OF CANDU NUCLEAR REACTORS TO SOUTH KOREA AND ARGENTINA

In which Canada insisted that the deal be consummated and negotiated through an agent when South Korea said it didn't want one. The agent cost $20 million. The Argentinian deal resulted in a loss of some $120 million to Canada due to price miscalculation and the "agent" was unknown to Canada except by an unlisted bank account in Lichtenstein. The agent in the South Korean deal lives in Israel, has an unlisted number, and no fixed address.

4. THE AIRPORT AT MIRABEL

Cost some $1.5 billion even though no one wanted it and certainly it wasn't needed and isn't used. It is such a white elephant that that has become the official symbol.

5. FUNDS FOR CIDA (Canadian International Development Agency)

From $150 million in 1968 to a billion dollars in 1978, with enormous amounts going to a couple of score of one-party dictatorships (Communist and otherwise, Tanzania, Algeria, Zaire, etc.) and "humane" aid to terrorist groups, and waste reaching epic proportions (milk cows to Uganda where Idi Amin celebrated by consuming them in one huge barbecue).

6. THE PRIME MINISTER'S SWIMMING POOL

A small but significant scandal is the PM's $200,000 swimming pool paid for by anonymous Ontario businessmen. The donors got tax exemption and were "persuaded" not to tell anyone what happened.

7. THE 1974 ELECTION

The cynical "scandal" of Trudeau winning the 1974 election by ridiculing the Tories' wage-price controls and promising to "wrestle inflation to the ground" without controls — and then implementing controls when the election was won. It is matched by Trudeau telling the world that "separatism is dead" in Quebec, six months before René Lévesque's separatist Parti Québécois won a massive victory over the Liberals.

8. MISCELLANEOUS

Impropriety in the Trudeau Cabinet is endemic — and versatile and varied. From improper contacts with judges over charges against a Liberal colleague (Drury, Chrétien, Lalonde, Ouelette); Marchand's suspended driver's licence and its hasty return after Cabinet questions were asked of the parole board (Allmand); Supply Minister Goyer's girlfriend flying falsely and freely on an Air Canada pass; Transport Minister Otto Lang's penchant for private government planes over Air-Canada scheduled flights to Grey Cup football games; Lalonde and Danson flying their kids on military aircraft for European holidays; freeloads for ministers to Israel courtesy of Quebec distillers.

9. GRANTS OF TAXPAYERS' MONEY

Via the Canada Council, LIP, and Opportunities for Youth — billions wasted with no returns. These resulted in no great works of art or literature, no meaningful jobs produced. Dirty poems that don't rhyme but win cash awards, Satanist groups, seagull enumerators, and Dracula home movies and hippie-hitchhikers are among the achievements.

10. THE LAST DISASTER

As for greatest individual disaster of the Trudeau era — how about that all-purpose Trudeau campaign organizer who once wanted Paul Hellyer for PM and who was once fired as a weekly columnist for *The Toronto Sun* (his column also appeared under the byline of other Cabinet Ministers) — Senator Keith Davey?

Peter Worthington
Editor
The Toronto Sun

THE 10 GREATEST FEDERAL EXPENDITURES IN CANADA

	Expenditure (millions of dollars)

1. Public Debt Charges
   Interest, bond discounts, premiums
   and commissions, and servicing costs
	5,350.0

2. Old Age Security Pension	4,777.9
3. National Defence	3,794.7
4. Payment to Provinces	2,879.5
5. Family Allowances	2,152.8
6. Central Mortgage and Housing	1,638.6
7. Share of Hospital Insurance	1,500.3
8. Unemployment Insurance Commission	1,376.5
9. Post Office	1,236.8
10. Transport	1,098.3

Statistics Canada

THE 10 COUNTRIES FOR WHOM CANADA HAS PROVIDED THE MOST EMERGENCY RELIEF *

		Purpose	*$*
1.	Angola	Humanitarian assistance	2,000,000
2.	Lebanon	Food and medical assistance for victims of Lebanon's civil war	890,000
3.	Portugal	Housing for returnees to Portugal from Angola	230,000
4.	Morocco and Mauritania	Relief for displaced Saharoui peoples	150,000
5.	Jamaica	Relief for fire victims	107,000
6.	Turkey	Earthquake relief	100,000
7.	Romania	Earthquake relief	100,000
8.	Lebanon	U.N. Secretary General's Special Appeal for Lebanon	100,000
9.	Zaire and Sudan	Haemorrhagic fever epidemic control	90,000
10.	Chile	Humanitarian assistance for political detainees and their families	62,907

*Figures are for 1977.

Statistics Canada

THE 10 MOST DECISIVE FEDERAL ELECTIONS IN CANADIAN HISTORY

Prime Minister and Leader of the Opposition	Party	Date	Number of votes	Percentage of votes
1. W.L.M. King	Liberal	March 26,	2,381,443	51.5
R. Manion	Conservative	1940	1,416,230	30.7
2. J. Diefenbaker	Conservative	March 31,	3,908,633	53.6
L.B. Pearson	Liberal	1958	2,447,909	33.6
3. L. St. Laurent	Liberal	June 27,	2,897,662	49.5
G. Drew	Conservative	1949	1,736,226	29.7
4. L. St. Laurent	Liberal	Aug, 10	2,751,307	48.8
G. Drew	Conservative	1953	1,749,579	31.0
5. W.L.M. King	Liberal	Oct. 14,	1,975,841	44.8
R. Bennett	Conservative	1935	1,305,565	29.6
6. P.E. Trudeau	Liberal	June 25,	3,696,875	45.5
R. Stanfield	Conservative	1968	2,554,765	31.4
7. W.L.M. King	Liberal	June 11,	2,146,330	40.9
J. Bracken	Conservative	1945	1,435,747	27.4
8. L. St. Laurent	Liberal	June 10,	2,702,573	40.9
J. Diefenbaker	Conservative	1957	2,572,926	38.9
9. W.L.M. King	Liberal	Dec. 6,	1,272,660	40.7
A. Meighen	Conservative	1921	945,681	30.3
10. J.A. Macdonald	Conservative	March 5,	397,731	51.1
W. Laurier	Liberal	1891	366,817	47.1

THE 10 CLOSEST
FEDERAL ELECTIONS
IN CANADIAN HISTORY

Prime Minister and Leader of the Opposition	Party	Date	Number of votes	Percentage of votes
1. J. Diefenbaker	Conservative	June 18,	2,865,582	37.3
L.B. Pearson	Liberal	1962	2,861,834	37.2
2. J.A. Macdonald	Conservative	July-Sept.,	159,006	49.9
A. Mackenzie	Liberal	1872	156,365	49.1
3. W.L.M. King	Liberal	Sept. 14,	1,500,302	46.1
A. Meighen	Conservative	1926	1,474,283	45.3
4. C. Tupper	Conservative	June 23,	414,838	46.1
W. Laurier	Liberal	1896	405,185	45.1
5. J.A. Macdonald	Conservative	Feb. 22,	362,632	50.2
E. Blake	Liberal	1897	352,184	48.7
6. J.A. Macdonald	Conservative	Aug-Sept.,	134,269	51.1
G. Brown	Liberal	1867	131,364	49.0
7. R. Borden	Conservative	Sept. 21,	666,074	50.9
W. Laurier	Liberal	1911	623,554	47.7
8. W. Laurier	Liberal	Oct. 26,	592,596	50.4
R. Borden	Conservative	1908	550,351	46.9
9. P.E. Trudeau	Liberal	Oct. 30,	3,718,000	38.5
R. Stanfield	Conservative	1972	3,384,000	35.0
10. R. Bennett	Conservative	July 28,	1,903,815	48.8
W.L.M. King	Liberal	1930	1,761,352	45.2